The Venice Adriana

by Ethan Mordden

The Venice Adriana

Ethan Mordden

St. Martin's Press

New York

Design by Songhee Kim

Library of Congress Cataloging-in-Publication Data

Mordden, Ethan.
    The Venice Adriana : a novel / Ethan Mordden. —
1st ed.
        p.   cm.
    ISBN 0-312-18202-3
    I. Title.
PS3563.07717V4   1998
813'.54—dc21   97-39714
                                                          CIP

First Edition: February 1998

10   9   8   7   6   5   4   3   2   1

To Michael

———————————

Acknowledgments

To my thrilling agent, Joe Spieler; at St. Martin's, to my ever trusty copy editor, Benjamin Dreyer, to Mikel Wadewitz, Meg Drislane, and my wise editor, Keith Kahla.

No zé bel quel ch'è bel,

ma quel che piaze.

_____

Beauty lies not in what is beautiful,

but in what gives one pleasure.

—CARLO GOLDONI

1

Italian Boys Are Ruthless Flirts

There was a church school on the Zattere that I liked to walk past in the warm half of the year, for through the open windows I could hear children reciting those now inspiriting, now bewildering mottoes that Catholics are raised on. I would catch the nun's wearily officious "The love of the tree," followed by the class's merrily dutiful repetition. "The sorrow that is heaven," the nun would continue, to the kids' echo; and "The mortification of vanity," "The tears of the olive," "All fear what is true," and, the nun's voice rising in the confidence of one made sensible of a great riddle, "Repentance is infinite."

How often, returning across the Accademia Bridge from errands around the Piazza, the Merceria, and American Express, I'd walk a bit out of my way, down the Rio San Trovaso and then east along the Giudecca Canal, to sample once more this inveigling liturgy. These were leisurely, stimulating days, when I lived in the world's loveliest city in the most pleasurable employ of the greatest singer of the age—of all time, some say: Adriana Grafanas.

Many an afternoon did I come home musing on the children's anthems, turning in on Rio Terrà dei Catecumeni, down to number 127, through the ancient door into the courtyard of our many neighbors. There would be a "Ciao, Marco" from whatever kids were around, perhaps a savory bow from il Professore or a brisk "Bondì" from Siora Varin, her eyes on her unpredictable old mother, just then, perhaps, pulling the basket of communication up to their third-floor apartment. In it would be bread, medicine, legal documentations to fuel Siora Varin's explosive relationships with the bureaucrats of the civil service, who—so she swore—spent their entire careers in cafés.

Home and unpacked, I'd take a book into the garden—one of the most secret in all Venice—and sip coffee while listening to the peace of the place. Sometimes Adriana, in the house, would be vocalizing, and I'd come in and play for her while she ran through a solo, always from the toughest roles—Lucia, Norma, Violetta. She insisted. Midphrase, she'd cut out, pensive and hurt, feeling her stomach muscles, her throat, the ridge along the back of her neck, as if, like a doctor in the Middle Ages, she could solve the problem metaphysically, or through leeching or spells. "No," she would say, with profound regret, "così non va bene," though of course she spoke perfect English, my language and, well into her late teens, hers as well, for though she was of Greek family and had lived in Italy for fifteen years, she was a New Yorker, born and raised in Manhattan.

Così non va bene. No, that doesn't work well. Nothing was working well for Adriana in the days when I knew her. The voice with which she had more or less re-created the very mission of opera, from the raising of pretty noises into the bitter generosity of emotional communication, was in shreds. The fierce self-belief that had enabled her to storm the fortress of opera, as an unlovely outcast who relentlessly demanded to be named its queen, was evaporating, dazed, and exhausted. She would consider a hundred projects as if she had her whole life before her, yet in the end she'd sign no more than a contract or two, and usually squirm out of those. She was terrified—yes, of a thousand things, but especially of appearing on stage. The theatre had been her life, but now, with her instrument gone bust and her command put to ridicule, it had become her death.

Let us not stand upon the fraud of ceremony: you know Adriana, *knew* her. She was, pretty much, the most famous woman in the Western world. Adriana Grafanas of the scandals and the temperament; of the now-you-see-me, now-you-don't cancellations; of the "Yes, tonight she was filth but last week she was heaven, weren't you there?"; of the news flashes and whisper columns. In the 1950s, when a woman made headlines, you knew she was big.

They spoke of her "corporation," of some gala entourage, I suppose to inflame the popular view of her as arrogant and despotic. No: There were no more in that tender little two-story house at number 127—Wally Toscanini's property, in fact, rented to Adriana without lease, con onore— than Adriana and the Actor she loved, the odious International Gossip she tolerated, and me, Mark Trigger, who had come to Venice to ghost Adriana's autobiography.

It was quite an opportunity for an uncredentialed young man working as assistant to an editor in a New York publishing house. I got it, truly, by fluke: my boss, who specialized in tell-all autobiographies of the illiterate famous, had acquired the memoirs of a noted prizefighter, unique for his cultural pretensions—he would embellish locker-room interviews with paeans to Eugene O'Neill and Charles de Gaulle—and for being a white man in a sport that was becoming almost exclusively a black man's field. Three "literary advisers" (so my boss always termed it, in a kind and not cynical way) had worked with the author, one after the other; still, the manuscript was a mess: overlong, grandiose, and drunk on its own mythology.

"Here," said my boss one afternoon, dropping the pages on my desk. "See what you can do with it."

I fixed it, through what you might call "creative cutting": dropping the pompous Theory of Sport passages and the dreary details about who was at a party to concentrate on what this athlete was made of—what drove him first into and then to the top of such perilous work, how friends supported and adversaries assailed him, what it felt like to be, for a time, the absolute of his kind. Finally, I deleted the closing page, on the power of "God's everlasting love, which has always shielded me," because there is no God.

Two weeks I spent on this project, every night and all weekend, because I was ambitious, as any youth from the sticks must be when crashing the cultural capital. My boss liked what I did, and because I had mastered Italian in college and was a trained musician, he sent me off to Venice and Adriana when she, too, signed to write her life for him. I was to spend the summer of 1961 shaping what she had already written and laying down guidelines for her continuation; but it turned out that she had not set a single word on paper, though of course this was the time of her semiretirement from the stage, after she had broken with her poor deluded old thing of a husband and more or less run off with a notoriously romantic actor—Greek, like Adriana—as the reporters and photographers of every discovered country gave chase and told all . . . even, sometimes, the truth.

Adriana had plenty of free time for working on her book, but it wasn't easy to get her to concentrate on it. When the Actor was away, she fretted; when he was handy, she fawned upon him like a bride. Finally I placed a call to my boss to tell him that I didn't think we were making sufficient progress and maybe I should—if I had to—come home. I made the call at the post office, feeling like a spy for a foreign power back in the golden age of this rigidly opulent, excruciatingly secretive city; and I cannot tell you how relieved I was when he told me to stay on as long as I had to. "Talk to her friends," he urged me. "Talk to her enemies." Whatever else happened, I was to *get that book!* Apparently, this liaison with the Actor had made Adriana bigger than ever.

"We'll best-sell easy," said my boss.

So I stayed on in Venice, and became absorbed into Adriana's household as something between a secretary and a fan; and I was absorbed into Venice, too, as I knew I must be from the moment I walked off the rapido, through Santa Lucia Station, and out onto the banks of the Grand Canal and thought, as everyone always does, God, the damn thing really *is* built on water!

Adriana's house was landlocked, though there was a back entrance on the Rio delle Fornaci that always gave me the shivers, for once you left the canal you walked down a very dead alley past a danger-high-voltage warning skull. Once through the back gate, however, you were safe in Adriana's garden, facing the house. It was a new one, postwar, a cherishable advantage in a city where people generally lived in buildings centuries old. Entering, you were spang in the dining room. To the right, the living room, the kitchen behind it to the left. Upstairs, first on the right was my room, then that of the Gossip, then the sala nobile, a suite of enclosures for Adriana and the Actor.

There was one nonresident I should mention, Deodata the housekeeper, what they call "a gem." I liked to check in with her now and again of a day: singing radio pop (especially "Never on Sunday," which she called simply "Domenica") as she did the laundry in the barren yard behind the house; grumbling over the food grease and crumbs in the Gossip's room; decrusting that strange little Italian white bread, quartering the oranges, scrambling the eggs, and brewing the coffee for my breakfast. The others luxuriated in their beds, but I liked to get up and see how the day might go, get a sense of its evolving patterns. In the kitchen, Deodata would sit with me and help me puzzle out the *Gazzetino,* the local paper composed in the growly, flowing Venetian dialect. She lived somewhere nearby and had been with Adriana—"la Siora"—almost from the beginning, way back when Adriana had just married Ambarazzi. "No, Signor Trigga," Deodata liked to say, with a conspiratorial smile, "the journalists ask and ask about the Siora. Shocking things, they ask. When she was married, it was always one thing—do they sleep as man and woman? Because el Paron was so much older, of course. But never did I speak to them. Never. I am all the Siora's secrets, dasseno."

It was in the mornings that I would make some assault on the Book, if only to justify the (modest) salary my boss was paying. I had determined not to lay out the typical catalogue (Chapter 1: I Am Born), for Adriana's life was anything but typical, even for an opera singer. A unique life, I told her, needs a unique chronicle. "Bravo," she said. "Ecco l'artistico, l'audace." I wanted to focus on her work—she liked that—and I planned to jump dramatically into the narrative during her early adulthood, when, alone and near penniless, she made her first visit to Italy to sing Aida at the Arena in Verona in 1947. She liked that even better, because she had had a difficult youth and didn't like to speak of it.

"Still," I said, "somewhere in the book we'll have to deal with your family background."

"Certo," she replied, as vaguely as possible.

Or was it hokey to start as the young hopeful enters upon her great trial, full of self-interest yet lacking self-confidence, ungainly and over-weight and possessed of a voice so distinctive that it was as evil as it was beautiful? I toyed with the notion of opening the book later in her life, at the terrible era of the scandals in the late 1950s—the "Edinburgh Walk-out," when she blithely canceled her last performance of *Maria Stuarda*, claiming exhaustion, then flew home to reign idolized at the Gossip's Par-venu Ball at the Palazzo Barbaro; then the physical assault on a reporter in New York, from which she escaped in a sympathetic millionaire's pri-vate plane, the police, two minutes late, shaking their fists on the tarmac; then the infamous cancellation of *I Puritani* in Rome at the first intermis-sion, which turned all Italy against her because the country's president, Giovanni Gronchi, was in the audience.

I would then illuminate the legend. Adriana had been announced for that last Edinburgh *Maria Stuarda* without her permission or even her knowledge, and it was thus not a cancellation. I assure you, she would much rather have been singing Donizetti than heating up the Gossip's ridiculous ball—nothing cheered Adriana more than great music, and nothing dimmed her more than socializing, particularly with idiots. But she owed the Gossip for many a favor, and just as she never stopped coming at those who had hindered her advance, she never—well, hardly ever—stopped thanking those who had assisted it.

As for the New York incident: yes, she did deck the reporter with her handbag, and down he went. It was a case of pure assault. You've seen the photos. But listen: He had made an intolerable pest of himself, insisting on getting a Story while Adriana kept telling him that she had nothing to say. She hated people who won't take no for an answer; so do I. And why did Adriana have to deal with this nuisance herself? Where was good old Ambarazzi when you needed him?

Now Rome. She dropped out of the *Puritani* because she was in terrible vocal shape. The management had not bothered to hire a substitute, on the idea that no one can substitute for Grafanas. But she warned them, two days before, that she was not in satisfactory voice. Bad throat, inflammations, strenuous high notes. She could not, must not. They were panicked and intransigent. La Grafanas must sing. She can do it—how many times has she concocted a triumph out of the ingredients of certain disaster? She was famous for it: as in the Naples *Tosca* in 1957, when a restless public began to whistle not only her misfired high notes but, by the middle of Act 2, virtually her every line. It was sport. Then came "Vissi d'arte," which she sang not at Scarpia but at her real tormentor, the audience: "Never did I harm a living soul.... I gave my songs to the stars in heaven, that they might shine the brighter." Moving to the edge of the stage, with every eye and ear in the house utterly mesmerized, she fell on her knees and begged them, "Why do you repay me thus?"

And of course they screamed for her then. It was love—because once more she had *seized* the triumph, raped it, really, as a man would. So, foolishly, Adriana let them talk her into going on in that Rome *Puritani*, but it went so badly that after the first act she left the theatre. Just gathered up her stuff and walked, while the opera-house officials stood about, pleading and wringing their hands. After an interminable wait, the audience was sent home. Now, interminable intermissions are routine in Italy, and performances there are very often canceled, because if the unions aren't manifesting themselves, the chandeliers suddenly need cleaning. Yet on this one night, everyone reacted as if Rome had suffered an unspeakable indignity. *In the presence of President Gronchi!* As if heads of state have rights more special than those of the rest of the house?

Well, all that began to seem more discouraging than dramatic. I thought of starting the book with a different Adriana, not embattled but ecstatic: Adriana as the Actor's sweetheart. Tosca, in "Vissi d'arte," says, "I lived for art, I lived for love"—but in fact Adriana had been living entirely *on* art, and now proposed to give it up entirely for love, for the Actor's devotion, and empathy, and beauty, and power. He made her feel, for once in that vexed and rowdy life, that she was worthy, redeemable, blessed. Oh, I know you've heard that he was an opportunist who vaulted onto the world stage by using her prestige and connections, that he gave her fuck and she gave him fame. And that much is true; but there is more than one truth.

I know exactly when to begin: during Adriana's Venice Normas in the spring of 1962, one of the last completed stage performances of her life. This was the day of the third Norma, I believe. As always, Adriana left for the theatre very early in the evening, her face drawn and her body rigidly upright, as if only the most formidable concentration would enable her to peel an onion, much less get through the toughest role in opera. A delegation from the Fenice escorted her to the theatre, though whether as bodyguards and flatterers or simply to make certain she would show up is hard to say.

Neither the Actor nor the Gossip was in sight; I was in the garden, reading. As Adriana and the men left (through the back entrance, to a motorboat waiting in the canal), il Professore came out of his house, approached, and, at my sign of welcome, entered the garden. This was not unusual. He often dropped in for a talk in his dark suits and apologetic ties. But on this day, to my alarmed delight, he had with him the Young Man.

This was an implausibly handsome chap I often saw in il Professore's company: about nineteen or twenty, tall and "well planted," as the Italians phrase it, with a methodical walk and impish eyes. To the others in the courtyard he was "el nevodo," il Professore's nephew; but to me he was a night dream—now Sinbad, then Perceval, iconic, demanding, promising. I had often seen but never met him, till one morning when Siora Varin's antique mother, annoyed at the stray cat that was always rushing into the courtyard when someone opened the street door, started shouting in her unique patois, a dialect of a dialect. I had picked up some rudimentary Venetian, but somewhere between old Signora Varin's toothlessness and her enthusiasm, all words dissolved into a fog of sound. "Sti ga' da Veneza!" she screamed, among other things. The cats of Venice! "Me refarò co tu!" I'll fix you! Just then, the Young Man appeared at il Professore's first-floor window. I was looking at him as he stared at Signora Varin, but she scrambled out of view and suddenly he was staring at me. I don't know how long I looked at him. He was shirtless, his hair tousled and his eyes sleepy, exactly as he had looked the previous night as Saint Sebastian being led to the stake by doubtful but obedient soldiers.

Then Signora Varin reappeared at the window and hurled down at that harmless cat a mousetrap, which snapped closed on its fur just below the back of its neck, throwing the animal into a frenzy of racing around and jumping awkwardly against walls as it tried to shake off its pain. I chased after the cat to pull the trap off, but the poor thing seemed to be everywhere at once, even when I cornered it. Then I felt a hand on my shoulder turning me aside: it was the Young Man, who leaped forward, grabbed the trap, and with a wrench freed the cat.

Signora Varin was still yelling as the cat paced into a corner, shivering and trying to lick the spot where the trap had bit but otherwise its old complacent self. The Young Man had tossed the trap away and was looking up at il Professore, there at his window and mildly reproaching the

Young Man for dishonoring the courtyard with such "unfulfilled attire" and assuring me that only an emergency of humanitarian concern could possibly have led to such a spectacle as this.

"Vieni qua," il Professore concluded, leaving the window, "e non dico niente." Come upstairs and that's the end of it. Not yet: because the Young Man paused at his doorway and gave me the familiar Italian gesture of shaking his right hand with the first three fingers bunched, as if to say, Well, what can you do? Then he smiled.

I smiled back, and he went upstairs.

His name was Vieri. Thus il Professore introduced him—without calling him "nephew," I noticed—on that evening of the third Norma, and Vieri was still smiling at me, and still silent. He was in a suit now, sized quite large for him, which only added to his appeal as the unruly bumpkin, I thought, forever coached in the finesse of self-transformation and forever breaking his training. "From Naples," il Professore explained, confirming my perception, "that incorrigible Inferno of the South. Though his name belongs to the region of—"

"Americano," Vieri interrupted. "You like me?"

Il Professore admonished Vieri with a hand on the boy's arm; piano, piano.

"The name is Tuscan," il Professore explained. "Florence, Siena, Prato. A somewhat aspiring name, one might say."

"Deluxe," Vieri added, in English.

The attentive Deodata appeared with a tray of coffee and biscotti.

"Madonna sings tonight, yes?" il Professore asked, as we sorted out the cups and so on.

"Norma."

"One of her greatest roles. Masterly. Historical. She is always re-forming our notion of what music can be. And yet." His expression grew sympathetic. "They say her powers diminish themselves."

I said nothing.

Il Professore nodded. "Your loyalty is praiseworthy. Molto valido. One is irresistibly reminded of the conflicted atmosphere at the court of the sixteenth-century tyrant of Padua, Golo the Louche, whose urgent rede-velopment of agricultural practices and extensive building projects vastly energized his subjects, yet whose Saturday noontime poetry recitals nau-seated all who attended."

"Adriana doesn't nauseate anyone," I began.

"No, perdonatemi. I did not intend such precise correspondence. I want to say that one certain greatness can forgive another certain failure. The true artist can survive a regrettable performance or two." Hand on heart, he added, "It is here, in the soul, that we are to be judged."

Vieri took il Professore's hand and placed it on his own much younger heart. "Here is Vieri," he said. "I am from the bassi napoletani. Dark, noisy, crowded places. Everyone is all over everyone else. For many years I am there, wanting better life. Now I am here—the sun, the life of roses, the easy time." He grinned. "Who knows what is next for Vieri?"

It was not easy for me to follow his dialect, and il Professore, noting my befuddlement, said, "The new television is teaching Vieri the national language, and I was hoping, my dear young American friend, that you would teach him as well. English."

At my glance of surprise, he added, "You will name your fee, ben certo."

Vieri patted il Professore's arm, saying, "The Professore will pay."

"I wouldn't know how to teach English," I said, sipping coffee and longing to simply say yes. This cursed fear of showing hunger. "I just speak it."

"Those things in our lives that are of real significance," il Professore observed with some gravity, "come naturally to us. It is only the superficial that is acquired by technology."

There was a pause. Then Vieri said, "I want to be like America."

"Strong," said il Professore. "Proud. Free of conscience. He has seen all too many American movies, of course, and now he envisions himself as a cowboy and bank robber."

Vieri looked seriously at me. "I want to know you, Americano," he said.

His hand touched my hand, pulled on the fingers, gently importunate. When I turned from him to glance momentarily at il Professore, the old man said, "No, look at Vieri," and I did, and Vieri winked at me.

"He flirts," il Professore remarked. "All the most beautiful Italian boys are ruthless flirts. With the girls, with each other. With stones, clouds, fire. Vieri would flirt with the Colosseum, and the next day, in the *Corriere della Sera* you would read that the Colosseum had moved to Venice." He extended his hands to me. "So you see—we are all helpless in his grip, and we must give him what he needs."

I was astonished at il Professore's directness, at the nonchalance with which he not only produced Vieri but doted upon him before me. When I first arrived at number 127, I took il Professore for another of those discreetly mournful shades hovering at the edge of an academic Elysium, with his stiff, archaic dress, his absurd references to literary and historical trivia, his tidy little bachelor's annuity, and somewhere in there, I supposed, a risible monograph on some demented Renaissance pope. But as our buon giornos gave way to little chats in the courtyard, then to full-length conversaziones in the garden, I realized that here was a man of humor and passion. He was not just educated but *bright*, and it was merely his tease to mask a vivacious personality behind the brittle tact of the university veteran. Still, never before had il Professore taken me so casually into his confidence—for now, surely, Vieri was no nephew.

"I know your duties for Signora Adriana are many," il Professore went on, blandly now, as he took out a handkerchief and began polishing his spectacles. "You are an invaluable member of the household—not unlike, it may be, an alchemist at the court of Dorian the Furtive, whose fascination with the dark arts brought him the awe of all Modena and the interdiction of several popes."

I laughed. Then Vieri laughed, chomping on a biscuit. Il Professore laughed, too. Three friends.

"Yet it was this same Dorian," he went on, "who, late in life, repentant in his cloister, said, 'It is better to make history, but it is best to enjoy the simpler pleasures.' I believe you would enjoy teaching Vieri to speak English, and I will naturally reimburse you, quite handsomely, I insist, for your time. Vieri will be a good student. To converse in English like a gangster is all his dream."

We made a deal, the two of them departed, and I went out into the dusk for a walk. I was keyed up, anticipatory and triumphant. It was like flying. I needed to talk about it—to wonder why il Professore was letting his façade slip and to parse for myself exactly the strains of manly ease and know-it-all innocence that combine to make a Vieri. I needed to exult to someone, because I was at the top of my days, in Venice with Adriana and capable. I had wandered off recklessly, without a destination, beelining through the least distinguished sections of Santa Croce and Cannaregio, skirting the town's center of trudging tourists with their pleas for help. "San Marco? San Marco?" they would ask, lost, even doomed, till they were safely back in St. Mark's Square. Like a birthright Venetian, I would point and cry, "Sempre drito," straight ahead. But there is no straight in Venice; it's a maze. There is no one path; we must choose. And, as I say, there is no God; we are all guilty of our lives.

2

Later That Night

The Gossip returned first. I was in the dining room, the table covered with Adriana's press clippings, which I had been trying to get into order and paste down in a fancy scrapbook almost since I had arrived in Venice. I looked up at the sound of the key in the lock, and the Gossip staggered in, paused in the doorway, fiddled with the train of her gown, cried *"Oh,"* and dropped definitively into a chair.

"Oh," she repeated.

I was trying to remember which stack held the Lucrezia Borgias, where I had filed the Mozarts.

"Aren't you going to *ask* me?" she said, pulling herself up to an imperious height, which is not easy to do when you're an insidious dwarf.

"I gather it didn't go well," I said, adding to my Curiosities pile a magazine item about Adriana's "weekend recipes." (Adriana was no cook.

I once found her dispiritedly rummaging through Deodata's bread tray, looking for toast.)

"Disaster," the Gossip hissed. She delicately touched her neck, moved her head from side to side, gripped the edge of the table. She was ready to begin. "I could see that *all* was not *well* when I entered the theatre. I heard grumblings, arguments." A warning hand flipped the air. "An enemy claque was *out* in *force!* Oh, the auditorium was *crackling* with a case of the furies! Some had come for art, to be sure," she primly admitted. "Gondolas, Tintoretto, romance. Our lovely Venice. But *some* had come to the theatre to . . . Oh! I need a sudden drinkie, don't you know, to calm my nerves!"

She ran off to the bar in the living room, and I heard the dainty swish of liquor in crystal.

"Where was I?" she asked, reentering. *"Oh!"* as she settled back down at the table. "My delicious Adriana *thrown* to the *wolves!* Of course"—she pursed her lips, a cashier confronted by a suspicious-looking bill—"she was in *execrable* voice! Couldn't hit a dearie note, I say. How they whistled and shouted after the 'Casta diva,' how they howled!"

She paused, eyes wide, to show me the horror of a spectator at a martyrdom. "The *chaste goddess,* don't you know," she whispered.

"Adriana always had trouble with the first aria," I told her. "But after that, she would simply take over the opera."

"Terrifying!" the Gossip screamed, rocking back and forth in a mourning motion. "With that Florence Cossotto pouring out her glorious voice for all to hear!" She leaned forward confidentially. "You know I like to sit up close." She lightly tapped at her cheeks. *"Here's* where the drama is seen. In those beautiful Adriana eyes. And I was watching, I can tell you. Yes. I watched Adriana, to test her feelings, as that Cossotto stole everything but the Stonehenge, or whatever they had on that stage. *What* a voice, is all I can say. High notes like candy!" Now the Gossip sagged a bit, showing me despair. "My poor Adriana. . . . *Oh!"*

She rose.

"Is the chicken left from last night? Never mind, I'll see to it." She bustled out, her voice fading. "I'll find it, no fear. I'll hunt it down. I'm unstoppable, there's no end to me."

That much was true. A party pianist and sycophant to the great and near great in the 1920s, Erna Keating called in all her favors one day in the 1930s and found herself a social columnist on one of New York's more drastic tabloids. In the growing world of café society, she played entrepreneuse, fixer, and blackmailer, most adept at getting up an impressive guest list for your soirée, for a fee or a favor. In national syndication by the 1940s, she became one of America's arbiters of taste in cultural matters— though, curiously, she was more influential when boosting one of her darlings than when trying to degrade the opposition. After a tumultuous interview with Marlon Brando during the Broadway run of *A Streetcar Named Desire,* Keating made herself ridiculous attacking not his nonconformist attire or his coarse verbal delivery but his acting—this in a performance that was clearly destined to mark a watershed in theatre history! She made comparable gaffes with Arturo Toscanini, Katharine Hepburn, and even Elvis Presley. She had at first attacked Adriana, too, helping to promote the notion of a feud between Adriana and Renata Tebaldi, at the time the other most famous soprano active in the Italian repertory. The Gossip called them "the Tigress" and "the Saint." Then, one night, Adriana and the Gossip met at a ball, and Adriana courted her. And the Gossip, who was sixty, hideous, and momentously fat, fell helplessly in love.

"That ludicrous demon," Adriana called her, with an indulgent smile. "I took all the poison out of her, didn't I?" But why was the Gossip in residence, for weeks at a time, in Adriana's house?

"The curses they shouted, I say to you," the Gossip continued, waddling in with plate piled high. Then she fixed me with a look (as she always did when sharing a bit of common knowledge as if it were oracular revelation), said, "Italians are very vocal at the opera," and sat down to dig in.

" 'Go back to America' " was the next thing she told me.

I begged her pardon.

"That's what they shouted," she explained, tearing into a chicken wing. "As if Adriana had come from America in any true sense."

"She was born there," I said. "She spent her first two decades, almost, in New York."

So busy feigning shock that she stopped eating, the Gossip replied, "She doesn't *sound* American. She doesn't *look* American. She doesn't *act* American, with that chic little waistline and her Paris styles. *No,*" she decided, returning to the chicken. "Once a Greek, always a Greek. That blood runs deep."

There was a buzz from the street door, and with a nod of her head the Gossip urged me to answer it. "That'll be the Prince," she said.

This was Prince Ion Eduard of Romania, a star of the demimonde who allowed the Gossip to play the satellite in return for adoring references in her column. I suppose he's pretty much forgotten now, but in the early 1960s he was notable, especially for his ability to live brilliantly on no income that anyone knew of and for his penchant for marrying, every five years or so, a famous beauty, each one from a different country. His wife at this time was French and a princess in her own right, Anne-Marie Bonaparte, whom *Le Monde* termed "the most elegant woman in the world" and whom *Paris Match*, retaliating, called "the modern Helen," but whom *Oggi,* in conclusion, set forth as "donnissima": the ultimate woman. There were those who thought the Prince handsome, witty, and charming.

"Prince! *Prince!*" cried the Gossip, heaving out of her chair to crumple at him as he came in. "Was there ever such a catastrophe for our precious Adriana? How the theatre stank tonight!"

"It was the breath of the Graces," said the Prince, suavely pulling out a paper-thin gold case and lighter, selecting a cigarette, and rapping it relentlessly on the table; that whole European smoking thing.

"I simply ran out, I couldn't stay," the Gossip went on, working from him to me and back. Now a gulp of her drinkie. "She humiliates us *all* when she falls this low." A wave of her fingers in the air, the schoolmarm who Said So. "Twilight of the Gods, don't you see."

The Prince said, "She is a magnificent racehorse who will die on the track. What power is in her, what a will to succeed! I was entranced." He turned to me. "You didn't come tonight?"

"I saw the dress and the prima."

"Bene, sì. Americans are always *seeing* a thing. One *hears* opera, no?"

"What abuse I heard tonight," said the Gossip, between chomps. "Oh, her reign is over. I know it, yes."

"No one can replace her," said the Prince.

"Not even la Stupenda?" the Gossip sang out: meaning Joan Sutherland, the Australian phenomenon who had, three years before this, suddenly turned up as a spectacular Lucia di Lammermoor at her home house, Covent Garden. She was now buying the world as the next dramatic coloratura—like Adriana's, a throwback voice redolent of golden-age ontology, of the very purpose of vocal music—and was often touted as Adriana's superior. Adriana had the guts, this intelligence ran; but Sutherland had the voice.

"You cannot challenge the unique," said the Prince, "and this Adriana surely is."

"Oh ho," the Gossip replied, emptying her glass. "After tonight—"

"I must go," the Prince said. He truly *took leave* of one, studying you as he shook hands, considering, warning, perhaps encouraging you. Funny—you never knew why he was leaving any more than you knew why he had come.

The Gossip went up to bed, and I went on sorting Adriana's press cuttings, marveling at how thorough someone had been. It seemed as if Adriana's every appearance was documented, from her debut in Verona on. Who had gone to this trouble? Ambarazzi, her cast-off manager and husband? Deodata? Surely not Adriana—she claimed never to have read her reviews, though she seemed as aware of them as the condemned man is of the firing squad.

This will be great for my book, I was thinking. This is the whole career and even some of the life, page by page. Then I happened upon a review of a performance in Venice of *Adriana Lecouvreur*, Francesco Cilèa's opera about the tumultuous last days of one of France's greatest actresses. The real-life Adriana Lecouvreur revolutionized poetic tragedy with her naturalistic delivery of the classic alexandrine stanzas, carried on a famous affair with a dashing prince, may have been poisoned, and died in Voltaire's arms. Rachel, Bernhardt, Duse, and Modjeska played a stage version of her life, and it was this play that Cilèa twisted into an opera. Divas love it, yet everyone scorns it but me: I love it, too. Perhaps I am intrigued by the tale of an artist who cannot enjoy the beauty that she creates. Perhaps I enjoy its look at backstage life, fascinating to all who, like me, are stage-struck but lack the thespian gift. Maybe I just like the music.

The review was clipped from *The New York Times*: March 3, 1949, page 39, less than two years after Verona. There was an eye-filling photograph of Adriana in the title role: heavy, as she was in those days, even lugubrious—anything but the most glamorous actress in Paris. The headline read NEW YORKER EXCELS, and the short piece barely mentioned Adriana's colleagues—Gianni Raimondi as the prince charming, Giulietta Simionato as Adriana's vicious rival for his love, and Saturno Meletti as the poor old capocomico who secretly adores Adriana—to focus on the local girl making good. "The young Miss Grafanas sang with gusto and nuance," the reviewer wrote, "balancing the character's vigorous personality with her romantic yearnings, to the cheers of the Fenice public." *No, no,* I was thinking. She isn't vigorous; she's tender, elegiac, private. But she lives on art, and art is res publica, so she must develop a phony vigor to survive. And gusto and nuance—what's that, a comedy team?

Still, it was highly agreeable to find Adriana in a forgotten performance of my just about favorite opera. She very seldom sang this so-called verismo repertory, preferring the holier sancta of Bellini, Donizetti, and Verdi. Of course she was a terrific Tosca, and she did, in her early days, sing a number of unaccustomed roles, including Wagner, in Italian. New Yorker excels, I kept thinking, enjoying that provincial view of a career that was to be unique for its lack of patria. A Greek raised in America reinvented Italian opera.

Shuffling the clippings, I murmured, "New Yorker excels." Then I heard the Actor say, in English, "What New Yorker?"

He was in the open doorway, taking off his suit jacket, tired but game and wry and smiling. "Adrì? She is New Yorker, sure." For a Greek, his Italian was surprisingly near to faultless and his awkward English nonetheless fluent and improving by the day.

As he loosened his tie, he came around the table to look over my shoulder at the clipping. "*New York Times!*" he said, impressed. "Yes, it is necessary to know, in a new country, what are the important newspapers, important writers."

"Is the U.S. your new country?"

"Well," he said, "sure," pulling up a chair as he pulled off his tie. "A young Greek wants to be movie star, right? He come to Italy to be successful," little pauses, choosing his words, "then he come to America to be famous." He flashed the grin that notoriously brightened many a dark evening for his countless women fans from Finland to Portugal. "But first I clean up my English tongue."

"Everyone loves America today," I noted.

He shrugged. "People with nothing love the place of everything, no? Greece is friendly, beautiful place, but you are all the time hungry and bored. You go to movies, and what is it, always? *Italian* movies and *American* movies. Beautiful women, sexy ways, adventure, plenty, I *love* it. I think, *Italy*. A great movie business, always needing handsome man, a little dangerous, a little not too young, and a little romantic and sad. Ecco?"

I nodded. Nik Acropoli was a guy born to be seen on the grand scale: virile and funny, lean and tense, a dark man with a glow, something between boyish and turbulent. He played, most often, Sartrean drifters with Shakespearean destinies, a rich mix, but he was also good at farcical comedy—one of his first big films was an adaptation from Feydeau in which he attempted to seduce, inadequately and with increasing despair, every woman in the cast. He was, by all accounts, a respectful colleague and a fleet study, as much a boon to producers as he was a gift to his public.

"Besides," he went on, "Italy is mostly Greek, anyway. You know that, Mark? Greeks discovered Italy. It was Greek colony before even Roman Empire."

"How'd you learn the language?"

"Oh, so easy. I steal a self-teach book and study. I steal another, always I am learning. Then I come here, work however, any jobs." He pointed at me for a mark-my-words kind of thing. "It is not so difficult, if you know what you want. When someone gets in the path, you walk around, keep still going. Sure, you have the looks, so people want to know you, help you out. How to behave, how to dress."

He touched my shoulder and smiled, signaling the presentation of an essential lesson.

"You cannot go through life with a villager way of thinking. Where all other ways are no good ways. You know this? Seeing the world like every-one else where you live, as if there is no other way to see. Like my grand-mother—tough, old, and so stubborn. She always buys vegetables two streets down from our house. That's her job, the vegetables. One day, no vegetables. She says there are none in all Athens. But I go to *next* market, nine streets down. *Vegetables,* Mark! It's stupid, no? She has *always* to *one* market, so there can be no other?" He shook his head, laughing. "What is English word for this?"

" 'Provincialism.' "

"Too long, that word."

"Italians call it 'campanilismo.' "

"Also too long, for simple idea. As you go into the world, you must expand like panorama, containing many things that you learn." Warming to his lesson, he patted my back energetically. "For example—what do you think happens tonight during the intermission?"

He paused for emphasis, his face open, trusting. I liked him.

"Sure, this intermission is so long, and we are all enjoying the hospitality of the taverna in the campo. It is many people I am meeting, producers, directors, who knows?" He roared out a laugh, drunk on dolce vita. "Everyone is smiles, promising things. Then this."

He rose, turned the chair around, and sat again, chest to chairback, as if only the most casual pose could naturalize the extraordinary tale he had to tell.

"This lady, very elegant, very blond, very jewels. She is a producer's wife. She is talking with me, serious but not patient. You know this type? As if she is important with important message to tell me. Quick, I must listen. But what she says! She wants to put her mouth on me in the certain place, you know? And when I throw out, I am to catch my hand to it, so she can lick it off my fingers!"

He seemed amazed, bewildered; or maybe just bemused.

"Then she showed me what she means! Licking my fingers as she looked at my face, the whole fingers in her mouth, Mark! Slowly, slowly, licking, as all could see!"

He held a hand before me, the fingers splayed, then swallowed the thumb and slowly pulled it through the grip of his lips. Then the forefinger, the middle finger.

"Sure, Mark, where I am from, in Greece, such a lady would be banned. Not to be spoken, not even to be seen. But the customs are not so in Hollywood. The women are bold. So I must adapt to the customs. I am not a villager. Son mondano . . . What is that word, English?"

" 'Sophisticated.' "

"Another too long," he laughed.

He had never spoken so intimately to me before, and I felt flattered, as we always are when someone with power shares a confidence. It is praise to be thought worthy of trust. And I must speculate that this tale of the producer's randy wife was not braggadocio. Nik's earthiness was naïve rather than bullying; he wasn't smirking but just telling what had happened.

"Maybe this lady want to enjoy me and forget," he said. "Or is this to be how they cast movies in America? Because . . ." He let out an appraising moan. "She had the lot, you know?"

"How did the opera go tonight?"

He shook his head, serious now. "When Adrí returns, you must not mention. She was not in bella figura."

"She knows what kind of voice she's in, whether I mention it or not. Anyway," I went on, emboldened by his intimate air, "it's less her voice she's worried about than your love."

"To worry?" he asked. "But why?"

"She fears she'll lose you."

"Of course she will," he said, surprised. "Love is always to be lost. How can it be the sex forever? It is wonder for a time, then it is homework. Adrì, she understands."

"She *doesn't,* is my point. What she wants is—"

"Father, son, brother, fiancé, dream, and God," he concluded, resting his hand upon my head. "Such ideals! And all I am thinking of is, What is possible, what is the salary, who—*whom*—do I enact?" He straightened up, shrugging. "It is all the working. It is a job."

"That's not how Adriana sees it."

"She is *Greek,* Mark!" he cried. "She knows what is real and what is not real. Please, Mark. Love is not control. Love is respect. That respect never dies, sure." How he was smiling then! "You are not more lovers, but you have shared something deep and true, and you must be ever more devoted. No?"

"Yeah? How come divorces are so acrimonious, and suddenly deep and true lovers hate each other?"

"That's the fault of marriage, old chap," he said, lighting a cigarette. "Such those false hopes."

"But the children—"

"Could you see Adrì and me with children, Mark?"

I couldn't see either of these two self-inventors with so much as a Betsy Wetsy doll, and I said so.

"Ecco," he answered.

"Besides," he thought.

"Consider," he went on. "Women. The different tastes and sizes." He leaned back, his eyes lidded, a lazy grin shaping up. "La rossa, che figura imponente, e che grandi occhi a lei!" The redhead, stacked and wide-eyed. "Ovvero la bionda, snella, snella e sì nuda, tutta nuda per me." The blonde, slim and [I'm] in the nude for love. "E la nera, avida, splendida, tutta amante." The dark lady, utterly given to passion. His eyes were nearly closed now; his lips were moist on the cigarette. "Beh," he said. "The taste of the kisses, you know? To sample so many. How can we deny ourselves this pleasure? The sweetness of the nipples, but also the center of the woman, her secret taste. The whole sample of her. I cannot be shy." His eyes opened, and he let out a low whistle. "There is no other way than to know her in this manner. The full taste. E perfino, when a woman gives herself totally to you, you see her joy in entrusting to you all, all of her being. This is like when my Adriana is wild and full, dark, Greek, crazy for what is true, the truest thing, the love, Mark."

He smiled and hit my shoulder lightly as he exhaled smoke. "I tell you this," he said, "because I like you and I know you respect her *absolute*. Yes?"

"Yes."

"What would they say in America here, to agree? The brothers, a pact on it?"

"They would say, 'Good man.'"

"I say that! And they shake hands, no? Americans are always hands."

"Yes, they shake." He already had my hand in a titanic grip. "Easy, though."

"Sì, and soon she comes. Be gentle, yes?"

"New Yorker excels."

He heard it, absorbed it, and dismissed it. Tousling my hair, he said, "I always trust you to be smooth with her. It is correct to say this?"

"It is correct."

He paused, nodded, and went upstairs, and I continued shaping the scrapbook, sorting through the odd news bit on a Fiordiligi here and an Aida there, through interviews conducted with some rigidly insipid phantom calling herself Adriana Grafanas, through photo montages of her coaching sessions, boutique outfits, and vacation home on Lake Garda. Some of her performances, especially those from her first years in Italy, were sparsely covered, while other performances were written up in virtually every major paper. And listen. While the *Corriere della Sera* found her Lucia "in beautiful voice, with commanding technique," the *Süddeutsche Zeitung* called her "tentative and distracted," while the Paris *Herald Tribune* saw "an artist of imposing presence but disappointing characterization." The London *Times* said that she "acted entirely with the voice, moving awkwardly"; *Der Spiegel* thought her "a natural on the stage, but in terrible voice." All this from one performance: was everyone imagining his own Adriana?

Suddenly I was blasted by a high note from somewhere outside: Adriana had returned. After a moment or so there came another high note, like the first very certain of pitch and carefully husbanded past the huge wobble that generally afflicted her high notes these days. I saw her trudging through the garden in the dark; as she reached the door, she emitted a third note and stepped inside.

"You see?" she cried. "I *have* the lousy high C, don't I? Then why didn't I have it tonight in the theatre?"

Pulling off her coat and scarf, she sat opposite me at the table, holding the coat against her as if she were still cold. "What's this, some scrapbook?"

"Yours."

"There'll be choice stories to add to it tonight," she informed me, quite bitterly. "At the curtain, they threw *turnips* onto the stage." She paused, I suppose for me to express shock. "Well," she added parenthetically, "I presume they were turnips. Who knows what a turnip looks like? Boris Christoff says they were turnips, and who should know better than a Bulgarian peasant?" She shook her head, nursing her wound, then slapped the table. "You can see it was planned, can't you? Nobody *brings* turnips to the opera by chance! They were *hoping* I'd be terrible!"

"Were you? Could you be?"

"Those stinkers are insulting Bellini when they attack me. It is the *music* they offend. What am I? The humble servant of creative genius! I am Norma, Violetta, Lucia. I am *music*. My name? I have no name. I am a wisp of art. Am I wrong?"

"You aren't humble. You are very aware of your greatness."

She almost smiled. "You are always right, and one day that will make me terribly angry."

"Rule for Opera Divas Number Three: 'Never slam a supporter.' "

"What is Number Two?"

" 'Come on like Godzilla and go off like a dying swan.' "

She was skeptical. "And Number One?"

" 'Always wear comfortable shoes.' "

She nodded enthusiastically at that, missing the joke, as usual. She had virtually no sense of humor.

"At least it happened in Venice," she said. "La mia Serenissima. From the start, they loved me here. I heard many in the audience shouting down the enemies tonight."

"It was that stormy?"

"There are certain places. Mexico City, London, Dallas. The public is warm. They want the best, but they forgive the most. Cologne, Berlin, Chicago, New York. But in *Milan*, tonight, they would have dragged me into the piazza and burned me alive. They would have inhaled my screams of agony with smiles!"

"Why don't you give up these tough parts?" I asked. "Take a break. Santuzza, Nedda, Mimì . . ."

"That isn't music," she said, rising, wandering about the dining room, examining the wall prints as if she'd never seen them before.

"You know what's music, and easy, and great theatre, and my favorite opera?" I said.

"*Norma* is everyone's favorite opera," she replied, as a high-school kitchenaire tells the principal, "All teenagers clamor for tuna-noodle casserole."

"*Adriana Lecouvreur*," I told her.

"Verismo," she said, dismissing it with a sweep of her hand. "Pop music. 'Stormy Weather.' 'Volare.' 'Granada.' *La Bohème*."

"Think of the attention you'd get—a new role!"

"I've sung it."

"I know," I said, holding up the *Times* clipping. She stared at it, not moving—I mean, moving neither toward it nor away from it, as if it were perhaps irrelevant to her but surely important to anybody else.

" 'NEW YORKER EXCELS,' " she read out, reaching for it now.

"It's a catchy headline," I said. "But you're not a New Yorker, I guess. You're not anything—neither truly Western nor truly Eastern, if Greece could be thought of as . . ." She wasn't listening: she was reading. She ran her fingers along the lines of newsprint as if checking them for accuracy; she felt the photograph, rapt and wistful, forgiving her turbulent past.

"I remember this," she said, sitting again. "Suddenly the lousy soprano got pregnant and couldn't bear to sing, and I learned the role in four days. Easy music, but so many *words*. The prima was a radio broadcast, and I was in such voice! The *best*, bravissima. I recall all this." She laughed. "I was thinking, They'll hear me, now, Italy. They'll know. Such wonderful colleagues, too—Giulietta, tanta cara. That Gianni Raimondi, fresh from his debut in some ridiculous little crossroads outside of Bologna. We were both twenty-six. *Beautiful* voice, and big wide eyes as if he didn't know what I would do next. Saturno, playing the whole opera to me like a hungry sheepdog."

She put down the clipping and faced me.

"I could love such people," she said. "But every time I opened myself to others, they would betray me! Comments to the press, trying to outsing me, grabbing extra bows!"

"Who cares?" I said. "Only the music matters."

"In a symphony, maybe," she snapped back, hey eyes dark. "In opera it is flair, élan, cachet. I will *destroy* those who try to block my advance! They will never sing with me again! I will hunt them from La Scala, the Met, Covent Garden! I am everywhere! I am opera itself!"

She rose, throwing away the coat and scarf, stalking the room. "That *Adriana Lecouvreur* was broadcast in the States, and my *mother* heard it, and she wrote to me, nagging and nagging, as she always does, *nagging* my father to his death, your family were dung farmers, you are not worthy of me, always out chasing the young pretties, nag, nag, *nagging* me for my ugly face and my big stupid body that no man will ever want and *nagging* my refusal to kowtow to *nagging* till I cannot be in a room with her for two minutes before I am screaming to let me *nagging* alone and why *wouldn't* he chase young pretties with that vicious idiot lying in wait for him at home, drunk on the litany of crimes she can *nag* and *nag* and *nag* him for, and that is what they sound like on nights like this one with their turnips and shouting, one great *nagging* because you were not beautiful in the sound, and you were not glamorous for the men, and you were *not* what I was *planning* to *love!*"

Out of breath, she held the back of a chair and shouted *"Nagging! Nagging! Nagging!"* over and over till she was spent, panting but in control. I hadn't moved through any of this.

At length she gently went on, "You know what they say of Greeks? We always pay our debts. If we owe favors, we give favors. If we owe revenge, we take revenge. Always, Greeks. And always I have paid, except for one thing. I have never apologized. Never, to anyone. And I have been wrong." She sighed. "That, too, is Greek."

"You have your own way of saying sorry," I said. "Chicago, 1955. *La Traviata*, Act Two. Something goes wrong backstage and they ask Tito

Gobbi to spin out his curtain calls while they fix it. You find out, call him to your dressing room, and roast him for spoiling your *Traviata*. He explains what the problem was, reminds you that it's Verdi's *Traviata*, and lets you off with a warning. One act later, you're in bed, ready to die, and Gobbi makes his entrance. Turning upstage, you say, in a little girl voice, 'Tito, you're not still mad at me, are you?' "

"Dio, this boy is everywhere!" she murmured.

I said, "You're so lovely when you relax."

She approached me and touched my cheek. "You are one of those few who love without asking for anything, no? Everything I do pleases you. Like my . . ."

Father, I believe she would have said, but she turned briskly away, saying, "Well, if I ever have to apologize to you, I'll make it dramatic. From beyond the grave, would you like that? An apology from Norma, Medea!" She glanced upward, an opera chorus fearing the arrival of an offended deity. "A wind," she said. "The doors and shutters bang open. A presence, quelque chose in the air. All in the room are frozen still in terror. But *you* know, Mark. However, I will not materialize." She sounded coquettish. "I'll give you a sign. And I'll apologize, and have you, and forgive you."

Ignoring that odd remark, I said, "Deodata left soup for you. And zucca barucca." (That's grilled pumpkin, a Venetian specialty. And the soup was a magnificent brodo in vino, boiled down from a pound of beef to utter honey.) "Come on to the kitchen."

Adriana let out one last speculative C—right on target but, yes, wobbly; very wobbly—and, shaking her head, followed me.

"I spoke to Manfredi today," I said, reheating Adriana's supper. "I made an appointment to see him next week. In Verona."

"No music critics in my book!"

"We have to size up the enemy's artillery in order to disarm him."

"That swine," she said, sitting at the kitchen table, a goddess in her Parisian couture. Having passed her youth as the Girl No Boy Wanted,

Adriana ran her maturity as the Woman You Daren't Forget. Cinderella went around in ashes but for a single night; Adriana went around dressed for the ball. No, wait: she just put on her glasses.

"Now I can see," she said. "What is this place?"

"Adriana, *will* you? It's the kitchen."

"Oh yes": the pope noticing the church of a disreputable saint in Calabria.

"I'm organizing your clippings," I said, stirring the soup. "Organizing your life."

"It is not life, it is love!" she cried, suddenly deciding to be joyous. "How I know that now!"

"It's both."

"It can never be both at once," she insisted. "What does a young American know? What did *I* know—ha!—as a young girl transported from New York to Greece in 1937? And this with a world war gathering! Do you see now that my mother is an idiot? What dangers we underwent! In New York, my father ran a pharmacy, and my brother and I wondered what toppings to order for our ice-cream cones. In Athens, my brother helped me pick out Nazis to seduce for potatoes so we wouldn't starve. An *idiot*, my mother! Europe in 1937, and *why?* For revenge on my father for tiring of her. But who wouldn't tire of an idiot?"

"You can have the pumpkin cold with the hot soup," I said, serving it up. "Like Norma—cool and passionate at once."

"You nice young man," she said, taking up her spoon but not yet digging in. "You don't belittle. You don't nag. When you like, you like."

"Come on, the soup."

"This Friday is lunch with Ercolani. About his film on the House of Atreus."

I nodded.

"You're opposed?" she asked.

"Not to a lunch."

"This bouillon is delicious. I must find out what brand of cubes Deodata uses, for my Paris Toscas."

"Adriana, you know you won't make a movie, with Ercolani or anyone else."

"We'll see. I am always fascinated by Clytemnestra. So wrong, so righteous. Yet the world sees her as a villain. Her husband kills their daughter, she avenges this, the mother, and who is guilty? The *woman*, never the man! *Ha!*"

"Adriana, what do you do? Why are you great? What are you loved for?"

She smiled. "This nonsense."

"Answer," I begged.

"What do I do? I sing."

"Right. And Ercolani isn't proposing a musical, is he?"

"Just to talk to him, what harm? They say my voice is breaking apart, anyway. It's this or dishwashing, hmm? Oh, that look on you! But you're all set to write my book, no?"

"I am."

"You'll tell the truth, bien sûr. How lurid and calculating I am." She was angry, snarling. "How I swallowed a tapeworm to lose all that weight."

I was alarmed at her sudden change of tone; but then; after a poor performance she could turn on a dime.

"Well, it's documented, isn't it?" she went on. "When I slimmed, they said, Oh, she thinks she's so great. When I learned a role in four days, they said, She's showing off. When I sang brilliantly, they said, But what a wobble! You'll mention that, of course."

She slammed the table with her spoon so hard the plates jumped. "Of course you'll tell them how I tortured my mother and lured Ambarazzi into a sexless marriage, the poor Don Pasquale. Tell how I drove that little Elsie Dinsmore of a Renata Tebaldi out of Milan—out of Italy! Because

I was not content to share La Scala, was I? I had to be assoluta, you'll tell them! Yes, *nag* them, till they know. You'll write how I sing like a man. Well, what are you so shocked about? I scream and attack and have inferior singers fired. I show my passions. Women are gracious, men are demanding? No? I *will*, I *will*, I *will*—a man!"

"Calma, calma," I told her.

"Don't tell me that!" she cried, sweeping the supper off the table with a furious wave of her arm. "Don't you dare ask me for calm after this. We want the truth, you must see that, you insufferably forgiving little toad. I will *guide* you to the truth. Ask that critic Manfredi, and ask my old teacher in Athens, Gilda da Coservo, and what about that great maestro who *created* me! That senile old..." She paused, touched a hand to her forehead as if feeling for warmth there. "Now I've hurt you," she said, staring at me. "Is it that I am cruel because that is all anyone has ever been to me, or am I cruel because that is how I am?"

She was very pale, and she smiled, looking down at the spilled food.

"I have made such, such a mess," she whispered, as she fell to the floor.

"No," said the Actor, suddenly there, ahead of me to hold her, comforting, strong, pulling her up to face him and see what love looks like.

"No," she whispered, trying to turn away, because love stings the uninitiated.

"Sì, sì, tesoro." He stroked her hair, held her close.

"I can't bear that you see me like this."

"See you?" he said, in English. "I heard you. They heard you in Cremona. Come, you cannot this. La mia diva, tu. No, not to cry, now. Why to cry? Bella tu sei. Tu sei gioconda." Beautiful. Happy.

"Amore," she breathed out, not moving, so bitterly happy.

He had come down in his shorts, the sexiest male star in Italian cinema, worth the price. She clung to him. He winked at me—it's all over—and carried her upstairs.

Then the house was still.

3

The
Dead City

In the mid-1950s, there was a toy called Robby the Robot that surged across the floor, arms pumping and body glassy with green light. At intervals, one would pull a chain at the back of his neck and he would grate out a paragraph of mechanical chat.

As English instructor, I devised comparable paragraphs for Vieri to master. At a party: "How are you, my name is Vieri. I am fine, I like your hairstyle." At the store: "I want to buy stamps, salt, jazz recordings, cuff links, decadent French novels." At the communal swimming pool: "Shall we have a race? I have lost my towel. You send me. Do you want to make love?"

Vieri laughed a lot and enjoyed his lessons. We worked mornings in the garden, as il Professore, nodding approval, passed through the court-

yard on some errand. Then, one day, Vieri jumped up and said—in English—"I will now show you something!"

He took me up along the Zattere to Rio San Trovaso, to a big wooden
building with the incongruous look of a Swiss chalet. "Oh-de-lay-e-hu," I
yodeled, as Vieri dragged me over a bridge and up to the squero, the
traditional Venetian boatyard—for so this was, one of the few remaining
workshops catering to ailing boats. The patients were lying everywhere; it
was a gondola hospital.

"Zormano, e n'ebben, ove sei?" Vieri called out, as we approached.

"Ciao, Vieri," a voice replied. "Cossa co tu?"

Out of the building came a man in his late twenties, wearing work-
stained clothes. He grabbed Vieri by the neck and gave him a shake like
a warily indulgent older brother.

"No, Zorman', ascolta," said Vieri, laughing. "Ascoltatemi!" Stepping
back and assuming the air of an eccellenza, a commendatore, Vieri cried,
"Ow ara *you*? Uhmy *name* is Vieri! Iya *am* za cow*boy* of Texas!"

Nodding his head in admiration and making the familiar shaking of
the fingers, the man said to me, "Beh, sto bravo fio, eh?" He's a fine young
man, isn't he?

Vieri introduced us; Zormano's father ran this squero, which Vieri frequented as an admirer of the motorboats Zormano tended.

"Zorman' takes me for rides," Vieri explained, back in his peculiar Italian. "He shows me how to handle the boats. And Mark," he added, answering Zormano's glance of inquiry, "is my English teacher."

"Ai, Vieri, tu," said the man, resting an arm around the preening Vieri's
shoulder. "This one," the man told me, "will make himself into something,
you will see. Not like my lazy brothers, who pass the day drinking coffee
and borrowing money. And the way he treats the boats—like a brigand
treats a princess!"

"I will drive a motorboat for the Danieli Hotel," said Vieri, "and you
will see how those American tourists will like me." Serious again, he said,
" 'Ello, sir, 'ave you losta your towel?"

I laughed.

"He is good at English?" Zormano asked, patting Vieri's back.

"He just got started," I said, to reassure them both. "But he's picking it up with great speed." "Prestissimo" was the word I used, and Zormano repeated it proudly, whereupon the two of them broke into a mock fist-fight, the kind my school friends got into back home when they had crushes on each other.

"Eh, Zorman', will you take us for a ride?" asked Vieri, as the battle subsided in laughter and looks.

Checking his watch, Zormano said he had a tourist pickup to make on Burano, well to the east of the lagoon; we could come along, but we'd have to take the vaporetto back.

"I can't," I said. "I've got an important lunch with my boss and some people on Torcello. In fact, I ought to be—"

"Burano's next door," said Zormano. "I could drop you on the way."

"Sì, Mark?" said Vieri, eagerly. "I will show you Torcello while we wait for your party. I know it well."

Laughing, Zormano said, "Vieri's been taking girls to the fields there, that's my guess. Eh, mi fio?"

"Chissà?" Vieri replied, telling nothing. But he dared a grin at me when Zormano turned away.

"Let me change my clothes," said Zormano, heading back inside. "These tourists, they all want to ride with the doge on the Bucintor', eh?"

So I phoned the house and told Deodata that I'd be waiting for Adriana and company on the wharf at Torcello, and, Zormano at the wheel, we took off into the Giudecca Canal, breezing into the Basin of St. Mark with a shower of white water and breaching the city at Santa Maria della Pietà. Modestly chugging along between decrepit back walls and the occasional campo, we broke full water just east of the cemetery island of San Michele so that Zormano could take the deep channel that cuts northeast through the lagoon, coming out midway between Mazzorbo and Torcello. All the way, Vieri excitedly pointed out to me the use of the instruments on the boat's control panel, and he roared with joy as we overtook a vaporetto plowing grandly through the bright, wet noon air.

"They will never get there!" he cried, staring, with a touch of disapproval, at the vaporetto passengers as we sped by. "They are too slow! They have no goal!"

"Everyone has some destination," Zormano observed philosophically.

"But to *grab* for it, eh? That is best. Not to wait so patiently like that. Mark, I am so glad we are going to Torcello. I will teach *you*, now, sì? Sì, Mark?"

"Sì, Vieri."

"Everything good is happening to me," he noted quietly.

Zormano was smiling. "Ai, Vieri," he said, shaking his head at the youth's energy and confidence and delight.

I had never been to Torcello, and was expecting a waterfront of houses and shops and people typical of the lagoon settlements I'd seen. But Zormano dropped us off at an empty little dock with nothing before us but fields and trees, a paved walk along a puddle of a canal, and, in the distance, the roofs of two ancient churches and a grumpy campanile.

"Come," said Vieri, taking my hand and leading me down the walk. We passed a few houses that clearly had nothing behind them but open space and finally reached a little square walled in by unprepossessingly official-looking buildings and the churches I had glimpsed when we arrived. Besides us, the place was deserted.

"It's a ghost town," I said.

"This is really the oldest part of Venice, il Professore says. That cathedral"—Vieri pointed at what looked like a Spanish stable topped by a stark yellow Romanesque cloister—"goes back to 639 A.D.!"

"The church may have been founded then," I said, "but surely the edifice itself has been rebuilt several times—"

"Oh, bene, yes, they rebuild it, if you like. But think how old it must be here, Mark. See—ruins!" There were circular markings in the grass and some large rocks of a ceremonial nature. Sitting on one, Vieri said,

"Here is the throne of a great man, condemning enemies to a wicked death. They were very rude to him before he had power, so now of course he must take a noble revenge."

"What about Christian forgiveness?"

"Saints do that for us. Come, Mark, see inside!"

I expected the church to be closed, as everything but the trattorias are at lunchtime in Italy, but it was not yet noon and we had a few minutes. The interior looked Byzantine, as does so much of old Venice—the Venice of the age when Constantinople was the cultural wellhead of the Western world and Rome had become the barbarians' Skid Road. Brilliant gold-and-blue mosaics filled the eye in a painter's light of haloes and sunbeams, and figures of the Virgin, of Christ and His apostles, stood forth with such strength that they might have been posters, perhaps cave paintings. I was transfixed; Vieri had to pull me out (urged on by the sexton, who appeared from nowhere, tapping on his watch).

"You see, Mark?" Vieri asked, as I came to, in the daylit square. "All over the islands of this Torcello were many houses and churches. A whole kingdom, my Mark Americano. Rich, powerful place. But up in that campanile, they can see the *new* place growing up—the tallest towers, the wealthiest manufacturers, the most notable harbor. The *Rialto*, Mark!"

I smiled. "Vieri, they haven't called it that for centuries."

"That's what il Professore calls it. Venice is the whole lagoon, but where *we* live, this is the Rialto."

Italian-style, I put an arm around him; but he lightly pulled away. "No, Mark, listen," he said. "We learn from this. Because Torcello was the king of the lagoon, but then came..." He was thinking of something. "Yes! Historical considerations!"

"Which ones?"

"I don't remember. But think—all that glory, and now this." He turned, his outstretched arms emphasizing the loveless nothing that was, today, Torcello. "Campo vuoto, Mark. No *life*. Il Professore, he says, 'Va piano, va sano.' " Don't make a big noise and you'll live longer.

We started back to the dock. "Tell me how you met il Professore," I said. "If I'm not prying."

"No, I am glad to tell it to someone. It is not good, secrets, you know? And it is a happy story, because that was not a joyous time for me, in Rome. Il Professore saved me."

"But you're from Naples."

"Sì. The biggest, poorest family in the whole place. Ten children, Mark, and when I am sixteen, they say, You have to go out now as your brothers did. Find your own way, and if you get a job with the FIAT, send money home."

"They threw you out on the street?"

He shrugged. "They had no choice. My father, he's always out of work. But some of my friends, you know, they say, Turi, you're handsome, you could sell it."

"Turi?"

"That was my name, Salvatore. They also say, You have to go to Rome, that's where they buy for big money. The Piazza di Spagna, they told me. You'll make it easy, Turi. But I don't have the money to go to Rome third-class. I don't have the money to *walk* to Rome."

"Wait—you were just going to...do this? Sell yourself?"

"What else can I do, Mark? I am not American college, like you. I am a young, naïve boy."

He smiled at me; I wondered, Does he know how appealing he is? Or does it just fall out of him?

"Perfino," he went on, "all my friends work overtime cheating tourists, and instead of a good-bye party they give me the money. So I am in Rome."

We had reached the water, and stood there, silent for a bit.

"Where would these people eat lunch?" he asked. "Are you going to nibble on the candles in the church?"

"There's a fancy taverna nearby, I gather."

He nodded.

"So," I said, "you arrived in Rome . . ."

"Ah. That was a bad time for me. Yes, there are plenty of frosci to look you over, maybe take you to dinner and then to bed. But—"

"Frosci?"

"Omosesuali. Finocchi, also, we call them. Soft. Not fighting, you know, Mark?"

"You'd be surprised."

"But the other boys were not kind to me. A man is talking to you. He is alone, his wife is dead, his children are all in the north. Now he says, Would you care for a little something to eat, I know a nice place? Suddenly Licinio comes over and tells the man, I know this boy, he is much trouble, you had better beware. He has the sex disease, he will rob you, something. Or some man would say, I want to see you fucking a girl and I would touch you then, wet and hot. I am thinking, How would the *girl* feel? Who is this girl that is willing? It is not nice, Mark. But il Professore, *he* was nice. He bought me a jacket and took me to the opera!"

"What did you go to?"

"I don't know. *The Knight Had a Rose?* Very nice but long."

He was scanning the horizon as if waiting for his own lunch party, his own boat, a transfer to something exciting.

"Did you ever meet a man named Ercolani?" I asked. "A movie director? Because he lives in Rome and I understand he fancies the Piazza di Spagna boys. Or even more dangerous kids. In the outlying districts."

"Oh, the borgate. Mark, that is praying for harm. They say, Sure, I fuck you, bend over. Then drops a weight on your head. Good-bye!" Vieri sang out.

"Ercolani's coming to lunch. That's why I—"

"It is only first names in that world. For protection. Not even the real first name. Or isn't it funny that all the men are called Giovanni?" He shrugged. "And I am Vieri. I heard it in a café on the Via Veneto once.

Such a name!, I think. Who has this name? I turn and see a man, so elegant and rich. Movie star, I think. He winks at me. To give me his name, I guess."

"Ercolani's first name is Giampaolo. And he's such a professional non-conformist that he's probably very open about his identity, even in the borgate."

"No, I don't know him," Vieri said, still searching the vista. "Will the buona diva be in his movie?"

"Surely not. But she likes to be courted."

Vieri gave me a poke, because there was Adriana's motorboat gliding down the channel. She was, as always, figged out to the nth, with a pagoda-like hat covered in a relentless silk veil. She looked like a priestess.

"I did not ever give them any power over me, Mark," Vieri assured me, his eyes on Adriana's boat. "Some days I went hungry. But I never let them fork me."

As the boat neared, I looked at the two men with Adriana. Ercolani, lean, intense, and, as always, dapper, sat next to her. Behind them was a fair man in his late thirties, also well-dressed. From the looks on all three faces, I sensed that they had had a somewhat less than sunny trip, and as the driver moored his craft, Adriana called out, "Sta bene, Mark," in her growly I-don't-like-anything-that's-going-on-here voice, and with that kill-all-the-hostages set of her features that made her seem so ungracious to strangers. The boatman jumped onto the dock to help the passengers dis-embark, and we made the introductions. Ercolani's friend turned out to be someone from the Film Festival who was going to collaborate with Ercolani on the script; anywhere but in Italy that would be viewed as an inflammatory conflict of interest. Ercolani made a sort of blasé little fuss over Vieri while Adriana briskly grabbed my arm and pulled me up the walk for what she called "a confidence."

"Mark," she whispered, "thank heaven you're here, because I have heard more philosophy and politics in the last hour . . ."

"Yes, Ercolani's a Marxist, you know."

She looked at me as if I had better be joking or a lunatic. "What are his movies like?"

"Sexy, violent, symbolic, and very artistic."

"Don't be ridiculous, Mark. How can anything be both violent and artistic?"

"Opera is."

She gave me another look, then turned back to find Ercolani strolling with Vieri, an arm around the boy's shoulder, as Ercolani's friend followed.

"And what is your *student* doing in our lunch?" Adriana went on, clearly exasperated but sparing me the full measure of her irritation. She did this too rarely, and with very few people, I noticed. Her chosen.

We were lunching outdoors at the Locanda Cipriani, where cognoscenti came to bask in the romantic torpor of this moribund island. Wine, cheese, pasta—even the bread—tasted different there, one was told, though the tavern itself was a modern construction, and there was an ultrachic swimming pool nearby.

Adriana followed the maître d'hôtel to the table, leading us all as if *we* were the women, while our neighbors buzzed and the host did that groveling thing. There was silence after we sat. Vieri, I know, was utterly bewildered to have been asked along, Ercolani was drinking in Adriana's features, and his friend was deferentially waiting for someone else to start off. Adriana shot me a *do something!* look, and I blurted out, "Bene, parliamo . . . del teatro." Let's talk theatre.

"Good, Mark," she whispered as the menus were passed around. But Ercolani managed to jump from Aeschylus to Pirandello to Dario Fo, whose satirical revue had just been closed by the authorities, precipitating skirmishes between students and police.

"You think I sympathize with the students?" Ercolani asked us all. "Già, in part, despite a certain, we can say, *exhibitionistic* quality to their protest. But what of the policemen, working-class men with families to maintain? These are people entirely innocent of history—yet they are trapped in a historical conjunction of the forces for liberalism, free expression, progress [he wagged his head to the left], and the forces for traditionalism, repression, stability [to the right] that they cannot understand. I sympathize with the police, too. E, perfino, they look so handsome and confused in their uniforms, strangely irresistible."

Adriana shot me another look, so I said, "Now we change the subject to the opera."

"An excellent choice," Adriana muttered again.

"No," said Ercolani in his crisp, detached manner. "It's too much opera. In Italy, the first art was church architecture. The second art was painting. The third art was music. But the *present* art is cinema. This is why I have come to you, Madama." Here he fixed Adriana with a look so articulate of love and awe that she was almost uneasy. "To bring the genius of your art to mine."

The table was quiet. Adriana liked praise, but she didn't like being stared at this intensely, and she made another silent appeal to me. I was out of ideas, though, and I turned to Vieri, who broke into his English catechism, addressing each of us in turn: "Yes, I am Vieri. I want to buy a towel. Shall we like your hairstyle? Do you want to make love?"

Ercolani and his friend just looked at Vieri, but Adriana threw her head back and laughed in that absurdly lengthy and delirious way people sometimes use when they're really letting off steam or decanting an anxiety. (Think of Garbo in *Ninotchka*.) The rest of us politely waited it out, but Vieri looked pleased, and I noted the other diners around us conferring, to get the story straight so they could tell it properly and be thought allknowing.

Everything ran smoothly after that: less because the ice had broken than because the dam had burst. We were all talking, all at once, idea after idea, notion upon notion; and Ercolani finally got specific about his movie, which greatly interested Adriana, if only for the afternoon.

"These Greek myths," Ercolani explained, "which we so commonly view as tales of murder, betrayal, incest, rape... What are they really? They are about *history*—about how political civilization overwhelms religious barbarism. Why else does the film begin with Tantalos eager to have his own son chopped up for the exquisite brodo he will serve at the famous banquet that launches the saga? The gods are attending, and it is right to give them something splendid. It is piety. And why does the film end with Orestes so unhappy at having to kill his mother to avenge his father's murder? Because *now* it is lawless to shed blood, especially one's own."

He held his hands out before us, as if to say, Now you see how art works. "Hmm," said Adriana, deep in thought, probably about what she would wear to the next cocktail party. She didn't like themes about her work; she liked working.

"So of course we will film the first sequences at the edge of the known world," Ercolani went on. "Those places where they live virtually as Tantalos did—Yemen, Africa. And we shoot the final sequences against the background of the Baroque palazzo—Palladio, Sansovino. The rhetoricians, one might say, of state power."

Turning to his friend, he said, "Perhaps you, lo Scenarista, have something to add."

"It is about glory," said his friend, eager but cool, prepared for this moment. "About people who live their whole lives as a gesture. People of naturally heroic character, incapable of dishonesty or compromise."

"But why me?" Adriana asked.

"*That's* why," Ercolani replied. "You are of this heroic character. You are Clytemnestra."

I hate to say it, but Adriana could be flattered; and when she was, she got all smiley and phony in a way that wouldn't have fooled your deaf and blind grandmother. Pressing his advance, Ercolani added, "It's about youth—most of the characters in the myth were teenagers at the time of their greatness." He turned to Vieri. "Like this boy. The perfect Orestes—sturdy, trusting, uncertain. Everyone finds him interesting, but what do they want from him?"

He turned to Adriana. "Come, may I? A little demonstration."

He led us out of the restaurant, to a meadow between the tavern and the pool—to our fellow diners' undisguised fascination—and proceeded to direct a sample scene, Vieri as Orestes and Adriana as Clytemnestra, while lo Scenarista and I looked on. Well, this was some stunt designed to win Adriana over. It *was,* clearly. For Ercolani, it was something between an audition and Flaunting It. He wanted to show Adriana that he was sharp enough to turn a pleasant lad like Vieri into a noble warrior with the stature of a Hamlet before her eyes; and he wanted to show her how he would direct an opera singer.

"How long have you lived in Venice?" lo Scenarista asked me while Ercolani staged the reunion of Clytemnestra and Orestes: the mother taking two steps forward and one step back, the son immobile and dreading, then circling around the mother, who was now forgiving but, I have to say, defiant.

"I've been in Venice," I said, "less than a year."

"Peacemaker!" Ercolani cried to the mother, moving his chess pieces. Then, "War bringer!" he called, to the son.

"How do you like it?"

As I was forming the young, unworldly American's typically inadequate encomium to the polished sensations of the Old World, lo Scenarista said, "I hate it here."

"Embrace!" Ercolani cried. *"No!* As if really . . . Sì! Ora, pianti! Famiglia! Amore!" Tears, family, love.

Adriana and Vieri were in each other's arms; the restaurant was transfixed. "The fervor of enmity!" Ercolani cried. "The honesty of hatred! All fear what is owed!"

"Florence," lo Scenarista said to me, "where I come from? *That* is a city. Glorious for two thousand years. The mother of the Renaissance. The cultural capital of Italia. Dante, Boccaccio, i Medici . . ."

"Each now say one word only!" Ercolani told his players.

The mother said, "Amo." I love.

The son said, "Temo." I fear.

"Si ritiranno," Ercolani coolly ordered. The players exeunt. The mother

wonderingly touched her son's cheek; the son looked to the giver of laws—
Ercolani—for guidance. But Ercolani said nothing. Adriana stalked off,
and Vieri stood where he was, bewildered.

"Bravissimi," Ercolani called at them, as the diners behind us actually
burst into applause. Adriana must have enjoyed herself, for she did a little
saunter kind of thing as she came back and tilted her chin up to show off
her neckline.

"Venice has been in retirement for over four hundred years," lo Scenarista told me. "A tourists' museum. Dead, oh yes." He lit a cigarette. "Do
you know how much history Florence made in the War? It was a center
of partisan action, and probably the major confrontation between the
German retreat and the Allied advance in all Europe. What happened in
Venice? Six fools fell into canals during blackouts!"

Ercolani had called his actors back for a huddle.

"The greed," lo Scenarista went on. "The corruption. The debauchery.
That is Venice. In Florence, everyone was concerned with profound questions on the relationship between God and man. The idealism. The role
of the state and the church in our life on earth. The nobility, the vitality!"
Squashing his cigarette, though it was scarcely lit, he chanted:

> La maggior don che Dio per sua larghezza
> Fesse creando ed alla sua bontate
> Più conformato e quel ch'è più apprezza,
> Fu della volontà la libertate.

(Which means, very roughly, "God's greatest gift to men, most valuable because it is most like Himself, was free will.") Lo Scenarista then gazed about,
at the greenery and the sky, as if . . . I don't know, communing with God's
vast nature, I suppose. "The *Commedia*," he finally said. "*Il Paradiso*."

Ercolani was running the exit again, and it was remarkable how much
more he had suddenly drawn out of what was, to all one's sensible surmise,
a self-protected musician who had never seen a movie, let alone been in

one, and an affable teenager of no artistry one knew of. Adriana had become Vieri's mother; Vieri had become Adriana's son, lover, and killer.

"One word only," Ercolani urged them.

"Lo voglio," Vieri shouted, cheating a little on the quota. I *will* this!

"Tutto per te," Adriana whimpered, weeping. For you, my child, anything. She tried to take his hand, but he furiously drew back, and, her features contorted, she raised her hand and would, I believe, have slapped him if Ercolani had not stopped her. He was pensive and satisfied. "Yes," he began. "Tutti questi miti . . . all history, you see . . . is produced by the hatred between the generations." He smiled. "E fine!" he cried. *Cut!*

Adriana was impressed, Vieri quite proud of himself, and Ercolani smug in, I must admit, a suavely unirritating way. We had done well, all of us, and it was a relatively merry crew that rode back to town, Vieri up front with the driver, Adriana with Ercolani, and I and lo Scenarista in the backseat.

"Well, they have a new anecdote to tell about the irrepressible Grafanas theatricality," I said as we turned into the channel and sped for home. "Rehearsing Greek tragedy on a meadow in Torcello."

"Do you know what is Terronia?" lo Scenarista asked. "It is the southern half of l'Italia. All rocks, huts, and animals. The people there are like a living dead. They eat roots and grass. They'd fuck cows if they could find one. Brothers marry sisters. We say 'Terronia,' meaning 'Big Ugly Stupid Land.' And who come from it are Terroni, you understand?"

He meant Vieri, and I said, "Take it easy, okay?"

Ignoring that, he went on, in a really resentful tone, "That boy is good-looking, oh yes, but in such a brutal way. For true beauty, you must apply to Michelangelo's David, of course. The elegance." He lit another cigarette. "You must not criticize the Maestro for paying this boy attention. This is typical of his bold voyage into the depths of corrupt society in his search for realism. He is a brilliant man, a genius, who says, 'The one thing that gives greatness to man is the fact that he will die.'"

"Look—" I began; but Adriana turned around and told us, laughing, "See, Vieri is steering the boat!"

And, with a little more this and some that, we managed to get back stimulated and content. The driver dropped us at the Salute, so Adriana, Vieri, and I came home by the street entrance, running into il Professore at the door. Adriana kissed Vieri and called him "caro." Then she pleaded with il Professore to join us for tea some afternoon. He was charmed, and shot me a subtle glance full of questions. I shrugged happily.

"Ben, sior barba," said Vieri, Venetian for Okay, uncle, let's go in.

Adriana was like some bride, twirling around and laughing. "Boy, you really enjoyed yourself," I said.

"Precisely how famous is this Ercolani?" she asked.

"Very."

"Is he married?"

"No, he's..." Should I? Well, this is Italy. "He's a homosexual."

She frowned and turned away, though many of her most influential collaborators were homosexual: the stage directors Amforto della Torre and Franco Zeffirelli, the conductors Leonard Bernstein and Nicola Inzenier—even, if you will, the photographer Luciana Costitù, who fell into Adriana's ambit after her fabulous weight loss, when she was starting to look the way Audrey Hepburn felt: or is it feel the way Audrey Hepburn looked?

"Why is it, everywhere I go, there is a ridiculous homosexual in charge?" Adriana wondered. "Why aren't they all in a cave?"

She didn't know about me, and I know I should have spoken up, but this was 1962 and we did things differently then.

4

The Critic

"Well," he began, in the intricate study of his I thought much too showy apartment in Padua, all tiny signed photographs in silver frames and old bound scores and the demonstration-level sound system, too American for Italy. "Well, *well*, well," he continued, slipping in a smile. "La Grafanas . . . Beh, ecco: She's not a voice, she's una fenomena dello spettacolo." A showbiz phenomenon. "She likes to be thought of as an opera singer, sì— but what does she mostly sing? Concerts! Three or four arias at most, a couple of overtures for the orchestra . . . Tell me, what has this to do with the art developed to the levels of Rossini, Bellini, Donizetti, Verdi? This has to do with making profit and playing to the arena public come to gawk at the famous."

He waited; I waited, too.

"No," he said. "This is about the *appearance* of a star. It is very much an American Hollywood thing."

He stirred his coffee, grinning as if to say, Protect her if you can.

"She has made history," I began, hating him for making me defend the unimpeachable. "Her reign at La Scala, for—"

"Oh, but yes!" he cried. "The cinema master della Torre directs, and she enters in toe shoes and, oh, those substantial Benois sets! It's so direly amusing—but is this opera, or sensation? The wondrous—oh no, really, the shocking—use of the principals in *Maria Stuarda* as an audience at the sidelines. Queen Elizabeth looking on in the execution scene, as her courtiers clinked flagons, cin-cin. Or that Hollywood *Puritani*—no, don't accuse me with your anguished stare, for that is what we all called it, with the principals decked out for Cinecittà. Or, then, that regrettably naturalistic *Rigoletto*, with the Act Two duet played as if a father were truly confronting his dishonored daughter. I will never forget seeing Tito Gobbi throwing away his jester's scepter, brashly hurling it onto the floor, in disgust at . . . You understand, he wasn't anymore the protagonist of Verdi's opera, but an angry father who—"

"That's exactly what's happening!" I told him. "The father thinks *he* is dishonored, failing to consider how his daughter must feel when—"

"That is not opera," he smiled out. "We are used to hearing the great works in certain ways. We are used to certain voices. Your Adriana—"

"She is not my—"

"Lo spettacolo!" he repeated. "Fans and headlines! Let us remember the very beginning of the Mercadante revival. Naples, March 1953. The first performance of *Le Due Illustri Rivali* in the twentieth century. Mercadante, our lost maestro. All musical Italy trained down to hear. And what is everyone talking of? The two *offstage* rivals, Adriana Grafanas and Renata Tebaldi, battling it out in the same theatre. No one is discussing lo stile Mercadantesco, with his revolutionary emphasis on ensemble, his moto drammatico, so swift and compelling, Verdiano before there was

Verdi. No, it is all gossip about the prime donne. Outside the theatre, as I was going in, I heard a fan exulting to a friend, 'Adriana e la Tebaldi nella stessa tragedia!'"

He extended his arms outward, mute with an inexpressible disdain.

"How was the performance?" I asked.

"Or consider that famous *Hoffman*, her second appearance at La Scala, after the debut as Luisa Miller."

"Wait, did you hear that Luisa Miller?"

He nodded, and I had him. Adriana's Luisa—sung this one season at La Scala—was legendary. "How was it?" I asked.

"The *singing* was stupendous, the comportment ugly, the voice irrational. Let us return to the *Hoffmann*."

"The *singing* was stupendous . . . No, stop"—because he was waving impatiently at me—"but the *voice* was irrational?"

"No one doubts her technical mastery. It is the sensuality of the timbre that I question. Its appeal as sheer sound. After all, Joan Sutherland has both the technique and the appeal."

"Adriana made Joan Sutherland possible," I felt bound to assert, "by reopening the Rossini-Bellini-Donizetti repertory for the many and various Sutherlands *and*"—he was going to interrupt here, but I plowed on—"no, I say, *and* by reestablishing the dramatic-coloratura as the essential singer of these composers' operas."

"The essential soprano, yes. The tenors and basses are still faking their way through the scores. And do you really believe that it was la Grafanas who breathed the spark of life back into those . . . *ashen* masters? I pray you pardon my sarcasm."

He bowed like a mandarin in the emperor's pleasure garden, coming upon a foe who is unaware that he is to be beheaded in half an hour. I bowed right back.

"The old works were revived," he said, "not because la Grafanas appeared but because contemporary composers had failed to supply the theatres with worthy art. You must not forget the Italian tradition of the opera d'obbligo, the brand-new piece that brings excitement to the season. At your Metropolitan, it is *Tosca* on Monday, *Lohengrin* Tuesday, and *Carmen* Wednesday. In Italy, we know these works already, and must balance them with novelty. We have heard nothing new *and* listenable since Benjamin Britten's *Peter Grimes,* so it was correct for impresarios and musicologists to exhume the forgotten but often quite extraordinary work of these nineteenth-century masters. I myself helped prepare the edition of Bellini's *Beatrice di Tenda* for La Scala just last year."

"Who sang that?" I asked.

"La Stupenda, of course."

"So this whole thing is Sutherland versus Grafanas, huh? That isn't music criticism. That's idolatry."

"Ma vedo chi parla," he replied contentedly. Look who's talking.

"No," I said, "because I see room for both singers. You want them mutually exclusive."

"Opera," he observed, "may *possibly* have room for the outlandish voice protected by imposing musicianship, or by a dynamic stage presence. But opera does not have room for the outlandish voice that has been *falling to pieces year by year by year!*"

He rose, went to the piano, and began touching the framed photographs as he called off their subjects' names. "Dusolina Giannini, Zinka Milanov, Ebe Stignani, Gina Cigna. Giuseppina Cobelli, the greatest Isolde and Eboli of the century. Margherita Carosio, whom la Grafanas replaced in the famous Venice *Lucia*s—but did she replace her sweetness, her charm, her lovability? Maria Caniglia, Rosetta Pampanini, Lina Pagliughi, Mafalda Favero. All beloved. Because their song was beautiful. And, perhaps most beloved of all, Toti dal Monte."

"Who came backstage after Adriana's Scala Lucia to announce—in tears, I should add—that not till that night did she understand what this role, one she had been famous for, was all about."

"These were opera singers," he went on, smiling that troublesome smile, so confident and so wrong. "They sang opera, not a couple of arias on television. They sang for decades, getting better year by year, till they sadly realized that they had passed their summit and bravely bade us farewell. Your Grafanas's voice has been deteriorating from her first night."

"Oh, you just—"

"Do not underestimate me, please," he said. "In 1947: La Gioconda, Modena. In 1948: Turandot, Naples; Isolde, Genoa. In 1949: Kundry, Florence and Bologna. In 1950: Isolde and Lucia in Venice, and Grafanas is famous—the Wagnerian who sang Donizetti, the newspapers called her! In 1951: Milan, Rome, Genoa, Venice, Florence, Mantua! I was there, I heard, I saw, I remember. Yes, the critiques, too, I remember, for the mask must be torn from the impostor's face. I admire your enthusiasm for what you love, because that is how one stays youthful. But you have mistaken yourself. Because she is so vigorous, so definitive, you believe her to be—"

"Definitive! You admit it?"

"Of herself. Now I skip to, hmm, 1958: Rome, half a *Puritani*. Milan: a revival of *Maria Stuarda*. London: a warmed-over *Tosca*, squally and pinched. Already, barely a decade after her debut, the voice is at a third of its former strength, the color of the middle voice is dim, and the wobble on the high notes is unforgivable."

"Not unforgivable," I said. "Momentarily annoying."

"Bene. But why is la Stupenda never momentarily annoying?"

"Joan Sutherland is never even momentarily exciting."

"There you are wrong." His voice went into reverie mode. "She is not *dramatic*, but she is certainly exciting. Many of those in the house, in her first years in Italy, had never heard such a voice. So lithe yet so big! The high D at half time in *Norma*—"

"Half time, you say. As if opera were—"

"Athletics? It is, in part. Isn't that why your Grafanas lost her voice? Can you imagine a wrestler walking into the ring after dropping fifty kilos? Voice is organs, hormones, vitamins. Eccoti, che canti." You are what you sing.

"But let's return," he said, "to that Scala *Hoffmann*. A golden age is upon us, we are told—at last, a soprano who can sing all three lead roles!"

"And she could!"

"Yes, and she asked, 'But will they pay me three times?'"

I was silent.

"Would Caniglia have thought of that? Carosio? Dal Monte?"

"They couldn't have pulled it off."

"I tell you, it is a case of lo spettacolo! The *business* of opera, not the music. More coffee?"

"Thank you, no."

"Please."

That European thing of Give in or you're being difficult.

"I don't want any," I said. "But weren't Adriana's *Hoffmann* heroines—"

"A brilliant Olympia, the robot—stiff, unyielding, alive only in the voice. A disastrous Giulietta, the courtesan, thick of voice and unbecomingly costumed. As Antonia...beautifully sung, but too grave and mature."

"But the showpiece of playing the different parts—"

"It was revelation. But of what? The ambition of Adriana Grafanas!"

"Did you never find her utterly first-rate?"

He thought for a moment. "In the early years, and always accepting the acrid quality of the voice," he allowed, "then, yes. She could be breathtaking. The Lady Macbeth, with true Verdian authority. The Kundry—yes, Wagner, but so expressive when sung this way. The Armida, for never before this had we heard such sheer volume and control in Rossini. And, of course, the Medea—a part, we recall, that was long thought unperformable because of its demands on the soprano."

"That was another of Adriana's distinguishing features, her ease in notorious monster parts. Turandot, la Gioconda..."

"But others have shown us beauty as well as ease. Italian opera goers have long memories, and we still celebrate the Turandot and Gioconda of the miraculous inglese, Eva Turner. *There* was strength combined with loveliness."

"Adriana is lovely, too—because she determined that she had to be and transformed herself."

"A ridiculous American idea. One does not become lovely—one does not become anything. One *is*. Otherwise, we are not speaking of talent, but of cosmetics."

"I will become," I promised. "I will transform. It is the national style."

He waved this nonsense away. "Isn't it interesting that it is the more eccentric, even lurid characters that seem to excite this performer? In the more standard roles, such as Desdemona or the *Trovatore* Leonora, she is quite ordinary. Without that disturbing personality to display, she must persuade strictly through the voice—and this she cannot do."

"Hold on, there. Whatever happens to Adriana now, and however many mere concerts she gives, she has had an undeniably important career. And no soprano can have a career in opera if she cannot sing."

"I did not say she cannot sing." He looked at me, sipped his coffee, sighed. "I *said* she has a vexatious voice. Listen to this story, if you please. At a Paris *Tosca*, just last year, in the third-act duet, your Adriana was approaching the perilous high note on 'Io quella lama li piantai nel cor.' "

This is Tosca recounting to her lover how she plunged a knife into Scarpia's heart, and Manfredi sang the phrase sotto voce for me.

"Everyone in the theatre can see that she dreads this note, and, indeed, she not only misses it but lets out such a ghastly shriek that she stops singing altogether. So . . . the orchestra simply breaks down—call it sympathy pains—and the public erupts in the usual riot of jeers from the unbelievers and heartening applause from her cohort. For a long, long time she stands immobile. What will happen? She signals the conductor that she will take up the music from the page before. 'No, no!' the fans cry. 'Yes, make her' is the judgment of the hostile faction. And *of course* this time she hits the C successfully and now the house truly *rocks* with cheers, as the adherents thrill and the enemies sulk in their seats." Eyebrows raised, he added, "She might have planned it."

I didn't think that worthy of a response.

"Now," he went on, "I ask you, is this about *Tosca*, or is this about la Grafanas herself? Lo spettacolo! Lo circo! Some, I grant, would call this 'opera at its most exciting.' I say it isn't opera. Because opera is not about the love of the audience, or the tears of the martyr. Opera is about beautiful song."

He reached for his coffee cup—no, it was empty. He gently pushed it away. He said, "I know many critics have attacked her as if they found her personally offensive. It must greatly distress her. They are like those who attend her performances precisely because they do hate her, because they hope she will fail so they can shout her out of music. But I am not so. I have the authority to support my contentions, and in any case I do not hope and do not shout. You say she is the nineteenth-century soprano revived. She is Giuditta Pasta, Maria Malibran. Maybe I wouldn't have liked them, either. Not everyone did, you know."

"Maybe I will have more coffee," I said.

"Sta bene," he said, leading me to the kitchen, "and we will look over my tapes and see if there is anything you'd like to hear."

"Anything with Adriana?"

He sighed. "The *Macbeth,* the *Luisa Miller,* the *Armida,* the *Alceste*—though Flagstad is infinitely superior, in a relay from Danish radio. Now, *that* is the voice for which—"

"You don't by any chance," I said, still in Adriana's camp, "have her *Adriana Lecouvreur,* do you?"

He stopped—posed, almost, coffee filter in one hand and electric grinder in the other. A somewhat modern man, in certain ways. "Why that one?"

"My favorite singer in my favorite opera."

He turned the grinder on. Then, spooning out the coffee, he said, "That's the *Adriana* from Venice, 1949. A very rare item. I know no one who owns it and only a few who've even heard it."

"Have you?"

"Certainly." Seeing my look, he added, "It's glorious, if you can bear that voice. The expressiveness is heartrending. Such nobiltà, fantasia, sfumatura." He fondled the very sound of these words as he spoke, as only Italians can. (How flat they play in English: nobility, fantasy, nuance.) "She actually suggests a woman to whom art is as important as love."

"Art *is* more important to Adriana."

"Rubbish. Women live for love alone. Anyway, if you're hunting for elusive Grafanas tapes, the one everyone's after is a Chicago *Trovatore*, with—"

"No, I want *my* Adriana. Tell me, is there anyone who could put me in touch with that tape?"

"I'm sorry, not to my knowledge. You know these collectors—they want exclusives. Somewhere, supposedly, there's a pirate with a tape of the Grafanas Isolde, from Genoa in 1948. Now, that even *I* would love."

Coffee cups refilled, we proceeded to the music room for a concert, all live performances from the bootleg underground. The Critic graciously emphasized Adriana, though he would then shadow her with (he reckoned) her superiors: Eva Turner in Turandot's Riddle Scene; bizarre snippets of Cobelli's La Scala Isolde that must have been taped at the bottom of Lake Garda; and the spectacular Scala *Ugonotti* of the previous year, with Sutherland, Simionato, Cossotto, Corelli, Tozzi, and Ghiaurov. Talking was forbidden during the music, but we passed some lively intermissions challenging each other's opinions. Then, as he retrieved a tape from the machine and boxed it with a conclusive gesture that told me the interview was finished, he said, "I hear Ghiringhelli is consulting with Madama over a possible return to La Scala next season. I hear *Le Nozze di Figaro*, *Manon*, *Semiramide*, even a revial of the *Ugonotti,* this time with la Grafanas. Ghiringhelli offered her the Queen—she said no, Valentine has the big scene. Ghiringhelli offered her Valentine—she said no, the Queen has the top line. Can her arrogance never be placated?"

I rose, saying, "Everyone's consulting. London, Paris, the Met—"

"La Scala is special. It was by becoming la regina della Scala that la Grafanas became assolutissima in opera. The quarrel with Ghiringhelli and her subsequent exile from the theatre must sorely hurt her. A return would seem as if . . ."

"As if she hadn't lost it?"

He smiled. "You put it well."

"Tell me why critics would feel threatened by her."

"Because most critics are ignorant frauds who managed to park themselves in their positions by fooling their publishers. They don't know music any more than I know aeronautics. They fear the imaginative, the unusual, because they do not know how to assess it. They regard anything out of the ordinary as a reproach to their own mediocrity. Listen to this very true story, which will frame my perception: the music critic of the most powerful newspaper in the world was a relentless foe of Adriana's. Was it because her obvious sense of command threatened his pathetically unconstructed ego? Was it because a new development in music brings out the authorities to debate, and he feared being made to look a fool? It was not because he didn't like the voice itself, because he had no idea what he liked or didn't like. Imagine a fraud like this man, who has no idea. Imagine his terror when something comes to town that must be understood. Not necessarily admired, I hasten to add. But understood, certamente. His idiot reviews report that she cannot sing. But she stays, she stays. She *returns*. She is more famous, more more famous. Illustrissima. He must, he knows, address what she represents, yet *he has no idea*."

He was smiling at me now as if we were the only two people who can get this joke. As if we had something in common.

"Meanwhile, he is having a record evening with a young friend of his. They play, they discuss. The friend, eager to . . . reeducate this critic, slyly puts on one of la Grafanas's first records, a 78. The critic is overwhelmed— who is this glorious singer? The 78 has fooled him, of course: he expected someone from the old days, one whom everyone has already typed. Imagine his embarrassment and fury at having been caught in such a revealing inconsistency."

It was leaving time, and we moved to the door. About to open it, he paused, looked at me, smiled once again, and said, "I will tell you something. If your idol continues to sing at her present disadvantage, snatching high notes as if defying the gods, now confronting and now soothing her public, weeping and canceling and collapsing . . . Well, they will make a saint of her. Because, like any martyr, she bears our pain."

As he opened the door, he said, "I admit it, we put her through hell. But watch. It will change. One day, an assault on la Grafanas will question even the most fundamental reputation."

"She bears her own pain, actually," I said, offering my hand.

Taking it, he said, "All pain is one. Thank you so much for coming today. I truly enjoyed it. Arrivederci."

And the great carved wooden door closed tight.

5

The Roots
That Clutch

I suppose I should say something about who I was sexually: I liked boys, trim boys, trim sweet deep-eyed quick-to-laugh come-on-you-know-you-like-me boys. I'd met a few, even knew some intimately, but had never been able to, so to say, make the scene with them. What scene? It was invisible then, a nameless rumor, or at least a very secret club.

Every now and then, someone would wave at you from a clubhouse window—for instance, when I slept over with my best friend, Kurt Carmines, and when we were in our pajamas he showed me how they judge the legs in girls' beauty contests, by running their hands up and down their calves. He asked to do this several times, and it got us breathless but nothing else.

Or when I spent a weekend with my cousin Tim, and I got up in the middle of the night for water and passed the open doorway of Tim's older brother Frank's room. The lights were on and so was Frank, nude, full-mast, and pulling on it while not only staring into the full-length mirror on his closet door but also spitting into it. He saw me and whirled around and I said, "Hi, Frank," as at a prom. He said, "Come here, you," and I ran away.

Not much to tell, huh? So when summer spilled in on us and all Venice took to the beach, I felt energized. The Lido is a highly touted beach, but what I loved about it was the quantity of Swedes interrupting their Grand Tour for an afternoon of warmth and water. Adriana maintained a cabana at the Excelsior, and as she almost never used it, Vieri and I were there all the time. He liked to hold races in the water, and have towel fights, and cut a deck of cards (as in American movies) to see who would pay for our end-of-the-day gelato, which were like tiny Good Humors. Sometimes, as we came out of the ocean. he would shake himself like a dog, grab me, and say, in English, "How much ayou like ame, Mark? This much?" (His hands close and his tone low.) "Or *this* much?" (His hands wide and his voice a shouting smile.) I felt I must be in love with him. I had to be: or why was I so triumphant in having impact on him? Vieri would say, "If you go back to America now, Mark, Vieri just..." He would make a throat-cutting gesture.

"I won't return to America," I promised, "till I'm absolutely finished here."

In Italy you never know whether someone loves or likes you: it's the same verb. Vieri would use it sorrowfully, lovingly, amazedly, his eyes wet and wide—and I would feel, for an exquisitely terrifying moment, that he was going to make some overt move so that our friendship could move onto the, uh, higher plane. But that comes later in the story.

The Gossip was often at the Lido, too, getting photographed with the Duke and Duchess of Windsor and shuffling around a lot of people she ardently referred to as "great ones," though they could fairly be termed so only in comparison with your Uncle Cornelius. No doubt that's why she most tensely doted on the Windsors. I suppose nowadays they are a picturesque footnote in social studies, but at the time they were hot copy.

"One feels so *vital* when the Windsors are by," the Gossip told me. Yet they were dead people. Their lives ended when he renounced the only throne that mattered in the Western world; scarcely a fly bite had happened to them since. Though the press mentioned them incessantly, they weren't news: they were tattle.

Two of the Gossip's genuine great ones were the Prince and Princess. She had virtually adopted them, rhapsodizing to all within her compass about the Princess's incredibly high-bred skin tone: "so *white*, my dear, that you can see the blue veins running right through her! And the body is so very *lavishly* constructed! She lets me sit in on her massage, don't you know—some strenuous Turk she found in Berlin, who gives the most . . . But, oh, to see her laid out on the table, so delicate yet so . . . very . . . physical." And the Gossip would stop there, quite quite still. You see, we all need to talk about our romances, even a pathetic little troll who is once again facing an unrequited obsession for a beauty of the great world.

I'll tell you who else liked the Princess: the Actor. On the beach, at Adriana's cabana, the two would cut themselves off from the rest of the world and converse in low, serious tones for hours, like people who are going to take time to get there but who will, when time comes, do it deep and slow, and that's what I call penetration.

Adriana avoided the beach but wanted verbatim reports on all that transpired there; she even (mildly) scolded me a few times when I said I was too busy to go.

"Busy teaching that *Vieri*, I suppose!" she railed.

"No, actually, we always hold his lessons on the beach now."

"Well, go teach him," she said, suddenly calma calma. "How will he learn when you are so negligent?"

I didn't like to go because I hated telling her about the Actor and the Princess. I admit I gentled all that down and concentrated on the antics of the Gossip.

"She's throwing a party for the Prince and Princess," I warned Adriana, "but wants you to host."

"If only I could," she said. "I have Amina to master." This was for a projected *L'Elisir d'Amore* in Lisbon that I knew would never happen.

"You learned that in four days," I said. "Last month."

"I learn everything in four days, true. But it is good to let a role grow into the voice over a period of time."

"Want to see the scrapbook? I finished it."

She smiled sadly. "You left it in the living room as a delightful surprise, but how could you know how rigid and . . . oh, how regrettable all that is to me today."

"You're only talking about the major career in postwar opera," I said.

"Built with such care," she answered, "and so wasted. Your scrapbook."

"No, yours. But it'll help me on your book, anyway."

"Tell me more about the beach. Nik—is he uproarious, like a perform-ing bear?"

Her tone was so tactfully casual, so very nearly successfully deceptive, that I realized that despite all I was leaving out of my reports, she sensed that the Princess was menacing her. What had she heard? The way the Actor X-ray-visioned his way through her clothes so understandingly that I'd have to term it an ontological casing of the joint? The way she looked when their sentences trailed off? Had the Gossip done some malicious blurting out?

"Tell me," Adriana begged. "For I love him so much that to hear of even his least . . . well, imposing undertaking . . . is my new music."

"They're right," I said. "You have a weird way of speaking your native language."

"My native language is opera. Whose pardon do I ask for that?"

"Boy, you won't show a soft side."

"Nik on the beach . . ." she prompted.

I shrugged. "You know how it is. Everyone's busy and nothing hap-pens."

"He talks . . ."

"Sure."

"The Princess, I hear, is a captivating conversationalist."

I was at the dining room table, she at the piano. We were each sort of working.

She said, "Nik told me that never in his life since he was twelve has he not been in love. Never once." Her voice was light and her style uninflected. "The Princess, is she nice to you?"

"She sort of ignores me."

"Is she nice to Nik?"

"Yes." I spoke evenly, but you should have seen those two on the sand, looking deep into each other and spotting the next stop.

"She is beautiful, as they say?"

I gave nothing. Couldn't.

She nodded. "Very, very beautiful, naturally so, whatever she wears, no makeup, no psychological preparation. She appears by magic and everyone is . . ." A tremolo on the keyboard. "Fetched by her, sì?"

"She's a woman on a beach," I said. The understatement—as we put it then—of the year.

"As Nik is a man on a beach?" she asked, ever so gently.

I nodded.

"È vana parola," she whispered, "che invano risuona!" Empty words are empty comfort.

"I guess I don't know anything about life," I said, "but after the glory you've known on stage, with all those people going out of their gourd to show you respect . . . How important can some man be?"

"You know," she said, "he is to stay in the apartment of this Prince and Princess in Rome when he is filming next month?"

"So?"

"You don't see her . . . dropping in?"

"You know what's crazy? In opera, you're the master of men—Medea, Norma, Tosca. You wipe up the floor with them. But the way you're talking now, you sound like . . ."

She turned to face me. "A slave of love?"

"Looks that way, lady."

She smiled. "I should learn to be wistful, like that American actress—you know, so mousy and poetic. She played Jeanne d'Arc in that Anouilh play in New York."

"Julie Harris."

"Yes, *wistful.* Then everyone would approve of me." She got up and struck a pose, the fingers of her right hand tastefully outlining her left cheekbones. "I'm so farouche, please love me," she mock pleaded.

"No," I told her. "Your greatest quality is that you made your own rules. You don't need anyone's approval."

She looked amazed at that, and I realized how wrong I must be. I had always thought that all she needed was freedom. I thought that's all anyone needs.

"All right, earn your keep," she said, sitting at the table, "and tell me about this House of Atreus."

"Oh, you'll want to read the *Oresteia*, and maybe—"

"Read? This is a movie, not a baccalaureate examination."

"Well, how do you normally get the background on a part?"

"Background? I just do it."

"So when you sang *The Tales of Hoffmann* you didn't read E. T. A. Hoffman's stories to—"

"What do *stories* have to do with singing Offenbach, may I ask?"

"Wow."

"The House of Atreus," she repeated, tapping her finger on the table for service.

"Well, it's this great dynastic saga about how your destiny is created by the actions of your ancestors—that you suffer for their sins."

She pondered this. "So," she said. "An evil parent will make you crazy with evil treatment?"

"No, it's not Freudian. It's not rational. An evil *great-grandparent,* even, who was dead before you were born, will destroy your life through the very shadow of his wickedness. It's as if certain sins are such an offense to the gods that the only expiation is for the entire bloodline to die out, in torture and despair."

"That's life in Greece, all right. Now tell the story."

"Too long. But the outline is, one, Tantalos serves his son to the gods at a banquet. This is bad enough—but then, two, his son, Pelops, while courting his wife-to-be, breaks his oath and murders the man who made the marriage possible. And by courtship I mean he has to beat her father at a chariot race or be killed himself. Anyway, the guy Pelops kills, with his dying breath—"

"That's the best way," Adriana put in.

"Well, *he* puts a curse on Pelops and all his line. So now the family is rotten to the core, and then, three, Pelops's son Atreus has another of those banquets, feeding to his brother, Thyestes, the flesh of Thyestes's children."

"And he gobbles them up?" she asked, getting into it.

"Unwittingly."

"They always say that."

"Anyway, Thyestes redoubles the curse, and by now this family is in big, big trouble. In fact, Thyestes sires a child by his own daughter—"

"Unwittingly, no doubt," Adriana sardonically put in.

"No, on oracular advice. But, obviously, their child, Aegisthos, will live as nothing but an instrument of revenge, and—"

"Now Clytemnestra," she breathed out.

"You sure love a good story, don't you? Clytemnestra was married at knifepoint to Agamemnon, the son of . . . Want to guess?"

"It has to be Atreus."

"Why?"

"That sews it up tight," she said. "Anyway, it's called the House of Atreus, isn't it? *Oh!*" She laughed. "I just got a joke, about six years late. It was during rehearsals for my Scala *Medea,* and suddenly the order came down that Rosanna Carteri would not sing Glauce after all. We were all on stage when this happens, it's very embarrassing. Ghiringhelli was no-where to be seen, of course. He did everything through minions. They walked Carteri around, cajoling her, explaining with this lie and that. She was a wonderful singer, actually too major for such a small role. Everyone thought *I* must have fired her, because she would...yes, *challenge* my reign. But in *Medea,* who cares who sings Glauce? *Medea* is not a two-soprano opera. Besides, if I had really wanted to hurt Carteri, I would have left her in the part but had them cut her aria. *That* is humiliating.

"Nevertheless. They kept trying to make light of what was happening, as if anyone in opera can be replaced for mysterious reasons. They told Carteri, 'We're one big happy family alla Scala, no?' And Carteri said, 'Yes—the House of Atreus.' Now we see what dark meaning she intended."

I scoffed. "Was it so dark as that? An opera company?"

"More than she knew."

"Okay, Clytemnestra. She has every reason to hate Agamemnon, because he sacrificed their daughter Iphigenia, in order to launch the Trojan War. And Aegisthos had every reason, too."

"So he and Clytemnestra become lovers and they kill Agamemnon."

I smiled. "How did you know?"

She shrugged. "I'm Greek."

"Now their son, Orestes, has to avenge his father's murder. But to do so, he must kill his mother. In myth, not to redeem blood murder is unforgivable: and to commit blood murder is unforgivable. He is trapped in a maddeningly sensible paradox—a fitting climax to the perfectly reasonable and utterly insane menu of Tantalos's banquet."

"Yes," Adriana agreed. "Yes, yes. Yes, yes, yes, because I am now killing *my* mother. With neglect, yes, but still. They want to pillory me for it. The *morons!* I send her money on the condition that she keeps her stupid idiot mouth closed. If she shuts her mouth, I'll support her. If she talks to the press—as, believe me, she *lives* to do—I'll let her starve in the street. So she has her choice. And *what does she do?*"

"You want to play Clytemnestra or not?"

"I want to play Orestes. But isn't this an old boring European scheme for a movie? Because the past is nothing—it's the present that shapes the future, no?"

"Right."

"Right—in the States. Everyone starts out fresh from birth in America. We believe we can turn into what we need to be. No?"

"You know, this is the first time I've heard you speak of America as a—"

"Americans don't have destinies," she said, piecing it together. "They have obsessions."

Deodata flowed in just then with a late-afternoon tray, and we dug in and moved on to other things. Suddenly Adriana said, "If I let my mother die in the street, they'll hate me, of course. You know how sacred mothers are in Italy."

"In America, too."

"But will I just endure some bad press, or will I inflict a curse upon myself?" She was smiling, biting around the edges of a biscuit. "Will I be ... playing chicken with destiny?"

"A family curse is like frostbite. You don't know you have it till it's already destroying you."

Deodata often told me how she wished la Siora would reconcile with her mother, but would immediately admit that if Adriana felt that alienated, there must be a reason. Deodata was, also, the only member of the household who took any notice of the scrapbook: she adored it. Many times, I would blunder into the kitchen to find her paging through it as a mystery buff traverses Agatha Christie. Deodata was vocal in reply to the forces that buffeted Adriana. To the rave reviews: "Bele parole." Well said. To the disparaging editorials: "Che scandolo da piazza." What a disgrace. To the bad reviews: "Bute parole." Ugly stuff.

"It's great to have everything together like that," I told Deodata one evening. "The whole Adriana. Of course, it's only the public Adriana." Conspiratorially, I added, "We have to know the private Adriana. I need interviews."

"From *me,* Signor Trigga?"

"The human interest angle. Come on," I urged.

"Gnente. Che bisogno ghe xe?" I'll tell nothing. Why should I?

I pulled my chair closer to hers for that comradely effect. "It's not enough to tell what Adriana is like as a singer. The reader has to ken the *person.* Or what's the point of the book? Everybody knows how great she is. Everyone with ears. Do you know there's a whole subindustry in tapes of her performances? The Covent Garden *Norma,* the La Scala *Norma,* the . . . I don't know *Norma.* It's a new idea. Any other singer's night at the opera vanishes into the ozone as the curtain falls, but Adriana is preserved."

"But why?"

"She's special."

"Ah, sì—"

"Not just because of the singing. She's special because . . . well, because it matters so much to her to be special. Look, fans write in from all over. They keep talking about these tapes. In America, they're starting to issue them on contraband records. Because it's too important to lose!"

"Madona!"

"They write in and ask if she knows where they can find the Mexico City *Puritani,* the Florence *Masnadieri,* the Scala *Luisa Miller.* Or they say, I *have* the *Puritani,* will you trade it for *I Racconti d'Hoffmann?* This is something new in opera, and it's because Adriana is new. We *have* to explain her!"

Deodata said nothing and looked miserable.

"Just give me some notes on her life with Ambarazzi."

"Oh, Signor Trigga! It is not right."

"Sure it is. I'm the priest, you confess."

She was outraged, though I got a shocked laugh out of her.

"Just a few observations," I begged. "The most innocent background touches. Like, did she really love that ridiculous old man?"

"Tu cattivo!" You wicked boy. "To speak so of the dead!"

"*Did* she love him?"

"Oh, yes, she loved, what else, they were married!"

"Does the Princess love the Prince?"

Deodata shrugged. "Francesi." The French, who knows what they'll do?

"It has been whispered," I said, "that Adriana was using Ambarazzi. That she married him so he would support her and serve as an aggressive agent with impresarios while she forged her career."

"Sior Mark! *Who* could . . . yes, *whisper*, I believe it, dasseno! To repeat such things about la Siora! She *adored* el Paron! When she left for an engagement abroad, she was heartbroken to part from him. And the letters she wrote— well, he showed them to me! He was so proud. And then, when she . . ."

Deodata trailed off, looking behind me. At the Gossip, I discovered.

"Just checking on the collation for tomorrow," said the Gossip. "Sur la plage? It's the first big do for our *sumptuous* Princess in Venice, and it *has* to be *right*."

"It will be right, Siora," said Deodata, after I had translated, getting up and going to the oven. "Would you like to inspect the chicken?"

"You know, the Prince has given me *absolute* authority in running this matinée, and I must be certain . . ."

Deodata looked at her; I hadn't moved.

"Yes," said the Gossip. "Yes, well . . . Oh, what's this?" she cried, slinking up to the scrapbook. She opened it. "Clippings! It's my world, don't you know?"

"You're right there in it," I said.

"Oh, it's all Adriana, I see. Yes. Well. Hmm. Music, la." She dropped the book closed. "Well, I'll see you all tomorrow on the Lido, see if I don't!"

Out she went, as Deodata and I shared a look.

"La xe una zentila veciazza," said Deodata, deadpan. What a nice old hag.

"She won't be with us much longer," I observed. "She has a new love." We left it at that.

Indeed, at the big do the next day, the Gossip was all over the Princess and could scarcely tend the reception itself, though every so often she took a swat at a flunky or yapped "That vase goes there" at some waiter. Cocktails and swimming at a cabana on the beach—it sounded amorphous to me, so showy yet so recreational. What was the etiquette for meeting a Princess while dripping wet in a towel? Was it preposterous, jazzy, or a panacea to swim in the sea on a Campari and soda?

Yet how quickly the party took shape, as carefully timed (I presumed) entrances brought forth the debonair Prince and his sumptuous Princess, both in white seared by red scarves; then the Actor, jaunty in lederhosen and the wide-mesh shirt that was to become the rage of Italian men's beachwear that year; then the Duke and Duchess, old but trim; then Adriana, graciously haughty and as festooned as a Maypole, like a slow introduction to and the allegro proper of a major romantic symphony going off at once; and the many guests began to circulate and the whole thing fanned out on the sand; and the paparazzi closed in.

I was at the water's edge with Vieri, watching passersby lurk and stare while I taught him how to chew gum American-style. Vieri was particularly taken with the method of parking chewed gum behind the ear during earnest interludes, then popping it back in your mouth. He liked to run into the surf shouting and splashing, dive deep down and come up streaking toward the wooden raft moored even with the end of the breakwater, mount the raft and attempt a handstand, then come barreling back to me at the shore. He would lunge out of the Adriatic like Dionysus on a tear, sleek and hot in his joy.

I would tell him, "You are beautiful." I couldn't help it. I didn't want to help it. I could make him laugh and need my teaching and admire me, yet he was a mystery in certain ways. I told myself that only respect for il Professore's primary rights to Vieri restrained me. In truth, like all young American gay men of the early 1960s, I didn't know the moves. Or: I could figure them out but had no idea how to reach them. Here's what I wanted to do: sit on the edge of a bed with Vieri in front of me, holding and feeling him, freeing his sweet nature to respond to me, kiss him and whisper evil teases into his ear till he was tender and completely yes, and then—because in love, less than the ultimate is nothing—I would, to use his term, fork him. But you can't just say May I, can you?

Il Professore joined us, a little too suited up for the beach, like Gustav von Aschenbach.

"They say it is the most lovely beach in the world," he told me, as Vieri dropped into the wet sand to dig and make mischief. "Glamorous. Revelatory. It is a beach of many tales. But did not your own T. S. Eliot write, 'Che sono le radici che s'avvinghiamo, che rami crescono da queste pietrose rovine'?"

" 'What roots cling, what branches grow from these rocky ruins'? Oh, *The Waste Land*! The original's a little different, but—"

"At such events as this," il Professore went on, indicating the V.I.P.s and hangers-on grouping and regrouping before us, "many all too miscreant characters slide out of the undergrowth to feed upon one."

"Everyone's after something," I said.

He nodded—then, noticing two appealing young women walking toward us at the waterline, and seeing (as I did) that they were looking at Vieri, il Professore quickly shot a checkup glance at him. Vieri, working on a sand castle, was grinning at the girls. Had they been Americans, they would have struck up a chat, but that is not the local style; they stopped and stood in the water, lazily patterning the sand with their toes as they glistened in the sun. Vieri stood up and took a step toward them, but then, feeling il Professore's eyes at his back, he shrugged and returned to his castle.

I was ready to follow up on our conversation, but il Professore was intent on the girls. He wanted them gone. His features stayed blank but, I knew, he was *willing* them off, like a conjurer who works without a wand. It took a minute or two, but seeing that Vieri was ignoring them, they wandered off whence they had come.

"It's about achieving," said a voice behind us. It was lo Scenarista. "All these various people, trading plans and building, creating, it seems to me." He, too, indicated the party. "The alchemy! The metamorphoses!"

I introduced him to il Professore, adding, "Of course you remember his nephew, Vieri," who looked up, smiling, as lo Scenarista sneered.

"Is Ercolani here?" I asked.

"No, in Rome. But many others are here, from la Mostra"—he meant the Venice Film Festival; the knowledgeable Venetian calls it nothing else—"and also Cannes."

"Yet our hostess is of the world of music," il Professore pointed out. "Here, at her party, one expects musicians, perhaps a party from our celebrated theatre, La Fenice. Centuries ago, such parties as this, in Venice, rang with the serenades of Monteverdi, Gabrieli, Cavalli. The gondolas swam through music."

"All the arts are one today," lo Scenarista replied, puffing out cigarette smoke as il Professore took a step backward, not impolitely. "It is for the greater glory of all things. There is no more Italian art, French art, German, oh *yes*. It is one amazing Europa."

"I would comprehend one Europe only with the greatest difficulty," il Professore replied. "I am scarcely used to one Italy, having spent all my days in the protecting, nurturing life of the lagoon."

"But you must know Florence."

"I have no need of Florence."

"No need?" Lo Scenarista laughed. Roared, actually. He was performing just a bit. "All Italians are by birth subject to the laws of Florence. The creativity, the intellect, the piety."

"Those are almost exactly the last words of the philosopher and black-mailer Cazzo di Giglio," il Professore announced, with a merry wink (at me), "before he was torn to pieces by mastiffs escaped from the private zoo of Cosimo the Crapulous."

I guess lo Scenarista was stunned, because I saw his mouth move but heard nothing. Anyway, the Actor came rushing down in the typically indecent Italian bathing suit, distracting us by roughhousing with Vieri, who tore after him into the sea.

"Quello Greco mi sembra un Ulisse," il Professore observed, looking after the Actor and Vieri. "Il mare l'affascina." That Greek is a Ulysses: the sea enchants him. Smiling, il Professore took his leave of me, ignoring lo Scenarista, and rejoined the party.

"His *nephew*," said lo Scenarista. "A Venetian has a nephew from Terronia, sì. The true aesthete *idealizes* beauty. He does not grab for it, shove in and deflower it."

"Isn't Ercolani notorious for his sexual escapades?" I asked.

"That is his glorious artistic struggle, as I have told you."

"He's very big on the Terroni you so dislike, too."

Lo Scenarista paused to collect his thoughts. "I do not understand this of him, it is true. The indignity. The impurity. These are people without a history, without a destiny. Yet he is impressed with your friend there." (Looking out to sea.) "He threatens to cast him as Orestes. But this is a prince, educated and heroic . . ."

He trailed off as one of the day's Swedes strode forth from the inexpensive cabanas at the back, heading for the water. Heavy-shouldered and long-waisted with skin like armor, he was some torrid Viking, houseproud on the most competitive beach in Europe, and I caught lo Scenarista taking him in.

"Is that your Orestes?" I asked, and he blushed. He said, "Come," took my arm, and led me a few paces to some men who were laughing and knowing and English. They were also effeminate in an aggressive way: a hostile softness, I thought. They said, "Oh, you're the one doing the book!," their eyes soaring to heaven. They said, "Well, we know some tasty stories, won't cost you much for all you'll get," with sidelong glances at one another and giggles on the sly. They said, "American men are the sexiest of all, the big ruthless beasts. We don't mean you, silly."

I just walked away. I was now at the party itself, in the thick, watching the Princess being the most desirable woman in the Western world, checking in with Adriana (she seemed tired); enjoying the Gossip as she cawed out "Those paparazzi are sampling the pâté!" and rushed off to repel them; and meeting this one and that. I was talking to the Prince and then the

Princess, ready to field that absurdly themeless yak one makes at these parties. Only the Princess said, "You are working with Adriana on her story of life. You are her eyes. What have you seen?"

Can I say this about her? She was what men most want: voluptuous yet tidy, long-lined, fair, and smooth as a cue ball. Her light brown hair tumbled in confident waves, her gaze took you in so comprehensively that you must win her approval or wither away, her mouth lay in a permanent half-smile, as if suggesting that life in her circle was as much blunt truth as feathery satire. I could see why women (except the smitten Gossip) would have no use for her, and why men (except my kind) would study her.

"What have I seen?" I repeated pensively. "I suppose this is one of those loaded European questions."

She laughed.

"I see *you,* anyway," I said amiably. Then I added (to my shame, but I have a tendency to blurt out unexpected confidences, probably in order to appear bohemian and unpredictable), "So does the Actor. See you, I mean. Adriana has been following your progress."

"She finds me threatening?" A reasonable question.

"No great artist can be threatened by matters irrelevant to art," I lied.

"She is sophisticated, philosophical? Self-centered, grasping? She sees all women as rivals?"

"Who wouldn't, with a guy like Nik?"

She laughed again, because I had thrown the last phrase out in English. "It is a sort of title for one of your Hollywood movies, I am thinking," she told me. "*A Guy Like Nik.*"

The Gossip joined us with a deep sigh. "Everyone wants a piece of me, you know," she announced. "It exhausts one fending them off. They must love me from afar. *Oh!* That insolent paparazzo is back at the pâté!" She clumped off to fix his clock.

"Cavolo," said the Princess, with delicacy. The word means "cabbage," but Italians use it to express dissatisfaction of almost every kind.

"Che cosa cavolo?" I asked.

Her hand waved ever so slightly around us. "Questa divina commedia."

But now came the big moment, as hostess Adriana made her official way over to her honored guest, the Princess. All grew silent, watchful, as the photographers leaped about the two stars, catching them from various angles. I wanted to move out of the way, but Adriana grabbed my arm as if to steady herself. Later, many of the attendees asked me what was said; I looked wry and replied, "When divas collide . . ." In fact, they had little to say.

One exchange caught me, when Adriana complained that she was prone to naps in the evening that would prostrate her and make it difficult for her to retire at a reasonable hour thereafter. The Princess said there was an excellent drug available to counter this.

"You understand," she warned, "it is contraband. It flutters the heart. But there is a doctor who can prescribe it, if you are properly recommended and have no history of trouble with the heart."

"I have no history," Adriana smiled out.

"The drug is called la Fleur," said the Princess. "There are those, I hear, who take it for pleasure. For the amusing tingle it provides."

"Have you tried it?"

The Princess said nothing—then, chin high, shook her head once, as if resisting more than denying. But now the Actor snuck up behind the two women, pressing their necks with wet hands to make them jump and cry out, like a schoolboy on a dare. These women were too cool to fall into his game; they were surprised but ironic, bemused. All Europe was watching.

Lo Scenarista had come up with the actor, and now we all chatted. The subjects were, in this order: la Mostra; the grand folly that is Cinecittà; Fellini; the mock-American policier that the Actor was about to make in Rome with Forzano; Humphrey Bogart; and Ercolani and the movie *he* was about to make (he fervently hoped) with Adriana, who did one of her preening "We'll see" numbers.

Then Vieri joined us, bearing a selection of seashells for the Princess. Lo Scenarista began steaming like a tea kettle as our Vieri explained to the Actor the authentic American method of chewing gum, as a tip for the Actor to take to Rome; then lo Scenarista blew his top, denouncing Vieri as an actor, a person, and a representative of a people.

"It is not effective!" he kept saying; and he pushed Vieri, who couldn't figure out what this was supposed to be but hunkered down into boxing stance—well, an American movie star's boxing stance, basically John Payne elucidated by William Holden with a patina of James Cagney—while lo Scenarista turned away in disgust.

"It is very intriguing," the Princess observed.

"Calmati," the Actor told Vieri.

"He does not even speak a proper Italian!" lo Scenarista cried.

"There is no such thing as Italian," I said, stepping in front of Vieri to stopper the trouble. "There are quite a number of Italian languages, and yours is no finer than his."

"I speak the language of Dante!"

"Let me to plug him, Mark!" Vieri shouted in English, jumping and punching behind me. "He will be taken for a ride and *then!*"

The Actor, too, went into boxing stance, merrily "fighting" Vieri down to the water. The Princess shrugged by moving only her eyebrows. The photographers and guests who had been greedily taking us in abandoned us. The hungry paparazzo got into the pâté again and the Gossip threw a slice of pumpkin at him. Adriana stared at the Princess, who seemed not to notice. One of the English guests sidled up to me, repeating the offer to sell me secret Adriana scandals; "Barbirolli, Sutherland, Sir David," he murmured. Adriana and the Windsors pretended to converse as cameras went off. The pâté-eating paparazzo dropped a marinated squid down the back of the Gossip's dress and one of his colleagues shot her trying to retrieve it. I looked toward the ocean, at Vieri and the Actor finishing off their boxing act with the Actor's long, hard right to the chin, Vieri's magnificent fall, a ten-count, and Vieri's bounding up to run full-tilt up the beach to throw his arms around me and whisper, "Grazie, Mark, you were on my side." I held on tight and felt so proud.

6

A Duel

At tea in the garden, I was telling il Professore about the trip with Vieri to Torcello. I asked him, "Is it really the oldest part of Venice?"

"No, there is Chioza, far off at the bottom of the lagoon, so old that no one knows where it came from. But what is Venice, really? It is not a matter of Roman or Byzantine trading ports, like Chioza. It is colonists from the mainland fleeing barbarian aggression from the north. They had to escape or die. So? What is necessary, you invent. Venice was invented— because it did not simply happen but was *devised*. The lagoon is impassable to strangers—treacherous, shallow except for certain channels of passage known only to the community. Venice, then, is both real and an illusion: the city you can see but cannot reach."

"What is necessary," I repeated, "you invent. Even yourself?"

"Have you heard that Vieri will now be a racing-car driver?"

"He really knows how to enjoy himself, doesn't he? He's so . . . so full of life. You must really adore him."

"Well, yes, certainly," he said, taking a sip of tea. "It will be unbearable when I lose him. There are many fine young fellows in Rome who wish to make the acquaintance of an only moderately demanding and finally all too tolerant commendatore com'io. But there is no other Vieri."

I was silent, startled, considering.

"Certo, I will lose him," il Professore continued. "Youth is eager for the next event. If I wanted someone who would stay, I would establish a ménage with someone like myself, an old ruin. But who would want someone like myself? Not I."

I was wondering exactly what he was un Professore of, but I didn't like to ask.

"Come sta la divina?" he asked, inspecting an angry-looking cake. Venice doesn't have great desserts.

"She says she has sung her last Norma, and the Aminas are canceled."

"Peccato—I would hear her practicing, and it sounded lovely."

"Some days it does, yes."

"Will she do this movie with Ercolani?"

"Well, she wouldn't have to sing, at least. And he's so . . . it's enticing."

"Do you know that Ercolani wrote a letter to Vieri, reaffirming this great cinema director's interest in casting our so appealing but admittedly inexperienced young man as Orestes?"

"What an incredible opportunity."

"Oh, I rejoice for him, ben certo. And mourn for myself. But I laugh, too, for one must. I have had good fortune, and count myself happy. What more, no?"

"Can I ask something . . . well, intimate?"

"About Vieri?"

"Yes."

"Prego."

"Without wanting to pry into what . . . well, arrangement you have with him, I've been wondering what his . . . I mean, what he . . . likes?"

Il Professore smiled. "You wish to learn what is the sexual interest of Vieri."

"Yes."

"This is an all too American thing, I believe, to insist on calling everything by a name. A category, yes? As if all in the world belonged to a certain political party and never veered from the party line. What is Vieri? A boy, full of impulses, excitements. Phases. I have taken him from a hard life into a pleasant one, so he is grateful and thus gives me unstintingly of his love. Later . . . who can say to whom he will be giving his love and for what reasons?"

"Uh, unstintingly?"

"Perhaps, some night, curiosity will draw you to visit our bedroom, as Gianciotto did that of his wife, Francesca, as she lay with her lover and brother-in-law, Paolo the Beautiful. Of such visits comes tragedy."

Just then lo Scenarista dropped in, seating himself while eyeing il Professore as Hannibal's elephants might have eyed the Alps.

"We were speaking," said il Professore, "of Francesca da Rimini—thus, by synecdoche, of the marvels of love."

"An unworthy harlot" was lo Scenarista's opinion, "who stole her prominence through the glorious verse of Dante. He treated her much too gently, too, *oh* yes."

"Gently?" asked il Professore, offering lo Scenarista the ugliest cake on the platter. "He consigned her to hell. And for what? For loving what is beautiful."

"For loving what is forbidden," lo Scenarista replied. "The *Commedia* is allegory on such grand scale that it can pity even as it judges. It is as vast as God. It contains the world." He turned to me. "Think of it— passing from hell through purgatory into paradise, in the most beautiful poetry ever written, a Florentine of the early Renaissance analyzes all Creation as if preparing an encyclopedia of the universe!"

"A bitter political refugee," il Professore corrected, on my other side, "spends his exile constructing a rationale for his grievances, putting his enemies in hell and building his faith on the beauty of an eight-year-old girl he glimpsed but never spoke to, and makes of Christianity a fascist state in which one yields all individuality in blind obedience to the Duce or suffers eternal torment."

"The *history*. The *piety*. The *poetry*."

"The poetry is stupendous," il Professore conceded. "The rest is gossip and hypocrisy. Worst of all"—he put this to me—"is his treatment of Brunetto Latini, Dante's own teacher, whom he plops into hell for the crime of being homosexual."

"It was a sin by the standards of Dante's culture," said lo Scenarista, getting a bit rattled, though I noticed he was eating his cake and took a refill on tea.

"There is no sin," il Professore remarked. "There is only rules for control of the people by a pope, an Emperor."

"Oh yes? And what poetry do you admire, signore?"

"I make no great claims for him, but as a Venetian, I have always enjoyed the work of Carlo Goldoni."

"Arlecchino," lo Scenarista scoffed. "Capocomico." A mountebank. A thespian.

"He wrote half-three-hundred plays, and that is epic. He accepted life as it is, without trying to codify behavior or humiliate personalities unlike his own, and that is Christian. He found joy in the everyday, and that is so basic it is miraculous. I am proud to add that Venice is the mother of Italian theatre."

"Florence," lo Scenarista snapped back, "is the mother of opera, the supreme form of theatre."

"Florence invented opera, sì, but Venice *re*invented it in superior form. In Florence it was elitist entertainment. Venice opened the first public opera houses, and blended into the ascetic Florentine style comic characters and ribald situations. And this, of course, reflects life, as all Venetian art does. Venice, where men were free. Florence, the city of tyrants."

"I Medici!"

"Exactly. The lords of fiduciary power. This is why I respond to Goldoni, who wrote of i popolani. Not of great men but of—"

"Great men make the world. Without them—"

"We would have freedom," il Professore inserted. "Great men are invariably tyrants."

I felt odd sitting between these two, silent, occasionally presiding over a tea pouring or signaling to Deodata for more of those hideous cakes.

"Your Dante," il Professore continued to lo Scenarista, "makes quite a show of free will. La libertate della volontà. He then proposes a cosmos in which one has the free will only to submit to someone else's ideas on how to live. That is neither free nor will. That is slavery."

"My Dante, eh?"

"Your Florence. You conjure up greatnesses, yet you speak in trifles."

Now quite annoyed, digging into his attaché, lo Scenarista told me, "I have brought Maestro Ercolani's cinema treatment for la Grafanas to review, if she would, please. Oh yes, you will see, for instance, just before Clytemnestra's entrance, a slight quotation of the first lines of the *Commedia*. It is so fitting—'Nel mezzo del cammin di nostra vita mi ritrovai per una selva oscura . . .' "

"La Grafanas may well be in the middle of the journey of her life," said il Professore, "but to find her in a dark forest is—"

"The *character,* not the actress!"

"But the wily public will see her as the character, so great is her cult today. One detects a disharmony in your treatment."

Lo Scenarista abruptly rose, gave me the treatment and a tiny bow, and started to walk out of the garden.

"Shall we consider Savonarola?" il Professore asked me.

Lo Scenarista's pace slowed. He hesitated, turned.

"This is a great man," il Professore went on, his tone, as it had been throughout the afternoon, patient, deceptively soothing. "A Dominican friar, a demagogue like our modern beasts Hitler and Mussolini, who harangues an entire city—a city, we must remember, that vaunts its individuality, a city of *great men*, as our amiable friend so recently reminded us ... Now, this friar bends a people to his will, forces them to renounce everything that is beautiful, stimulating, intellectual. Because *he* cannot use it, *they* must not have it. A man of God? Bene, certissimo. For that *is* God: the angry lord who says No. Who would want such a master? Yet this magnificent city bowed to the despot, finding spiritual ecstasy in his tirades at mass and holding the great bonfire of vanities, in which such all too worldly things as chessboards, musical instruments, paintings, and books were burned to ashes. Botticelli and Petrarca were among the artists so honored. They say that in all the town, only one man denounced this bonfire—in fact, made an offer of twenty thousand scudi for the lot, for some of the books were very rare editions and the paintings, of course, irreplaceable. The citizens ignored him. But who was this man, I ask? Un Veneziano, naturally. When everyone in Florence goes rabid with tyranny, who but a Venetian will keep his head?"

Here il Professore paused. Then, with a short glance at that curiously lurking Scenarista, he leaned closer to me and said, "As with all religious zealots, Savonarola's spirituality was a façade. It was not grace he wanted, but power. So, once his public duties were completed, he would exchange his plain robes for the luxurious dyed linens for which Florence was world famous, enjoy a feast of Medicean proportions, then meet with his many several concubines to—"

"This is falsehood!" lo Scenarista cried, approaching us. "This was never said, even by Savonarola's bitterest enemies!" He appealed to me with "You cannot believe these insinuations!"

"Bene," said il Professore. "I admit I made the last section up, as one peppers the risotto for a *special* guest."

"Savonarola made real for all the republic the concept of eternal life," lo Scenarista told us. "He authenticated salvation."

"This is your defense of a man who burned books ... and homosexuals, too, like your heavenly poet Dante? That is not even to mention that Savonarola was the worst traitor l'Italia has ever known, welcoming the invading French army simply because they appeared to fulfill his prophecy that the nation's sins would be punished by foreigners." To me, il Professore added, "The French invasion led to a giant battle in which most of Italy took part, and in which we were so sorely beaten that for centuries after, northern Europe looked upon our land as wolves consider a pen of sheep. This," he concluded, "is what comes of great men."

"So you ignore the Renaissance, which Florence gave to the world. Buon talento!" What a debater! "While Venetians were busy counting ducats on their trading wharves, the Florentines were virtually inventing the art of painting."

"Venice, as all know, was a city of painting genius."

"Venice," lo Scenarista countered, really moving in on his theme, "was called la Serenissima, yet her greed for power kept her always intriguing, spying, hating—"

"Rebuilding," said il Professore, still imperturbable. "Defending. Aspiring."

"Venice was a brothel."

"Venice is chaste. Her love is the sea. What we might remark about Florence, however ... Do enjoy one of Deodata's lavish pastries," he urged lo Scenarista with an impenitent grin, indicating the most lurid sweet on the plate. "Yes, Florence." To me: "Do you know that when the Florentines exiled a family, as they were all too ceaselessly doing, they would demolish the family's house? As if to eradicate the fact that they had existed at all. This is the way of great men. This is why my ideal of art is not a tapestry of murder and pillage but a vivacious farsa da Goldoni on the day-to-day reality of harmless, free-willing people."

At last, to lo Scenarista, he said, "You haven't touched your enchanting pastry."

Lo Scenarista rose abruptly and left us, and there followed a quaint silence. Then il Professore tasted his tea and leaned back in his chair to muse, "The great life? The quiet life? Can we enjoy both, or even either? I do not know. But I wish to invite you, some day, to tour this ineffable city with me. You have seen Venice, I know, but not in the company of a Venetian. That is an adventure not possibly to be omitted from the sage traveler's itinerary."

7

The E.M.I. Man

You may have forgotten about that book that I was supposed to write; believe me, *I* hadn't. I kept telling myself, Any day now. But came the day and there I was, running errands or goofing off or playing for Adriana's practice sessions or scratching out yet more notes or revising the outline: not writing. I actually lied to my boss in New York, telling him we had begun work and were already in Chapter 2. It's slow going, I warned him—she's a reluctant subject.

"Stay on her, kid," he told me.

But it really wasn't Adriana stalling me as much as it was I myself. I still couldn't see a clear way into this life of hers: Where does one pick up the thread in such a rich tapestry? What inspires the *needs* of an Adriana, you know?

Anyway, I got off the phone with my boss in midafternoon—I had to call him late because of the six-hour time difference—and went off to the railroad station to meet Hugh Drummond, the artists and repertoire man for Adriana's record label, E.M.I., who was about to become Adriana's producer. I had been on the run all day, and what I *really* wanted to do was go home and lie in the tub. But among the many duties that excused my not applying myself to the writing of the book were these diplomatic excursions. Drummond's train (from Milan) was on time, and I spotted him immediately out of my own idea of what an opera-loving A&R man who was single and in his mid-thirties would look like. Tall, I'd reckoned, with curvy reddish-brown hair and a good helping of that never-fail British irony about the mouth. Well, he wasn't so tall, but otherwise I was hammer on nails.

"Mr. Drummond?"

"Yes. You're Mark Trigger."

Note: a statement, not a question.

We shook and How are you.

"I'll be better," he said, "when I bite into a cup of coffee. The railway buffet was quite—no"—to a determined porter—"I am not in the slightest need of your assistance." Smiling, he said, "Come on, Yank. I know an excellent café not two streets from here."

"You don't want to go to your hotel first?"

"It's halfway to Istanbul. What I want is peace, a chair, and un caffè macchiato. Shall we?"

Well, I liked him straight off. I liked his dressy-rumpled look and razor-cut diction and his ability to hop from city to city bearing one slim suitcase. He was in Venice partly to close a deal to make recordings in, and using the forces of, La Fenice; but he had come mainly to persuade Adriana to expand into the French repertory with aria recitals and a complete Carmen, a role she had never sung onstage.

"Yes," I agreed. "The security to do retakes will . . ." I thought of something. "What happened to Walter Legge? Doesn't he produce all her records?"

Drummond made a whimsical face. "Don't you know there's a feud going on? Legge made a Verdi Requiem, which Grafanas has long wanted to do. She once told me that she believes it's the greatest music Verdi ever wrote. Ah, il caffè! Il con latte qua, ed io . . . Ta." As the waiter receded, Hugh said, "Heavenly Italy and its cafés," sipped, and put his cup down like a man blessed. "Meanwhile, Legge signed Elisabeth Mrs. Schwarz-kopf-Legge to sing the soprano in the Requiem and offered Grafanas the mezzo line. Of course, Schwarzkopf had already recorded the Requiem on her husband's first try, so it looks a little grabby, and besides, Grafanas plays seconda donna to *no one*. So she sends word to E.M.I. that her association with them is over, and *we* say, You can't, we have an exclusive contract with you. She says, Fine, but Walter Legge is out of my life, that's it, no discussion." He smiled, raising his cup in toast. "And here I am. Cheers!"

"Feuds are sort of a regular thing with Adriana," I said. "And they're almost always with the people who mean the most to her. Even without a formal declaration of war, she hasn't spoken to that famous old teacher of hers in Athens for years now. And there was a big breach with di Stefano in the 1950s. All right, he's lazy and temperamental, but he was probably her most supportive colleague."

"Her lover, too."

"He . . . was?"

Hugh nodded. "Sorry to interrupt, laddie. Carry on."

"Well, I was going to . . . Her lover?"

"Feuds," Hugh prompted.

"Okay. Because there's also Contramin. Her key conductor, right? The man who . . . well, let's say it: *instituted* her as the reembodiment of the fabled dramatic-coloraturas of the nineteenth century. She owes him, we all know that. But she's never made it up with him."

"She made it up with di Stefano fast enough."

"It makes me feel funny working for her—you know, when is it my turn?"

"Never, from what I hear." He grinned as his tidbit made its effect—
what exactly had he heard? " 'Whatever you do, win over the Yank, she
trusts him'—that's my field expedient. Because it's not going to be easy
enticing Grafanas into the studio, or anywhere. The offers she doesn't turn
down she 'considers' interminably, and the few she accepts she ends up
canceling."

"Who told you she trusts me?"

"E.M.I. have long arms and wide ears when they need to. It's a lucky
chance for me, at any rate. It's my promotion, after a decade of assisting
Legge."

"It's weird for Adriana to feud with the head of her recording company.
It's so reckless it's inspired."

"This is really the upshot of the feud that she intended to have with
Legge back in 1955, when he recorded *La Traviata* with Antonietta Stella
just as Grafanas had that incredible success with the Scala *Traviata* staged
by della Torre. She had established her supremacy as Norma and Lucia,
and Legge duly preserved them. Now she had added Violetta to her list,
she naturally expected Legge to preserve that, too. It was a contractual
problem, actually—she had recorded *Traviata* earlier for another firm—
and Legge should have waited for her to be free. What a reading that
would have been! But he had Victor and Decca *Traviata*s to challenge, so
he went ahead. And *she* decided to blame the recording's conductor, Contramin."

"Why him?"

"Legge was too powerful. Contramin was available."

"So why Legge now?"

"Now she can. I asked Contramin how he felt about it at the time, and
he shrugged and said, 'She's a little pazza.' " Crazy. "He was jolly about
it—might as well be, too, after all he's seen. But, say I, these legends about
how a particular figure influenced a singer like Grafanas get too legendary
to believe. Contramin taught her Verdi, Bellini. Contramin showed her
the Italian path to Wagner singing. Contramin led her into the dramatic-

coloratura Fach. If you live in the middle of all this, the *real* truths sneak into view."

"Like?"

"It was Contramin's *wife,* also a singer, who saw Grafanas's potential in the bel canto parts—at the time, Grafanas was specializing in Turandot and Isolde. And what about that vocal coach she worked with in her first years in Italy? No one even knows his name. Who's responsible for Grafanas? Contramin, de Sabata, della Torre, Zeffirelli, they say. Well, she learned from them, that's clear. But the author of Grafanas's career is Grafanas—I saw it happen. She isn't educated, but she has amazing instincts. Damn, but that was a smashing cup of. Shall we have another?"

As he signaled the waiter, Hugh said, "In real fact, it's Walter who might have been Grafanas's Svengali. His recordings introduced her to the States when she was little more than a rumor, and he emphasized her versatility from the top of the day. Well, his program was brilliant altogether. He wanted to enlist a troupe of specialists who would be top in anything, allowing him to widen the repertory of works on disc— Schwarzkopf and Nicolai Gedda in what-have-you from Lehár to Richard Strauss, Victoria de los Angeles for French and Spanish music, Grafanas to and fro in the Italian catalogue and going up and down in it. In the States, R.C.A. were creating studio replicas of humdrum nights at the Metropolitan, and in the U.K., Decca were grinding out some of the worst recordings imaginable—del Monaco raving away and *Manon* with a narrator putting his oar into everything. A *narrator!* Legge's idea was to synthesize performances so carefully cast that they would address the aficionado as outright classics from the day of release."

"That must be true," I said, "because almost all the albums I bought when I first got into opera were Angels. They seemed somehow more sophisticated than everything else."

"The only problem was, Walter was far more intrigued by the possibilities for the German repertory—which he loves—than the Italian, which he rather takes for granted. You know, his idea of a desert island disc is a Hugo Wolf recital. So he let Schwarzkopf do the gramophone premieres of pieces by Cornelius and Orff while he had Grafanas riding all the Italian war-horses, including things she wasn't especially notable in. Why didn't Walter record her Lady Macbeth and Luisa Miller or her astonishing Rossini and Bellini? Even her *Sonnambula,* when he finally did it, totally missed out the excitement we all felt at La Scala. Because Walter cut all the fireworks and passion. Those simply amazing embellishments in the cabalettas—*out.* The unbearably tender radiance of her first scene and the heartrending elegy of her last scene—*out.* 'You are not singing into a theatre, Adrì,' he kept telling her. 'You are singing into the listener's ear. Keep it tidy.' *Tidy* to a Medea whose entrance in the finale with the bloody knife was so terrifying that the chorus scrambled away from her as if they thought she had really murdered some children backstage. Oh, and speaking of that—why didn't Walter record her Medea? It was my first Grafanas, I have to say, right here in Venice, and I still call it the finest thing she ever did. That great rude voice just cascading out in fury! Yet when I first met her, a few years before, she was still a forlorn overweight young woman so embarrassed to be who she was that she kept her eyes on the floor and stayed in every night. Only when she was rehearsing or performing did she come alive."

"Was she easy to work with?"

"Exceptionally so. The most conscientious artist I ever met."

"It makes all those feuds really puzzling, doesn't it?"

"I always thought Ambarazzi put her up to all that."

My face must have gone a little wry on him, because he quickly dropped a hand on my arm and said, "Granted, Grafanas has her temperamental side."

"That's like saying, 'Granted, Vesuvius erupts.' "

"Well, but you didn't know her in her first days, when it was all seething *inside*, all suppressed. People think Ambarazzi built up her confidence with love and support, and that as her career became strong she became arrogant. Certainly, her personality underwent some sort of change—I saw her grow from whipped dog to sergeant major. But I think Ambarazzi played on her lack of confidence. He was the one who kept imagining conspiracies against her, who would spot Tebaldi in the audience and go running backstage to warn Grafanas that her rival was defaming her, who promised her that the costume designer had sworn to humiliate her."

"Really?"

"He was an impossible man. *Ghastly* so. We had someone like him when I was up at school, forever denouncing boys to the master or trying to play boys against one another. Every time he spoke, a bunch of us would murmur 'Sneak, sneak' in the background. Truth, now?"

"Truth."

"It was amazing that any impresario wanted to hire her after negotiating with Ambarazzi. It would be a hell of letters, phone calls, and telegrams, mostly unanswered. Finally, you thought you had a deal—and suddenly he'd add on a ton of demands. All ridiculous things, just to drive you barking. You know, before he started to really use his power, she had excellent relations with impresarios. Not Ghiringhelli or Bing, because they had no respect for talent. But Siciliani in Florence, Caraza-Campos in Mexico City, Lawrence Kelley in Chicago . . . and it can't be a coincidence that now Ambarazzi's dead, every impresario who closed his theatre to her suddenly wants her back."

"Why did she let him make things so difficult, though?"

"Given the world of hostile forces all bent upon the destruction of Adriana Grafanas, why shouldn't she?"

"All right, then: why was he so difficult in the first place?"

"Because *her* power gave *him* power. Everyone in music was at his feet, begging for a booking, and he exploited it."

"So they were made for each other. She thinks everyone's against her, and he proves it."

"Made for each other? She loathed him."

"No, she . . . *What*? She *married* him!"

"She was alone and penniless in a foreign country. No one would hear her, no one would hire her. Ambarazzi said, 'Marry me and you'll live comfortably while I become your agent. You'll sing and the world will bow before you.' "

"He was that prescient?"

Hugh laughed. "He couldn't have known it would turn out so well. He probably thought he had a second Caterina Mancini. Shall we move on? I'd like to drop off my bag and freshen up before I tackle la divina."

Heading down the Grand Canal on the no. 2 bus, I said, "You make Adriana and Ambarazzi sound like a pair of opportunists conning each other."

"No, he truly loved her, whatever else he did. And she must have tried to convince herself that she loved him, in some dubious way. She *acted* as if she adored him, at least at the start. But perhaps it only was an act. By the end, after she had met Nik Acropoli, she treated Ambarazzi like . . . Attend me. After one of the Scala *Lucrezia Borgia*s, a group of us were leaving the theatre together for supper at Biffi Scala. Someone had given her a little stuffed bear, and while passing out the street door, she dropped it. So now she is beaming at her fans as she hisses at her husband—I mean hisses like an enraged cat—'Pick it up, idiot!' In all, I'd call it a marriage of convenience, sexless and thoroughly lacking in that inlay of respect and sentiment that a genuine union thrives on."

"Sexless? I've been wondering about that."

"Of course, some very great artists function without sex. They put their energy into . . ."

He stopped because I was shaking my head. "Believe me," I said, "that's not Adriana. Have you ever met Nik?"

"I've seen a few of his films." Hugh smiled. "To be horribly candid, I wouldn't mind waking to find him prowling my room in his knickers."

I nodded, once again struck—as I had been throughout my European sojourn—by how much more open We were over here.

"There's another thing I need to be candid about," Hugh told me. "I will truly need your help in persuading Adriana to start recording again. Do I have it?"

I tried for something between blasé and innocent. "What's in it for me?"

"What do you want in it?"

"The Venice *Adriana*."

Hazy on what I'd said, he went, "Come again, Yank?"

"It's a tape. Of Adriana's performance, in Venice, of—"

"Oh, pirate opera."

"Fact is, it's my obsession, and I've been corresponding with a lot of Adriana's fans trying to find a copy. People know about it, but no one has it—except the general feeling is that A&R men in the record industry have the best access to these tapes. True?"

"Not in my case, and Walter frowns on that sort of thing. He complains that he drudges his genius away constructing a performance that outdoes opera-house routine, and yet all that the fans want is souvenirs of live performances."

"It's called the Real Thing."

"Terry McEwen, of Decca, could possibly help you out. He's got a sheerly *mad* collection of live material. I could call him for you."

"Would you?"

We were nearing the vaporetto stop—the busiest one in the city—and all about us came the rustling of tourists' maps being opened, to excited babble in a dozen languages.

"Let's do a deal," Hugh offered. "The Venice *Adriana* for an Adriana *Carmen*."

"Actually, I would have helped you anyway. But I want what's best for Adriana, and if she really is too afraid of going back into the studio, I won't attempt to cajole her. Still, I think *any* records made by Adriana Grafanas would be good for opera and for herself. Better than good. Excellent. Even necessary. Even essential."

"And so say all of us," he replied, and we shook on it.

8

Schmeiing
Around

Number 127 was in chaos when Hugh and I arrived, at about four-thirty that afternoon. In the courtyard, Siora Varin and il Professore were trying to hearten Siora Varin's ancient mother, who for some reason had decided to dare the trip downstairs with a basket of ridiculous pottery (that she had made? to sell?) and now couldn't get back up.

"La mare no xe zoveneta," was Siora Varin's astute assessment. The old girl's no lassie. Il Professore wondered if they should call the police or the carabinieri. "But no matter who shows up," he explained, "they'll say it's the *other* department's concern."

In the garden, the Gossip was huffing and puffing over her luggage, rummaging through now this, now that valise, I suppose to ascertain that she had pinched every last piece of the house silver. "No, *don't* try to stop me, I'm moving on," she told me. "The Princess has asked me to her gracious, secluded villa in Amalfi, and when royalty beckons...Oh, that big hulking neighbor boy *must* help me get my luggage to the station. Of course, I'd hire a motorboat, only—*You there!*" she called to il Professore, as I shot Hugh a you-don't-want-to-know look. I didn't bother introducing him to the Gossip: why slow, even for a moment, her progress out of our lives?

"Madama?" il Professore asked, approaching us.

Then Deodata came running out of the house in dismay. "Signor Trigga, a terrible thing! The bad news from America, la Siora becomes upset, and now she has vanished!"

"What bad news?"

"Come, come," the Gossip interjected to il Professore, "Tell that nephew of yours, or whatever he is, to come downstairs and help me with my bags. No, none of your Italian prevarications," she went on when he had no more than opened his mouth. "I've lost *far* too much time as it—"

"What bad news, Deodata?" I asked.

"Her godfather, from New York. He called last night to warn her, in case the newspapers...She did not tell you this morning?"

"I didn't see her this morning, I was out from—"

"If you *please,*" said the Gossip, with immense confidence. "Where is that boy to help me, and *right now?*"

"Vieri is not here, Madama."

"There is Dolfino, down the street at number 122," said Siora Varin, who had come forward, as would any sensible Italian, to enjoy the un-folding drama and perhaps take a small part. "True, he is a half-wit, with a harelip besides. But who needs cleverness and beauty when there is luggage to take?"

"Deodata, *what news?*"

"It was told yesterday in the scandalous New York press that la Siora's mother is so poor that she was put out of her flat and was then found sleeping in the street like an animal!"

"Holy cow!"

"What is this woman saying?" the Gossip demanded of me, about Siora
Varin. "Has she a nephew, too? Make her speak English."

"Why don't you go to hell?" I said.

The Gossip froze, thought it over, and decided to throw a tantrum; but
I had taken Deodata off to the side to get the rest of the story.

"What do you mean that Adriana has vanished?"

"This morning," Deodata said, "she told me she was going for a walk.
That is unusual, Signor Trigga—la Siora always takes the boat. And this
was long before lunch, so now I have telephoned to every place where she
might be—the opera, the modista, the special cafés . . . Over five hours she
is gone! I am fearful, Sior."

"Did she seem upset when she left?"

"No, but she was in her very quiet mood, when you feel lightning will
strike subito."

As I turned back to the others, the Gossip was just getting into third
gear. Ignoring her, I asked Hugh and il Professore to help me scour the
town for Adriana. Hugh said he'd take Dorsoduro, il Professore would
hunt around San Marco, and I would nose through San Polo—only half
the city but, at least, our half. I told Deodata to ring the police *and* the
carabinieri, the two men and I agreed to keep in touch through Deodata,
and we started to the street door with the Gossip following us, still screaming, till Siora Varin's mother beaned her with a particularly vile-looking
creamer and she sagged to the earth in tears.

"Mama!" Siora Varin cried. "Che strambazzo!" How could you?

"Sì, sì," said her mother, philosophically.

In the street, Hugh headed down to the Zattere while il Professore and
I went north, he to take the traghetto across the Grand Canal and I to
hire a gondola to take me to the Rialto Bridge. It seemed a long shot—
three men combing a city for one lone figure. But what else were we to
do? If Adriana had taken a walk, she might well be on the Zattere, or
somewhere near La Fenice for il Professore to find, or—in my territory—

near the Rialto, where she once told me she likes shopping because no one there ever recognized her.

I was not long arrived when I realized that I had it all wrong. The Rialto was in effect the flea market of Venice, all fish and flowers and hand-me-downs. It was what Adriana had come from, not what she would go to. So I ran back over the Bridge to the Merceria, Venice's Fifth Avenue. Ran? Venice in summer is so clogged with tourists—especially along the Merceria—that it was like swimming through peanut butter. Anyway, I didn't see her, not even trying on some rigidly madcap hat in a milliner's.

Then, as I reached the little square before the church of San Zulian, I came upon two young men squaring off for a fight. One was a real Capitan Spavento, a big strutting galoot to whom this was surely as much a performance as a contest. His (I thought) reluctant opponent was physically out of his league but determined not to run. The galoot had been carrying a crate of something and he brought it into his act, hefting it as if weight lifting to parade through the crowd so all could admire his expanded biceps.

"Just look!" he cried. "You'll see!" He even paused to make a statue of himself for a pair of camera-wielding Japanese tourists. "Ecco!"

The smaller guy was just standing, steeling himself, when a young woman broke out of the crowd. She seemed to be his sweetheart, and she began pleading with him, I assumed to come away. The galoot took her in and guffawed some remark to the crowd that I didn't catch; nobody laughed. Now the young woman turned her appeal to those in the square, begging them to prevent the fight. People were shouting. I heard "It was deliberate!" and "They are not fairly matched!"

Suddenly, with a hoarse cry of animal joy, the galoot charged the smaller man, and they locked in a punching frenzy as the young woman broke into sobs and the crowd called encouragement to its side of personal choice. The galoot's face, one big stupid snarl, read, "I do this for fun." The other's face, a fragile wall of determination, read, "No obstacle can subdue my guiltless will." And he *was* holding in there, pushing the galoot back and redoubling his advance—I can if I need to badly enough, or something like that—till, as if in one of those bossy pageants that old Venice was famous for, the doors of the church swung open and three priests came out in triangular formation.

The crowd, at first stunned silent, began to murmur as the father in the forefront moved quickly into the fight, stopping it through the sheer authority of his office and the instant shame of the combatants. The priest looked sternly from one to the other, apparently reckoning where to set praise and blame in the matter.

The two priests in the back line, their hands heavily gloved, were holding giant candles, which they waved at the crowd in slow, stately earnest. "The folly of independence," one chanted, and the other responded with "Resentment is vicious." Many of the spectators crossed themselves (a few on their knees), and the young woman approached the priest and whispered something to him. I wondered if this was a routine ceremony at San Zulian, vespers or whatever. The head priest now joined the hands of the hero and heroine and gently sent them on their way; to the galoot he boomed out, "Even the sinner demands justice," staring at him till he calmly reclaimed his crate and marched off.

Struck by a thought, I found a telephone and checked in with Deodata. No, la Siora was still missing. At the nearest bridge I found two boatmen accosting tourists with the usual "Gondola! Gondola!," made a deal with one of them, and rode off to Castello, which some say is the oldest part of the city, where the first trading boats docked their silks, dyes, and spices, the arts of the East. I got out at San Antonino and ran over the bridge and down the alleys to San Giorgio dei Greci, the Greek Orthodox church: and there I found Adriana.

She was sitting amid the huge wooden bleachers that line the nave, looking absurdly small—even insignificant—in the near-empty church. Her lips moved as if she was rehearsing for the thousandth time an angry conversation that she never quite got to have with some powerful enemy. Or she might have been praying, but very forcefully.

She smiled at me as I entered her distracted view, and I sat next to her and waited. It was a long time coming, but at length she patted my hand on the armrest, cleared her throat opera-style (a series of delicately spiraling grumps), and said, "We had many neighbors when I was a young girl, because we were always moving, especially when my father's pharmacy business was in trouble. The best of the neighbors were the Hegyis. Patty Hegyi was almost my own age, and I loved to go down the hall and visit because she had such lovely things—the clothes, the dolls. She let me dress her second-best doll, Lindabelle, and walk around her room in the most beautiful black satin pumps with a strap and a tiny black buckle across the center. Once I watched Mrs. Hegyi help Patty prepare for a party. It was the birthday of someone I didn't know, yet I so longed to go to this party, and to wear Patty's clothes, and have *my* mother dress me with such love and...Such love, you could see it on both their faces. Mrs. Hegyi called Patty her 'little princess.' You say, Of course, what else does a mother say?"

"My next-door neighbor," I said, "was Richie Goldenhart, and believe me, his mother never called him a prince. When I came over, Richie's mother would say, 'Oh, here's the other one, and now the two of them will schmei around all day.' That was her idea of original sin, schmeiing."

"But what could it mean?"

"I never really found out. I took it for granted, like wallpaper. When Richie and I would go to Skateland, his mother called that 'winter schmeiing.' Or when dinner wasn't ready she'd say, 'Go upstairs and schmei till it's time.' On high-school graduation day, she said, 'Richie schmeied the whole way, from freshman to senior, and now he'll schmei at college.'"

"Schmei..."

"I *think* it means to keep busy without accomplishing anything. Goofing off, really. Coasting."

"Like that Anna Moffo?"

I laughed. "No, like me, here in Venice. What have I been doing, after all? Schmeiing."

"I, too, have schmeied."

"No. Oh, lady, no. You've made history, and that is the opposite of schmeiing."

"I schmeied today. Is the house in an uproar? Were you looking for me?"

"No, I always come here," I said, dryly.

"Caro," she said. "I have been foolish about this news, but you see how infuriating it is that I cannot get my mother *out* of my *life*. I have cut her off, I have paid her hush money, and *still* she finds evil ways to come in!"

A passing priest gave us a paternally admonishing glance, and Adriana bowed her head. At length she whispered, "Perhaps another pill."

"What pill?"

Fishing in her handbag, she found a small lacquered wooden box with a flower painted on the top. "It is la Fleur," she told me. "I took up the Princess's suggestion, and the doctor was very reassuring. I took one this morning, and it seemed to calm me."

"So now you have what Patty Hegyi had, is that it? *You're* the princess?"

"Ah, well, the Princess wants what I have, no?"

"Nik."

"They might be together this minute, laughing. He loves to make laughter. So handsome, strong, exciting. My mother would love him. Greek mothers always want sons."

"Don't you have a brother?"

"Yes. George. Still in Athens."

"And did your mother . . . Are you sure you want to eat that thing?"

She held a pill between two fingers: tiny, white, innocent.

"I mean," I said, "who knows what's in it?"

"Peace . . . escape, oblivion."

I took the pill from her, saying, "You can't have peace, you're too important."

"I repent of my importance. I renounce it."

"What, the theatre?"

"I never think of it."

"Your fame."

"A mirage, of course. What does it cure?"

"Music, then. Your vocation."

"So disappointing, in the end."

"Your *loves*," I breathed out, in a risqué manner.

"Oh, who are they, I wonder?"

"I know what—let's go home and call Nik in Rome. He should just be getting back from work."

"The Princess will answer with a cruelly teasing laugh, and I . . . Well, if I weren't woozy on this silly pill of hers, I'd go down there and rip her pretty face apart."

"*That's* my girl. Come on and let's find a motorboat."

"No, I want to walk along the Riva." She rose and we started out. "It's so lovely and open, and I too seldom come here. Only when I get so angry that I entertain murderous thoughts. Then I beg God to forgive my wickedness."

"Does he?"

"He never says," she replied, taking my arm.

We neared the embankment at the Church of the Pietà, looking out onto the great basin made by the marriage of the Grand Canal and the Giudecca Canal. It was dusk, and the dimming light seemed to filter rare, unexploited colors among its golds and oranges and blues.

I telephoned Deodata and made my report, then rejoined Adriana. "The Gossip has decamped," I said as we strolled off toward San Marco among the hordes of people who throng the Riva, the only long, wide walkway in all Venice.

"Yes, I am happy for her," said Adriana carelessly. "She will never find what she seeks, but she knows how to enjoy looking for it."

"She says the Princess is in Amalfi or something."

"A few hours from Rome."

"But isn't the Prince still around?"

"That vicious homosexual toad," she said.

All right, now I had to speak. "Adriana," I began, "it kind of hurts my heart to hear you get so down on a guy just because of his sex life."

"You defend this practice? It is anormale, infame."

It was strange to hear her utter her usual excoriations in such a subdued tone—the effect of la Fleur, clearly.

I said, "Do you realize that if all the homosexuals who assisted in your career had never existed, you'd have been left with little more than make-weights and stooges?"

"Uffa, such creatures are often tormented geniuses. What else can they do?"

Okay, tormented genius. I gave up for now, and we crossed the Piazza silently, Adriana lost in thought and I enjoying the stir she created among some bystanders. She was, as always, dressed for stardom; people would stare even if they had no idea who she was.

"Schmeiing around," she suddenly said, as we passed San Moisè. "I have been guilty of this for too long. Now that I have visited my Father's house, I will be resolute."

That last bit sounded so loony I decided to ignore it. "Hugh Drummond arrived today. The E.M.I. guy? He wants you to record *Carmen*."

"I am looking at it," she said thoughtfully. "And I have been reading questa trama di Ercolani." The movie treatment. "It is quite well brought off, no?"

"He's another tormented genius, you know."

She just shrugged.

As we entered Campo Santa Maria Zobenigo, I saw a teenage couple in a doorway celebrating the near nighttime in the passionate embrace favored by the very young, the world's newest lovers. I thought of the couple from the fight at San Zulian, hoping they were as carefree and enchanted as this couple so apparently was. They broke as we neared them, the girl shyly turning away from the boy and he pressing his advantage. She stepped out of the doorway, ruffled and happy, and he, so happy too, darted a look at us.

It was Vieri, and his expression at once turned to surprise, then embarrassment. I kept on walking with Adriana from square to square, over the Accademia Bridge, then backtracking east to the Rio dei Fornaci and the back entrance from the canal. Adriana placed a call to the Actor, emoted and wept and remonstrated with him, then went to bed, supervised by an uncommonly bustling Deodata. I spoke with il Professore and Hugh both, then set up shop in the dining room in expectation of a social call. Well, I'd caught him at something, hadn't I?

I had plenty of time, it turned out, and I got on paper five potential ways to start Adriana's life story. I *will* make this happen, I told myself, reviewing and comparing. It was well after eleven when Vieri knocked.

9

Italian Boys Do More than Flirt

Vieri was one part sheepish, two parts bashful, and seven parts absolutely confident. He wanted to go upstairs to my room—to talk, he said. It is important, Mark. Just together, sì, Mark, now? Who could say no?

He had been in my room before, momentarily—following me in when we were about to go out and I needed something, say. This was his first real visit, then, and he went through the appropriate newcomer's ceremonies, commenting favorably on my knickknacks and studying the photographs.

My mother, my father, my sister. Our ski trip to Sugar Loaf. That summer on Cape Cod. Diantha's wedding. Christmas with a hundred Triggers.

"So beautiful, these all," Vieri said, gazing raptly at each picture in turn. "Many places to go, as in your American movies. The family love each other. They are all at the dinner table, making American jokes. It is very nice. Sì, Mark? La tua famiglia tutto gentile, meravigliosa?" Your family is wonderful?

"Mezzo, mezzo." Happy families are all alike.

"My family, it is not so wonderful there. Too many kids, too much Naples, poverty, disappointment." He sat on the bed, patting the space to his right. "Come, Mark, to sit with Vieri."

"Should I go down for some wine? Or would you like—"

"No, come here, you, Mark, please."

I sat with him, docile, friendly. He put his arm around my shoulder. "Sì, fremi, tu," he said. You're trembling.

"No."

"Ma sì."

His hand rested on the back of my neck, one finger gently trying the skin just at the hairline.

"You like Vieri, yes?"

"Yes."

"You wouldn't hurt Vieri, no, Mark?"

"Never."

"Now *you* be friendly to Vieri, Mark, with hands."

I put my arm around his shoulder, but he said, "No, closer, like brothers," and I tightened my grip.

"You see, Mark, it is one problem with il Professore, that he is always forgiving except when he knows that Vieri is with the girls. It is strange. Last year, at the Feast of the Redentore, I was out late with friends and came home so sbronzo—you know this word?"

"Drunk."

"Sì, and I fell into the televisione and it . . . come si dice?"

"Broke."

"Ed il Professore, he is so gentile, he says, Okay, Vieri, so young, so excited. Or when I slip just a little money from the dresser, he knows and says nothing. He loves Vieri, and those who love forgive."

"Can I have my arm back?"

"Sì, Mark. Be contento."

It was uncomfortable having to sit hooked up like that.

"But it is one thing that il Professore does not forgive, and that is girls. Do you know why?"

"Nope."

"*I* do not know. But he likes me to be with *you,* Mark. He likes very much that I am learning English. When the American movies come on our important new televisione, he is eager to see if I can know the story just by hearing, not reading the little words. You see how il Professore and Vieri enjoy to be together, and it would not be good to worry him about Vieri. Right, Mark?"

I didn't respond because I was staring at him and going over my many fantasies about him. Is this love?, I wondered, taking his hand.

"Right, Mark?"

"Right."

He smiled, and I thought, It *is* love, and I brushed his black hair back from his forehead. This beautiful boy.

"Yes, Mark, like brothers." He laughed. "Così anch' il Professore." He does that, too. "But he is disappointed that we are not having any lessons the last few days."

"I'm sorry, Vieri, I—"

"No, it is good, Mark. We have a lesson now, sì? You are excellent teacher, but you leave things away. Conversations at the restaurant, in the bank, this is all good, and Vieri knows you put in funny things not attaching ... 'Can I fuck you?' to the bank cashier. And so we laugh together, it is so witty. But many words I do not learn yet, Mark. Per esempio ..." He grabbed my arm just below the elbow. "What is this name? L'avambraccio?"

"The forearm."

He echoed me, this time closing my hand around his arm. "E questa?" he said.

"Skin."

He turned his hand palm up, wiggling his fingers. "E questi, i diti?"

"Fingers."

"Fingras," he said, drawing my hand to his mouth and, never taking his eyes off mine, sucking the length of my index finger with a slow, deep pull. I was, uh, on roller skates going off some ski jump into the black sky of Vieri.

He got up, closed the door, threw off his shoes, his shirt, and his pants. I got up, too, but he came over and sat me down again, as solicitous as a doctor, saying, "Ancora fremi tu. But you are not afraid of Vieri, sì?"

I felt very distant now from the vision of myself as an avuncular debauchee fondling and forking some amenable teen: I *was* afraid, because I was not in power and I didn't know what would happen and I was no more than a breath or two away from that flesh yet I still could not tell what was permitted.

"Now these, Mark," said Vieri, guiding my hand again to focus his approach. "I cappezzoli?"

"Nipples."

"This?"

"The stomach."

"Liscio, no? Soave?" Sleek, smooth. "You feel?"

"Sì, Vieri." My God.

"E questo?," circling it.

"The navel."

He had my fingers under the waistband of his shorts now. "Segreto," he whispered. "Amore. Già, l'ho duro." He was hard now, hypnotizing me, bringing me into his guilt to share it so I would not betray him to il Professore, but I would never have done that, and I had my hands on him now and pulled off his shorts and shoved him back on the bed to get my mouth on him, the most natural thing and a most logical fit though at first I gagged because I took too much at once but I soon got the, yes, hang of it and I was tasting him and wondering if each Vieri has a different taste, and I freed myself, tugging my clothes off while working on Vieri, but I had to get up to get my pants off so he jumped up, too, and we pulled the bedclothes back and jumped in but there was no forking, just licking and rolling around and little aching noises, now all calm and now in a frenzy, and I was kissing him and that must be the most intimate thing and Vieri is the most intimate boy, so affectionate that of course I was infinitely in love but they say you always think that when you have your first communal orgasm, especially at that moment when you're rising to the big blow and he's rising, too, skin to skin crashing all over the bed till you lift up soaring to the bull's-eye liscio soave Vieri boy so wet and hot who kicks his legs high and shouts "Cazzatràc!" as he shoots. Ay, Vieri, tu!

Then the panting down, thinking, Oh, I bet I can handle love, as you lie there holding him, trying to assume a protective air even though he ran the show. Then thinking, Well, I'm unsure of love, because after all there are considerations—il Professore, one's future, Adriana's book. Vieri shifts position, taking control again, and you think, Gosh, I fear love. (The folly of independence.) It all slides down. Then he gets up and goes to the window to gaze into the garden, peaceful in this noisiest of the world's great cities. We can't even hear the gondoliers' cries or the boat motors from here. He goes into a pocket and pulls out a folding knife.

"Vieni qui, Mark."

"Perchè?"

"Su, vieni, com'io dico."

I joined him at the window.

"Dammi la mano," he said, reaching for my hand.

"No."

"Daimo!" he cried, grabbing my wrist. "I will not hurt you! What do you think, after amore? It is sacred now." I was still fighting him, so he put the knife down and held me, sweetened me down to stillness, all skin, and I threw off everything but the wonder of him. Yes, *anything*, I thought, like a woman, accepting the loss of power for the return of love. Anything:

and he passed the knife blade across my thumb, pianissimo, and pulled it up to suck the wound. Then he cut himself and gave me his thumb to suck in turn.

"Brothers," he said. "Never to betray now, Mark. Each protects the other. Sì?"

"Sì."

We held each other a long time then, so long I might have dived right into him and come paddling slowly back to the surface, one great grin. Finally we broke and went to the bathroom to wash away the reek of our sin so il Professore would make no judgment upon us. It was a virtuous, lighthearted shower, and Vieri was soon on his way. At the door, he told me, "Ti amo, Mark," and this time I believe it meant "I love you."

1 0

All the World Hated Her

How dared you face il Professore? you must be thinking; but he seemed so unusually cheerful around me that I felt he had not only divined what we had done but approved of it. Vieri, too, treated me differently, with less respect but more intensity, especially when I disagreed with his opinions or thwarted his will. It was as if he liked me more but trusted me less. He was more physical as well, constantly leaping upon me at the beach to wrestle me to the sand and, whenever we parted, embracing me solemnly and whispering, "A fratù, Mark," the oath of the blood brotherhood or whatever it was. I always hoped he wouldn't hug me, because I would get an instant hard-on; but I did love the feel of him. We were not to have sex again: once, he explained, was necessary to show brotherly affection, but twice would be swindling il Professore.

Anyway, I had already started a whimsical little affair with Hugh

Drummond. Now that the Gossip had moved out, Adriana invited him to join us for the rest of his stay (most likely to judge whether or not she could rely on him), and as our bedrooms were next door to each other it seemed the most—well, not only natural but *honest* thing in the world. Besides, even though I bedded Hugh the very next night after my adventure with Vieri, he was only the second man I'd had in my whole twenty-four years, so I hardly thought of myself as, you know, a slut.

Hugh was quite a change from Vieri. "What precisely do you fancy?" he asked the first time, as if I'd eaten my way through some lavish menu and had two or three favorite dishes.

"I don't know," I said. "What do you fancy?" Which, I realized a moment too late, made me sound like a fool and a neophyte.

"Actually," said Hugh, ever so airily, "I really rather like to be buggered. Does that fit in with your plans?"

"Sure," I said, shooting a quick prayer to heaven to fortify my buggering skills. It turned out to be a relatively easy and absolutely pleasing operation, and I felt so grateful to Hugh for bringing out the man in me that I decided I was in love with him, too.

Hugh was steeply versed in the romantic arts; he knew terms for acts I had scarcely imagined. "Eton style," for instance, involved his resting on all fours. For "Harrow style" he stretched flat on his stomach. (When I suggested we try it with Hugh on his back, facing me, he said, with a mild reproach, "That's strictly for butcher's boys and other animals.") At first I thought, This is so European, so aristocratically decadent. But if Europe was decadent, why did I feel so invigorated?

Hugh and I would talk nights, after, and once I told him, "It's uncanny how easy it is to find . . . like-minded fellows here. This could never happen back home, you know."

"It happens all the time, lad."

"I never saw it."

"Were you in the midst of the music world back home?"

I shook my head.

"That's why," he said.

"No, because there's a whole European thing going on that America doesn't know about. Like that first day, when you made the remark about Nik. No American would have been so open."

"What had I to lose? I knew you were . . . of the fraternity, shall we say?"

"Maybe it's because everything is so much older here. Europeans are wiser?"

"Europeans are *too* old, Mark—hardened in their ancient ways. It takes a new people to discover fresh paths. That's what we admire about the States—no old debts to work off, no antiquated systems. We're the victims of tradition, cursed with it. You're the inventors of change."

A great advantage in our intimacy was that Hugh actively enlisted in the search for the *Adriana* tape, phoning Terry McEwen in London while I nervously hung about. McEwen said he'd been trying to trade for it for years with an *extremely suspect* character in St. John's Wood who *claimed* to own it but you *know these collectors*. He promised Hugh to take another stab at it, and when Hugh got off he told me, "I can't say how amusing it is seeing you so entranced by this ridiculously inanimate object. You're *living* with the woman—what do you want with a *tape* of her?"

"It's not the artist," I replied. "It's the art."

I kept wondering if Adriana would catch Hugh and me together, or at least dope out our guilty smiles of a morning. But I expect she was distracted by her tumultuous personal life—staging willowy yet tragic telephone scenes with the Actor in Rome, arranging through her godfather in New York for her mother's new living quarters, and grimly charming the reporters who haunted number 127's two entrances. She never chanced the street without either Hugh or me (or even Vieri) in tow, and she cursed the newspeople roundly once she had "given them something" and passed on her way. Still, I have to say that she handled them fairly, intelligently, and in the grand manner. It was exactly what they wanted.

"My mother," she would tell them, flashbulbs popping, "indulges in

dramatizations, as I'm sure you're all aware." Here she affected an indul-
gent smile. "I have always provided for her and I will continue to do so.
But she is only one of many projects. Now I am learning *Carmen*, the
Bizet masterpiece, for my next recording engagement."

"Isn't that a role for the mezzo-soprano, Madame Grafanas?" asked an
American reporter. "Does this mean you're losing your voice?"

"Many sopranos have sung Carmen," Adriana replied, keeping her temper. "Mary Garden, Geraldine Farrar, Rosa Ponselle, Maria Jeritza..."
She turned to me expectantly.

"Fatata de Ponce," I added—not a persuasive concoction, but no one
was listening to me, anyway.

"Will you sing Carmen on the stage, Madama Grafanas?"

"As soon as I have been graduated from castañet school."

They humored her with laughter and we went our way.

It was high season now, pushing into August, and the center of town
was so crowded with visitors that everyone at number 127 was sticking
close to home. So when il Professore found me in the garden and invited
me on a personal tour of the Serenissima, I begged off till he promised to
lead me through "calli ignoti," the secret parts of the city.

"Come va l'opera?" he asked, as we took off from the water entrance.
How's the book going?

"It's a struggle."

"Vieri speaks so much English now that he is giving tourists directions
at all times. You are an accomplished teacher."

"No, he's a neat student. He's so..." I trailed off uncomfortably, but il
Professore simply rejoined, "Yes, everyone befriends him. Who would not?
All know what is true."

I needed to tell il Professore of my relationship with Hugh; at least, I
had to tell *somebody,* and I thought il Professore would listen well. I held
back, though, as we marched through Dorsoduro to the San Barnaba
Canal—"a most famous spot," il Professore pointed out, "where your
American film star Katharine Hepburn fell into the water as part of a

movie scene. All the town marveled at her thespian commitment. I believe that Americans are all congenital cinemaphiles. I visualize the streets and parks deserted every evening as the population swells the theatres. Vieri, too, is avid for the movies. This week he has been three times to *L'Inferno dei Vivi,* an American attraction, naturalmente."

"*The Hell of the Living?*"

"He has enacted scenes for me. It is a Nazi camp for American prisoners-of-war, and your William Holden is unfairly suspected of spying for the Germans. There is much suspense, much terror, though Vieri says there is not enough shooting."

"Oh, *Stalag 17.* That's an oldie."

"Yes, three nights he has frequented this film—or so he says. It is not always certain where Vieri goes, and at times I need to expand slightly the disciplinary structure of the household." He smiled sardonically—or, no, in a blasé, capering manner—as always, testing me to see how readily I credited his tales. "Sometimes the best way to prove one's protection of a beautiful boy is to give him these extra loving attentions. And Vieri is very responsive. My dear young friend, you seem to be blushing."

"On with the tour," I suggested.

"We are already at our next stop," he announced, indicating a bridge without handrails.

"I hate that kind," I said. "So dangerous."

"Già. This is the Bridge of Fists, where, for centuries, opposing factions of young bravos would engage in fierce combat."

"Why?"

"Well, i Castellani lived in the eastern end of the city, and i Nicolotti in the western end."

"That's reason enough," I observed.

"It was, to them. Or were they descendants of settlers from two mainland cities recalling some ancient feud? Memories die slowly in a city as isolated as this. Resentments may fester for millennia."

We proceeded northward, to the square giving on to the Church of San

Rocco, the School of San Rocco, and the gigantic church of the Franciscan brothers. "This is one of my favorite spots in all Venice," said il Professore, nevertheless hurrying me along, "because one passes from some of the most sumptuous architecture to some of the meanest. . . . Ah, here we are—the all too uncomely Campo San Tomà, with its dismal little tabernacle. Can you imagine how dreary the mass must be in that little pissoir? Who would be saved?"

After crossing a bridge, we paused before an imposing palazzo, which il Professore presented to me rather as a Parisian might the Tomb of Napoléon, an American the Lincoln Memorial.

"What?" I asked. "Who?"

"This is the birthplace and now museum of Carlo Goldoni, our great Venetian national playwright I have so often had occasion to quote from."

"Yes, your . . . poet of the everyday."

"Ecco. Yes, for till this extraordinarily penetrating writer rose up in the eighteenth century—a century, one must note, of great democratic movements such as your own colonial revolution—all Venetian art was either of the highest or the lowest. It was Veronese, Titian, Tintoretto, glorious and idealistic. Or it was our sinful farce of the masks: Arlecchin, Truffaldin, Brighella, zesty yet idiotic. There must be something enlightening—no?—between the sacred and the profane, something touching, comical, and true, as our life is. It is said that when an Italian of any other city attended his first evening of Goldoni, he would be shocked for fifteen minutes at the reality, and exhilarated from then on—at the reality. Because our caro Goldoni had used art as no one had before: to show life as we live it. Shakespeare, Molière, Goldoni."

"Do we go in?"

"No, the thought is enough for today. Our next stop is a brothel."

We passed through Campo San Polo, then went into a labyrinth of calles and rogas till we reached a square dominated by a church devoted to John the Baptist—the Church of St. John the Headless, in fact. And just down an alley was a house that, il Professore assured me, was Europe's most celebrated bordello, whose women were not only lovely and cultivated but so intricately practiced that princes would book season tickets.

"Of course, Alfred the Uncouth of Holstein Minor became so attached to a votary of this office that he suffered a heart attack during his Venetian stay. It was deliciously hushed up, and they gave it out that he died of surfeit. Ah, il coco! Will you have a taste?"

A vendor was offering slices of fresh coconut for ten lire; il Professore and I munched as walked toward the Grand Canal, and I believed this was my moment to tell him of what Hugh and I were up to. Il Professore attended with the academic's administrative interest, shaping his analysis even as he listened. As we neared Venice's version of the Big Muddy, he said, "All people seek after sexual congress, because it is in this way that we contact the life-force. Yes, it must be so, no matter how perilous or forbidden. There are those who risk everything they have and are to enjoy this certain pleasure. But it is especially important to make contact through those to whom we are most intensely attracted, not through those we find ourselves merely in the company of. The union with the life-force must be estatico, terribile."

"Am I having inappropriate sex?"

"You are having what we Venetians call sex alla Milanese: inconsequential but convenient because it doesn't interfere with office hours. Look there, across the water—the house with the two doors."

"I see it."

"Palazzo Marcello. There, two generations ago, died a great Venetian, ma infatto an Englishman, who styled himself as Baron Crow. He was an angry and reckless man who made many, many enemies. That is one side. The other is that he very assiduously sought the love of Venetian boys of the rougher class."

"Terroni?"

"Ah, you know this term. Sì, terroni del nord. Terroni da piazza." Local toughs.

"Why is it always boys? Youth?"

"Beh, the life-force! We live on their energy!"

"You make it sound like..."

"La pirateria?"

"What about living on the energy of older men? An older brother fig-ure, or even a kind of erotic father who—"

"Such as Baron Crow? Or myself? What energy?"

"Or ... You know, some ... Hercules has energy. Or Nik Acropoli."

"He's past thirty!" said il Professore, almost scandalized.

"Well, the way he bunches up when his arms move, or ..." I stopped, because il Professore was politely rising above a look of nausea.

"Cavolo," I said.

"O davvero," he replied.

We were hard by a traghetto station, and we crossed the Grand Canal to arrive at San Marcuola. Then we hopped on a vaporetto to glide through the snaky center of town to San Marco.

"Bene, we needed a pause in our exertions," he explained. "Sitting, riding. Sì, riposare. But it is necessary to reflect upon the all too refulgent glory of the city, so confidently dramatized in the very rhetoric of these great merchant palaces. La Serenissima was always proud, unapologetic. You see this in the architecture—arrogant, beautiful, powerful in its ele-gance. In your Scenarista's beloved Florence, the palaces were like strong-holds. Powerful, sì, but ugly. The Palazzo Vecchio, the Palazzo Strozzi, the Bargello ... They look like prisons. Here, everything is open, natural. It was this so very pretentious lack of pretension that caused such outrage and jealousy in other Italian cities—even in Europe generally." He sighed, looked around us at this precarious nonesuch, then shook his head. "All the world hated her, for her independence, her defiance of traditions, her inventions. To mediocrity, genius is unforgivable."

We fell silent, drinking in the still parade of Gothic and Renaissance fronts; they must have stopped building this city in 1450 or something. "These noble houses," said—well, rang out—il Professore at last, "pro-duced all the Serenissima's doges, men of ability and intelligence but as seldom as possible great men. The city itself was great. And it is an odd thing—those doges who cast away the ducal cap before their death almost invariably retired to a monastery, as if it would have been unseemly for them to continue as public figures after their time of importance. Perhaps, in all, it is best for the formidable to die when they lose their powers. What is more useless in the world than an *ex*-doge? But, ah!, here is San Marco already. We go to the mosque."

" 'The mosque?' " I asked, though I knew what he meant: the basilica of San Marco, so Eastern with its onion domes and Greek-cross layout that it's like Christ playing Mohammed. "Venezia," il Professore murmured as we approached, "the city without a patria. Byzantium owned her allegiance at first, for Rome was then a ruin and Christianity had moved house. But Venice finally broke away from the mother city, and celebrated her independence by building the greatest Byzantine church in the world. Not the biggest, nor even the richest: the most ironical."

We stood before it, in the overrun Piazza with the cameras and vendors and yelling and those disgusting pigeons. It was hard to maintain one's historical perspective.

"You see," il Professore went on, in grave earnest, "it was Venice's destiny to remain Eastern even as she became herself. She was neither of East nor West. She was . . . free of loyalty. And, naturalmente, all who bear the terror of loyalty to a supreme power loathe the freethinker. That is why she was hated. And now . . . Look around you."

I did: at the tourists and the guides and the coco sellers, at the two opposing overpriced cafés filled to the last table, at the sheer droll romance of holiday schmeiing.

"Now," said il Professore, "everyone loves her. She is forgiven—*ah!,* another bite of our wonderful Venetian coco?"

"Sì, Sior."

11

Women Have an Idea—Men Have Only an Image

"It's a new regime from now on!" Adriana cried, bustling about the house to move furniture around, replace *these* antiques with *those,* lay out the specially ordered towels and sheets, and generally admonish all of us to Show Signs of Life. Deodata, thrilled to the core, planned a roast. Hugh got the promise of *Carmen* and four sides of French solos—"And I want that Otto Klemperer to conduct the Gluck arias! He said I was lousy as Iphigénie—now we'll see!" And I got grief for not having started the book.

"Where are your outlines?" she cried. "Your doodle pages?"

"I've got a *mountain* of—"

"And where does the book actually start, if I should wonder?"

That was always the problem, so I said nothing. No, wait—"Where do *you* think it should start?" I asked her.

For a moment, she seemed to tune out on me; then, energized, she said,

"We must begin at the first performances when I felt the audience respond to me! Oh, of course! The *Vespri*s and *Luisa Miller*s. That first Norma, in Mantua. Well, the third night, anyway. It was during the first duet with Adalgisa—Livia Pandolfi, a wonderful colleague. She spit a lot, but always upstage, nothing on the costume. I don't remember exactly when it came, but I heard all the audience sigh at me, they were listening so strongly. Or even my first Venice performances, the *Adriana*."

So of course I got tense.

"They had heard of me by then, and they were in a fierce 'let's see' mood. When it was announced that sweet little Gianni Raimondi was indisposed but would go on anyway, instead of grateful applause they were growling. Oh, I was so fearful! I thought, If only it could be Donizetti, Bellini, bel canto. This *ridiculous* Cilèa. Bombastic and repetitive, flogging his measly tunes to death. But I made those stinkers listen to the music, all the same! Do you know, when I came out in the fourth act, pale and messy, they cheered? Oh, not because they liked me! Because they had to, because I was that good. *That good,* Mark—and this is where the book should start, no?"

We were in her room, because she was suddenly packing for a trip in this whirlwind new phase of hers, considering dresses and shoes, hunting for jewelry, studying her hairdo in the mirror.

"That would be a great place to start," I said, "and if I could get my hands on a tape of that performance, we could—"

"I might have one somewhere."

"What?"

"Don't electrocute it, as my old teacher Gilda da Coservo used to say. *Sing* it. Now, give me your partly honest opinion of these new hats."

"You have a *tape* of that—"

"I have so many tapes, who cares for a tape? Really, Mark. People send them to me as if . . . This one, with the bow? They fall madly in love when Audrey Hepburn wears it. . . . Or they want things autographed, I always wonder what they...No, we must plan my book. Now, the cover: I'm Norma? Violetta? Medea with the knife?"

"You're Pandora closing her box on my dreams. Why haven't you told me about this tape be—"

"Mark, really. Tapes. You have to be *in* the house to appreciate a performance, not just hearing it later. What about this one? Lovely in the store, and suddenly it looks so red."

She's modeling a hat, and I'm feverish for the music.

"It's Jacques Fath, you know," she told the mirror. "And *this* is a—"

"Adriana, *where* are your tapes? Please!"

"In storage. That place all the way down the Zattere near San Sebastiano. Rats have probably nibbled everything to...Mark, *what,* for heaven's sake?"

"I want that tape! I want you at your best in your lost role, and don't ask me why, because you *know* why. Because it's special." I hesitated, then: "Everyone hated you once. Soon they'll all love you. Your music is why."

"My, these outbursts," she said, all business as she gathered up the hats and tidied around and then stood there taking me in with a scoffing eye. "Maybe I won't bring you to Rome with me, after all."

"I don't want to go to Rome. What Rome?"

"Everyone wants to go to Rome. Anyway, I'm going and you're going, surprise. Deodata! Come take the coffee things and did the Paris contracts come?"

"Paris?"

"Tosca," she said, "and don't look so shocked. I told them yes a long time ago."

"You would have canceled."

"Oh, you know me so well?"

"I have to, I'm the author of your book. And what's *that?*" I added, though I recognized the little box with the flower. "Are you still on that stuff?"

"It makes me feel better."

"It makes you drugged and strange and—"

"Don't tell me what to do!" she thundered.

Absolute silence and nobody moves.

"Okay, I'm sorry," I said.

"Like my *mother*—always checking and disapproving!"

"Right, I exceeded the speed limit, forget it."

She blew the anger away with a smile and a wave.

"So you don't like the hats?" she asked. "I hope you like your new suit, at least. The tailor brought it over himself. It's in your room."

"My . . . new suit for what?"

"For Rome. I won't have you escorting me around in those American high-school prom clothes of yours."

"We're really going to Rome?"

"Well, why should I be here when Nik is there, no? La donna italiana resta coll'amante." The Italian woman sticks with her man.

"Except you're both Greek," I said.

"Go try on your suit with one of the new shirts and ties and make sure you pack Ercolani's scenario. We have to discuss, to plan, we have to write a book." She tried on another hat. "What is the cure for schmeiing around?"

"Executing one's destiny."

She didn't like that, but she bore it, and I went down the hall and, yes, there was the new suit laid out on my bed, a handsome very-light-wool number in charcoal gray. And the shirts were snazzy and the ties were bright, so I marched confidently back into Adriana's room, and she let out a happy cry and put her arms around me. I am not terribly demonstrative, yet suddenly I was getting a lot of embracing done: but while I was kind of crazy about Vieri and fond of Hugh, Adriana I was in awe of, and it felt troubling to touch her, not unlike hugging a goddess. Our heads were bent together affectionately, and there was a gratitude thing going on, too.

It was a thank-you embrace: for being who you are. But all that was said (by me) was "Thank you for the suit."

Hugh was about to return to London, so he arranged to leave when we were leaving and we all had a party in the garden, charmed by Deodata's Dramatic Reading of a piece in the *Gazzetino* about all the activity promised in Adriana's 1962–63 season; and marred by Hugh's revelation (to me, aside) that Terry McEwen's suspicious collector in St. John's Wood turned out to have been deceiving everyone about having the Venice *Adriana*.

"Apparently," Hugh told me, somewhat amused, "Terry whipped through the man's stacks and catalogues, and caught him up for a phony, and utterly had him out." He gave me a grim smile. "So I haven't come through all glistening, have I?"

We hugged, right there in the garden before them all, and I realized that I must like Hugh considerably, all the more so—I was certain of this—because we had known each other so fundamentally. We would have been friendly in any case, but having sex made us . . . friends.

I told Hugh, "I hope we . . . I mean—"

"Of course we will," he said. "And I do have *something* for you, in the anyway, even if it's not your dodgy Venice *Adriana*."

I knew I'd love it, because he grinned as he handed me a large, flat package, one foot square.

"Records!" I cried.

"You'll be surprised. Actually, I'd bought them for myself, in Milan. But you'll want them more."

Siora Varin's mother had dared the ground floor again, and presented Hugh with another sample of her mysterious pottery as a going-away present. This number was, I believe, a bud vase. Everyone cheered when Hugh accepted it, and he was courtly with his thanks, though eventually he sidled up to me and said, sotto voce, "What does that lurid crone think I'm to do with this? And why me?"

"I think she has mistaken you for the Actor."

"Well, I'm flattered, in any event."

"Ah!" said il Professore, coming up. "Siorissima Varin has honored you with an exhumation. What a festal day!"

Hugh merrily waved the vase at Siora Varin as she passed. "Zà, el don," she remarked. Your lovely gift. "Bon viazzo, dasseno." Have a good trip.

"Madam," said Hugh, "I intend to drop this horror into the nearest canal."

"Troppo zentil," replied la Siora, with a bow. You're most kind.

Vieri, admiring my new suit, kept trying to stay in English while telling me of his progress in motorboat driving at Zormano's squero, though the vocabulary was too technical for him. Heck, I couldn't have done it in English myself.

"When you come back, Mark?" Vieri asked me. "There is much I have to tell you, sì?"

"I expect we'll be back in a few—"

"Molto importante, Mark. That I have to say, yes, Mark? Do you love Vieri? Do you miss me when you are go?"

He had this way of holding a searching glance on you while waiting for answers to his questions, eyes at eye level, mouth almost on mouth.

"Sure I'll miss you," I said.

"No, this is not . . . sincerità, Mark. It is segreto, amore, what I have to tell. Like us two," he added, very urgently. "Please believe."

"I do, I will, I promise,"

"A fratù, Mark," he said, solemnly holding me right in the middle of the party.

"Mark?" asked Hugh; "*Mark*," Adriana demanded; and I felt like Aeneas, drummed on to his goal by destiny: to Rome!

In those days, I should tell you, air travel was not as acculturated as it is now. People often took boats for long trips and trains for hops, so Adriana and I rode the rapido down the center of Italy, with, by chance, a first-class compartment all to ourselves.

We had scarcely passed Padua when Adriana broke out the rations that Deodata had prepared: cold baked chicken, cold pasta (penne all'amatriciana), and oranges, which Adriana peeled with casual expertise. She made much of the rare delight of picnicking on the train, though in fact what she really delighted in was saving money. Dining cars, restaurants, and the like were for times when others played host.

It was during the oranges that I pulled out and opened Hugh's present—an album box, so it was surely an opera. But as I pulled off the wrapping all I could see was black—no, there was something on one face, a photograph of Adriana as ... yes, Amina in *La Sonnambula,* in that Marie Taglioni ballet getup in the blankest white, with her hair pulled straight back, her hands crossed at her breast, and on her face the ravishing, victimized stare of the truly innocent brought to some terrifying realization. . . .

"What is that?" Adriana asked, cleaning her hands with one of those little packet things Europeans were so wild about, though they were too efficiently fantastical to be anything but an American invention.

The album spine read only "Grafanas Sonnambula Milan 55," and I said, very quietly, "It's your Amina from La Scala. Live, in the house. The real thing."

Curiously—not fascinated, but politely interested, as you might be by a friend's new charm bracelet—she opened the album, which held three plain-covered discs, no booklet. "Very nice," she said neutrally.

"It's better than nice—it's historical. Now it won't be just tapes for the underground elite, but *records* that anyone can buy! Right? See, they've finally decided to start preserving the wild magic. *This* is opera. Isn't it? Not those scaled-down studio jobs." She was just looking at me, wondering why I was so excited. "Authenticity," I told her. "Amore, segreto," I said. "The music of the future."

"But what recording firm is it?" she asked, peering at the uncommunicative cover as if she might have read its secret lettering if only she'd brought the right glasses. "When did I contract for this? What is my cachet?"

"The label is some guy turning these out in his basement, you didn't contract, and you won't get paid. You'll get something better: remembered for all time at your greatest."

She chirped out a sour laugh. "When it's over, it's over."

"No, that's my point. It can never be over as long as it's still there. Yes, *you'll* be over one day. *I'll* be over. But when I'm over, there'll be nothing. I might never have visited at all. But *this*"—I reclaimed the records, ready to treasure them for life—"and maybe the Covent Garden *Norma* and the La Scala *Luisa Miller* and *Hoffmann* and a *Medea* from somewhere and, heaven help me, the Venice *Adriana* . . . these will—"

"Don't talk nonsense, Mark, I've made plenty of records. Just ask Carteri and Carosio and that lovely Zinka Milanov who thinks there should be a law against anyone singing Norma but Zinka Milanov. Ask who's made more records, we'll see."

"No, but those are just—"

"Put that thing away and help me work my schedule out. I need a coach, an accompanist, and a confidant"—she pronounced it alla francese: *caw-fi-daw*—"ed eccoti. Now, there is Tosca, Paris, Ercolani, Clytemnestra, a certain book you haven't even started . . . and you're mooning over a lousy little production without even a libretto pamphlet, not to mention candids of the artistes at the recording sessions or looking glamorous as they dine at Biffi Scala. And I don't feel all that contenta myself, if you must know. I forgot to take la Fleur this morning in all the excitement, with everyone getting presents but me and you hugging that shifty-looking Vieri from the courtyard."

"He's not shifty," I said. Well, call him richly ambiguous. "And Hugh's giving you the present of your very own *Carmen,* in which you will be superb, even if it is a studio creation."

"I feel so alive," she suddenly breathed out. "As if we were flying in the *sky* to Rome. I feel Nik in my life. Have you ever been in love, Mark, young as you are?"

"I . . . don't . . ."

"When you will be, you will learn of a feeling that is quite quite more important than any other feeling you have known. You will be always thrilled because it will give you a calm you did not have before." She smiled. "A calm," she almost purred, "that lets you forgive almost every villain. And you will forgive yourself, and have someone to share with. That brightens the good news and sweetens the bad, you see. I can bear anything with Nik." She smiled again. "Yes, anything, you see. So I must, must not lose him. Anything."

Nik met us at the station with the usual host of reporters, tipped off by someone or other. This time Adriana was playing not the opulent diva but the enchanted princess, focusing her public's attention on what *she* wanted them to see: not the woman fighting for control but the woman who delights in ceding it to a redemptively overwhelming force.

Travel brochures speak of "whisking" one to a destination, but our cabdriver more truly hurled us to the Princess's apartment; it was a real shake-up after the gliding transports of Venice. All the way, Adriana and the Actor traded sappy endearments in mixed Italian and English. Odd that they never conversed in Greek: but then Nik favored English as the language of the culture he admired, Hollywood; and Adriana favored Italian as the language of the culture she had adopted, music.

Like the cab ride, the Princess's apartment offered quite some change from our cozy Venetian ways, being two floors' worth of an old palace on the Via Torino, not far from the Opera. Rugs were like tapestries, and the monster-size rooms boasted windows you could ride a gondola through. The place was a museum of marble and art; I truly felt an intruder in the bedroom assigned to me.

Adriana locked herself in to bathe and nap, but outside Rome was roaring, and I felt like an exploratory amble. Then the Actor said Giampaolo was coming around to take us all to dinner.

"*Ercolani* Giampaolo?" I asked, following him down a corridor into a lavish salon or whatever Europeans call those regal dens that are like Marlene Dietrich's idea of a family room. A massive table dominated, and upon it the Actor had spread a selection of eight-by-ten black-and-white glossies, drawn from his latest P.R. shoot. Lighting a cigarette, he urged me to tell him which ones I liked.

"You have the sharp eye, I know," he said. "You like to seem a not-knowing boy, yes this, but you quietly look right into everyone, I think."

The photographs, all taken on the beach, ran from Nik in a tuxedo, to Nik with the tie gone and the shirt front unfastened and the pants just starting to fall away, to Nik in mesh shorts so sheer he would have alarmed a nudist colony, to Nik raw.

"It is smart, yes?" he said. "Le sexy-hot."

"You look great. But isn't this a bit avant-garde? Who's going to print nude photos of anyone?"

"It is strategy. Somehow the photos get out, the press grab them, it is scandal, legendary."

I should probably say here that Nik was not only wildly handsome but in terrific shape, one of those big-shouldered, long-waisted guys who stay in tone with a little ocean swimming and a calcio match with the kids in the street. Big genitals, too. He was half hard in one of the nude shots.

"It is new way of keeping famous," he continued, moving the pictures around, trying the partly dressed Nik next to the nude, the erection atop the tuxedo. "It is not real you, but this *image* you."

"Then all your fame would be fake," I protested. "And it wouldn't be you they liked, it would be—"

"It *is* all fake, this," he said. "Today on the set I conquered many crooks, detectives, all after me. I sock this one, shoot that one, kick, turn, shoot again, like ballet, in tempo of music. But am I this hero? I am Greek boy from Athens! How do I meet such these crooks, detectives? When do I meet a gun? In movies. All is fake, performance. C'est la vie, it is all theatre."

"Not for Adriana. When she plays those big mad ladies, she turns into them."

"Oh, so Adrì is Medea, she kills her children? *What* children? And Norma, she burns up. But Adri is still now."

"I didn't mean literally. But it sure isn't fake the way she feels it."

He put his hand on the top of my back, looked off in the direction of Adriana's room—well, their room—lightly pounded me a bit as if wondering whether to spring something on me, then said, "We talk this man-to-man style, okay you?"

"Okay."

"Bravo, sit. In these big chairs, by the fireplace, we are great Roman lords, okay? So, you say to me—what for is Adrì so busy now? To do *Tosca* in Paris, records, this movie of Ercolani. It is wonderful, but why all now?"

"*Is* it wonderful? Or do you maybe resent it?"

He pauses, then: "I have not thought this. Do I? Beh. Perhaps, a little I like the woman to be empty and crashing down when I am not there. But I always know Adrì is different. She is exciting, why. So much in her, the love, the feelings, the anger, fascinating to watch. No, the busy is good, I think. I just wonder why now, suddenly."

"Maybe she's getting ready for you to leave."

"Beh."

He picked up the half-hard nude shot, showed it to me, and grinned.

"Yes, you're a stunner, Nik."

Through the house came Adriana's voice, humming "L'Amore è una cosa meravigliosa." "Love Is a Many-Splendored Thing," still a big hit at the time.

"You hear her?" said Nik. "The chosen one, I think." Aroused, an arm around my shoulder, he guided me toward the singing; he was like a big Vieri, older and smarter. He had figured life out.

Well, not all of life: "Tell me, Mark. This one thing—why do women want to love only one man forever? Men don't love one woman."

I said, "It is because women have an idea of men, while men have only an image of women."

"Is true?"

"I guess."

He smiled. "So young you know such philosophy? Then tell this—what is your image? All these others racing around in the run of love—Adriana, Nik is me, others, who knows? But Mark is so secret to us."

How often I'd been confronted with this. Got a girl, Mark? You want me to fix you up with Eleanor's cousin? Who're you taking to the prom? And you could not possibly hang by the sidelines. They allow no neutrality: you're part of it or you're queer. That's the choice you make. But the penalty for being part of it is to live so dishonestly that you become a corruption of yourself. They've burned in hell for less. And, you see, every so often in this life of ours, a moment comes when you can revise your choice. Some never seize it, never in all their days; they try to thrive on lies. Some grab it the first chance; what a relief. I had to work myself up to it, but I knew that *this* moment I would take.

So I looked at Nik straight on and said, "I like guys, Nik. And my image would probably make your nude photos blush."

"Yes, Mark, I know this. I was only teasing with you about love. I did not mean to cause you this." He was genuinely contrite, casing my eyes to see if he had hurt me. "You remember that first day when you come to Venice? Adrì liked you right from this. But if you weren't froscio, I would give you the boot. Or could I let the rival man be sleeping in my home when I am not?"

"Am I that obvious?"

"Not to most, I think. But I knew, because I am from life and I see what all things are. Remember, I told you, you have to be mondano. *Worldly*. Listening to others and this learning . . ."

These many years later, I can confess that I broke down, because I had never seized that moment before, except with someone else of the cloth, and I suddenly felt vulnerable and I don't know what else. Maybe limited. Yes, that sounds awful; but next to Nik, to whom all things desirable came as if drawn to their very source, I felt somewhat lacking in radiance. Nik held me, because that was how he assuaged pain: contact. And I held on, because I knew he was one of those ultra-rare figures that slip into one's life with neither blame nor praise but with acceptance. Adriana was in good hands, for the while.

12

The Chain of Life

Ercolani's dinner was one of those elegant catchalls, the kind you see photographed in the newspapers (as a rule) and wonder where they found a table big enough. There were: Ercolani and lo Scenarista; Adriana and Nik; some of Nik's co-players from his policier; Nik's agent (whom Nik was about to fire because he "can't arrange the Hollywood"); the agent's girl friend (Hungarian, beaming, mute); the girl friend's agent; and the co-players' dates. We took up an unseemly fraction of a chic restaurant, as pedestrians ogled us from the street and photographers dashed in, snapped, and raced out like bandits, though dinners like this are created on the very notion that photographers will publicize it. On one level, if it isn't shot—preserved, like Adriana's performances on pirate records—it might as well never have happened.

I was stuck down at the end of the table with lo Scenarista, but at least he was someone I knew—and in fine form, too, smacking away (verbally) at the "miserabili da café" that we had been lumped with and heaping encomiums upon his god, Ercolani.

"Searching, always" was lo Scenarista's view of the Ercolani approach to art and life. Indeed, they were one: "What he *is*," lo Scenarista told me, "is what he films. There is no selection. It is such honesty, oh yes."

"The art is the life, huh?"

"He has no choice," lo Scenarista told me with a sort of expert simplicity; I suppose he had made this speech before. "It is his destiny. Such films, personaggi, subjects as he treats are what he was born to confront. To reveal man as demonkind."

"Everyone has a choice," I said.

"Oh no, he is driven to it, born to be Ercolani."

"No one is driven to anything," I insisted. No, try this tack: "You admire his movies, don't you?"

"They are works of genius."

"If he has no choice and was simply born to the Calvinist assignment of living out his particular fate, then he cannot take credit for those films. He neither conceived nor executed them—his fate did. Right?"

"No!"

"But that's what you're saying."

He bent closer to me to rephrase his argument, but our attention was drawn to a tiny man in tails and white gloves who was clapping his hands and crying, over and over, "Signore, signori. Signore, signori."

As our table turned to him, he extended an arm to indicate two approaching figures: a very old, very short woman leading a doughy, middle-aged blind man who was laced up so tightly in his carnival duds that he might cascade into a puddle if you pulled a zipper.

"I hate this part," I told lo Scenarista, though I had no idea what part this was. I don't like surprises with people in creepy clothing. "Is this a regular entertainment at this place?"

"Eh," lo Scenarista replied. How should I know?

"Signore, signori. Signore, signori."

Why *our* table?, I was thinking, but the others seemed amused; I heard Adriana merrily cry, "What will it be?" as she grabbed the Actor's arm, showing the world how it feels to be distinguished, loved, and regaled by a freak show right at your restaurant table.

"Il figliuolo vede il futuro, la sorte, l'occasione," the little man in tails sang out in a high voice. The son foretells your fate. "La madre parla per lui, parla con voi." The mother does the talking. Okay; but he was shrilling this out in a neither-here-nor-there voice, one you'd use when trying to scare your sister in a cemetery. "La Commedia del Indovino Cieco e della Madre Chi Parla." The Act of the Blind Seer and the Mother Who Interprets for Him.

Making his way toward the middle of the table, the son began feeling faces, and none too gently. He had happened into a crowd of the Actor's chums, running his hands over them and making uncouth noises. The first face he abandoned soon enough, to its owner's relief (and puzzlement), the second he studied inconclusively, the third he barely touched. But the fourth, for some reason, brought on a smile and somewhat less disgusting noises than before. He paused, seeming to listen to his own private music, then nodded intently several times and babbled some more. His mother, hanging on his every sound, grandly held out her arms, smiled, and, as if translating for him, announced, "The child knows well its parents, but parents never understand the child. It is the chain of life forever repeated." Then she bowed to buzzing voices and light applause.

Adriana and the Actor, I noticed, were watching with the wonder of infants. (Adriana, at least, may have been acting somewhat.) But Ercolani was transfixed. Pointing this out to lo Scenarista, I asked, "Is he going to put them in the movie, too?"

"Sì, certamente," he replied, matter-of-factly, as if major art were always built on objets trouvés picked up among the mad vaudeville of Rome.

Traveling farther down the table, closer to us, the blind son reached an attractive young woman—the girl friend of someone's boy friend, if I got it right—who accepted the manhandling of her face rather well and inspired some of the blind son's most elated gushings. These his mother rephrased as "The heartless king thrives, the heartless queen languishes."

There was more applause this time, and laughter, especially from Adriana, who seemed to be having a fine time not taking any of this seriously while basking in the hot love of the paparazzi flashbulbs. But the blind son had come uncomfortably close to my end of the table, and I was just about to rise and get out of the way when he froze, attended once more to the room's psychic undertones or whatever, and frantically began to grope his way back up the table. At times he would halt, inhaling the air and sticking out his hands, fingers waving as if pulling invisible, crucial strings.

"Siamo qui," Ercolani called out. "Che volete di noi?" We're up here. What do you seek?

The blind son shook his head and began to move again, slowly now, toward the head of the table. He smiled and dribbled as he stalked, and Adriana grew wary. Our whole party seemed to sense that it was indeed she whom the blind son had picked up on his shortwave, and the atmosphere turned expectant, fearful.

"È quella donna?" the mother asked. Is it the woman? "Si trova là, guarda e attenda tranquillamente." She's there, happily waiting for you.

Adriana murmured something to the Actor. He got up and, just in time, pushed away the blind son, who let out a torrent of noise as he repeatedly tried to lunge at Adriana.

"It is dangerous to break the chain of life," his mother intoned—but people were calling for intervention by the management, and the three players were hustled out. The table got very animated then, everyone laughing nervously and comparing opinions; but Adriana was pale and trembling and the Actor genuinely irritated, and now the party broke up.

Some of us hung around outside making those dawdling farewells while Adriana and the Actor shared some words with Ercolani, then jumped into a cab.

"The chain of life," lo Scenarista mused as we watched them depart. He seemed buoyant. "It is a useful idea for the film, no? For it tells of the continuities from father to son. To the Greeks, this was fate. To Christian Europe, this was original sin—the ghost that no born mortal can evade."

Ercolani joined us, looking very pensive. "She wants to blame me for what happened," he told us. "But I persuaded her that it was her amazing energy that attracted the mage's intuitions. She drew him to her."

It's called la Fleur, I thought, apropos of her amazing energy—the sudden merriments followed by eruptions followed instantly by coy recoveries. It's not energy: it's a drug. The real energy was spent in building and then proclaiming her art, and that energy was dissolving, along with her voice.

"Some coffee?" lo Scenarista asked Ercolani. "La Duchessa? L'Urbe? Il Prego?"

"Fastidiosi," said Ercolani. Boring. "Our young American friend needs to see a less fanciful Roma." He looked meaningfully at lo Scenarista, who immediately seemed mortified, regretful, and ambivalent. What's going on? "Most great cities are no more than old famous cities," Ercolani continued, turning back to me. "They are places where everything happened hundreds of years ago. Rome is the oldest of all—yet it is very contemporary. Each day, new history is made."

"Do you want to go?" lo Scenarista asked me in a warning tone. "Do you feel you can see this?"

"I'm a stranger in Rome, right? I have to have adventures."

"Andiam," said Ercolani, waving at the last bit of our party as they headed off in another direction. Lo Scenarista and I packed into Ercolani's red Giulia G.T. and we drove to (I expected this from things il Professore had told me) the Piazza di Spagna—the Place of Boys, so to say. Ercolani parked, and we got out and strolled around as he pointed out features of the scene—the terribly nervous older gentleman pretending to be hypnotized by the posted menu of the English teahouse, the ruffianly youths who favored the eastern end of the square and the more socialized youths at the western end, the gentleman and stripling enjoying a leisurely conversation by the fountain.

"One negotiates quickly, in most cases," said Ercolani, "or the boy becomes suspicious."

"Do they discuss price only," I asked, "or—"

"Quick, see there," he interrupted, noting a lavish, bright-eyed, and fairly well dressed teen talking to a hopelessly moribund old guy. "You see Luca, such a beautiful cheat. Watch as he stares eagerly into the man's eyes, rests his hand on the man's shoulder, moves his lips as if bursting to kiss. Liar!" He laughed. "In fact, he does nothing. Or there is Denis— from Corsica, he says." Another laugh. "Is all love a lie? You pay plenty for nothing, some nights."

"Non e l'amore, questo," lo Scenarista muttered. This is not love.

"Perhaps not here," said Ercolani, gazing up the Spanish Steps toward the sky. "It has become bourgeois, predictable. Love should be rash, unexpected. The true lover is the one who upends you, shatters your ideals. Love is protean, mythic. Love is struggle. Love is everything you fear. It has no dignity. When you enter the room of love you are in control, but soon you cry, 'Turn me over!' "

"I beg you," lo Scenarista interposed, "to consider the mystification of our young friend."

"Sta bene," I told them. It's okay.

Lo Scenarista made a helpless gesture, but Ercolani, walking me back to his car with an arm around my shoulder, started asking me about America and our equivalents for (as he put it) "la vita." I had to ask if he meant Roman male prostitution or the lives of homosexuals in general. And of course it took forever to sort it out, because there were no terms for all this in 1962, in Italian or English. We were like doctors trying to define a condition that had yet to be documented.

Ercolani tried another approach: "When I was an infant, perhaps five or six, I organized lists in my head of all the boys I knew. There were two lists—those who were bello and those who were brutto." The hand-some and the ugly. He turned to lo Scenarista: "You?"

Lo Scenarista shook his head.

"It is necessary."

"I do not wish to tell."

"The process of honesty," Ercolani explained, "is a part of the creation of my movies."

Lo Scenarista shrugged.

"Beh. So?"

After a moment, lo Scenarista said, "It is about sin. The brothers found me ..."

"At what age? Engaged in what act? Describe your partner in exquisite detail. Were his ears pointed or curved? Did his nostrils flare like a pig's? Were you lo sposo or la sposa? Did you enjoy the guilt, taste the tears of Christ in your lover's cream?"

"Oh yes, I have *told* this story!"

"But not to our young American friend, having adventures."

Turning to me with an air of sheepish resignation, lo Scenarista said, "An older cadet at school forced me to taste of his member. To ... suck on it."

"And you frisked and capered at this first taste of love, eh?" said Er-colani, a droll line but very seriously uttered.

"I ... I was flattered by this attention. He was a very popular boy, very ... handsome."

"Confide in us as to a priest—how was he hung?"

Lo Scenarista paused as a pair of amiably thuggish teens scuttled past us. One nodded at Ercolani but regarded me with suspicion.

"Actually," I told lo Scenarista, "if you're uncomfortable with this story, don't—"

"No," he replied gently. "It is true that I should answer to my own past. Each of us bears his temptation, yes. From that day at school, this has been mine, and it is why I feel at times like a condemned man."

"Condemned to bliss," said Ercolani, as we got into the car.

"Condemned among the foremost," lo Scenarista corrected, "to shrivel in God's fire."

"In God's greatest gift!" Ercolani laughed out. "The love of the outlaw."

"It is *sin*."

"Sin," Ercolani declared, starting the motor, "is the child's sensation that he has offended his parents. This is expanded into the patriarchal state, in which the Church and lay authorities combine to convince the people that fathers must be obeyed or their love will be withdrawn."

Thinking of Adriana and her difficult childhood, I asked, "What if it is already withdrawn?"

"Then it is much easier to free oneself of their tyranny."

"Or much harder, because then the child is doomed to pursue the unattainable." Boldly, I went on, "Did your parents love you?"

"My father was devastating," Ercolani replied, which does not appear to answer the question.

We drove in silence for a bit. Then lo Scenarista said, "You aren't going to L'Aschenbach, are you? Oh yes, not!"

"Ma perchè no?"

L'Aschenbach turned out to be a café cast along lines laid down in the Piazza di Spagna: older paying gentlemen and working boys, though there were as well some colorful characters who operated on a different plane entirely.

For instance, there were Rita and Anita, irreproachable replicas of Hayworth and Ekberg who joined our table without invitation to regale Ercolani (in such vividly locked-up Roman dialect that I missed a lot) with the latest pranks of Sergio, Rolando, Giacometto, and, in particular, a certain Tonudo.

"Ah, Tonudo, sì," Ercolani chimed in, "with the wondrous poleaxe and no idea in that curly Apulian head what to do with it."

"Lo sistemerò io," Anita grunted out, in his own voice. I'll show him what to do with it. "Chi è lo tiscio?" she asked, about me, now the coy starlet, one hand delicately fingering her famous bosom. Who's this guy?

"Un amico d'Adriana Grafanas," Ercolani told them, adding, in a warning tone, "Eh, diplomatiche, badate." Be polite, girls.

And so they were, in their strenuously facetious way. Lo Scenarista looked utterly miserable and said not a word, but I was amused enough. Had Vieri been here during his Roman stay?, I wondered. Rita and Anita began cataloguing the boys on view, name after name, reviewing their fortes and faux pas, all the while constantly advising Ercolani to cast them in a movie or at least make one based on their lives. (Here they got into a mildly charming quarrel over whose life was more glamorous; as they resolved it, Rita claimed the more distinguished past but Anita anticipated the more brilliant future.)

Lo Scenarista had turned entirely away from us, leaning forward in his chair with his head almost in his lap. I tried to bring him into the party while Rita and Anita enjoyed ferocious debate as to whether blond or dark-haired men made better boy friends. "Why so glum?" I asked lo Scenarista.

He just shook his head. Behind us, Rita and Anita had reached a climax and, after ravaging each other with a load of arcane terms, pulled out fans and began ferociously rattling the air with them. Ercolani, however, had tuned them out to stare at a brooding young man nursing a coffee all by himself on the other side of the café. The young man acknowledged Ercolani with a slow nod, thought it over, then, taking his coffee, approached and sat at our table.

I was impressed by Ercolani's formality in this picturesque environment; he might have been dining with Alberto Moravia and Giorgio Bassani, though he would surely not have been gazing at them with the aching triumph of discovery that he presented to this young man. But then, once more, it is not artists that captivate us: it is art. Beauty. Surprise.

Ercolani suavely introduced us all to the newcomer, who nodded at lo Scenarista and me and looked with grim loathing at Rita and Anita.

"Uffa," said Anita calmly. "What fire."

"I'm scalded," Rita agreed. "Toss us the Campari bottle."

Ercolani told the young man, "You are very handsome. Very serious, very alone with your coffee. What do they call you?"

"I'm Ruccio."

"Ruccio, sì. Very, very handsome."

"Play it correctly, madamigella," Rita advised Ruccio, "and he'll make you a movie star."

"Like us," Anita helpfully added.

"Oh, I know who you are," Ruccio told Ercolani, matching his even tone. "Famous, with a sack of loot, smart with words. You like to be forked, then you turn a revolution and do the forking. All the kids know about Giampaolo Ercolani. But I am not like all, not so easy, eh?" He smiled. "I, Ruccio, say this to you."

"Accidenti," said Rita, fanning away. "Che guaio, tutti." Everybody watch out, here comes trouble.

Ercolani said, "I see you in the half-darkness, lying on the bed, face-down, wet, warm, peaceful, ready, happy. I inspect you. Like all beautiful boys, you have a dirty ass. You need attention, affection. Then you are compelled to show your soft side. It is wonderful when rough boys show their soft side to me."

"Why do you play these games?" lo Scenarista cried, turning around to face the table. "Why is the highest name in Italian cinema in this place, with these creatures?"

Anita favored lo Scenarista with the classic Italian gesture of disbelief, irony, and rejection: pulling down on the cheek muscles just below the center of the eye. But Rita smacked Anita with her fan, warning her with "Ecco la regina." Here comes the queen. I turned to see what she had seen—everyone did, except Ercolani and Ruccio, still engaged in their staring contest—and there, coming toward us in an air of almost elegiac languor, was an androgynous figure in dark slacks and a loose red silk

shirt, hair too long for a male and torso too slim for a female. Very dig-
nified, with a touch of evil blended into a quiet sense of command. Medea
unmarried?

"La Carlù," Rita breathed out.

"Dottore regista," la Carlù slyly and cordially called Ercolani—Sir Director—as (s)he sleeked into the chair next to Ruccio. "I see you have met
my love. My trove. My rigid prince who moans while dreaming."

"Don't talk to him," Ruccio told la Carlù.

"He is surly because I am late. But he is always surly, so I am always
late."

"The tougher the boy," Ercolani reasoned, "the sweeter his taste."

"Kiss me," la Carlù told Ruccio. He didn't, and when la Carlù reached
for him (with a sad smile), he pushed la Carlù away.

"What do you think of Ruccio for Agamemnon?" Ercolani asked lo
Scenarista; it was the first time Ercolani had taken his eyes off the boy.

Lo Scenarista was nearly speechless at this casual infiltration of wooing
rituals into the Higher Cinema. "We are considering the Inglese Bogarde!
Or Alessandro Metro! You liked his hat, remember?"

"Quel gigione," Ercolani answered. That ham. "I see the youth, power,
vitality of the story. Doom is interesting only when it stalks the most gifted.
You, mio caro, see slimy doddering kings with bad livers cringing at or-
acles. That has all been done, my friend. What says our young American?"

He had turned to me; I noticed that he was now in fact turning to
everyone but Ruccio. Changing his tack from showing need to playing
hard to get, perhaps.

"It's true," I said. "We always think of those old Greek characters
as . . . well, veterans of life. Casting for youth"—here I borrowed a leaf
from il Professore's text—"would bring your audience directly in touch
with the life-force."

"Già," said Ercolani. "The chain of life."

"*Art* is the chain of life," lo Scenarista insisted. "The themes. The enlightenment. The tales that stir the soul. Art is the life-force, not a . . . a fling with Signor Chimai that is gone in a moment."

"Adriana isn't young, though," I reminded Ercolani. "How would she fit in with all these Vieris?"

"She is la Madrone." The all-mother.

"We must go, tesoro," la Carlù told Ruccio, in honeyed tone.

"I will stay."

"No, caro." Legato, andante. "The friend I told you about is waiting for us. He is eager to meet you. It is important." She whispers, improvising. "Who knows what money? Or even a trip to the beach some weekend. He has a villa, anything may happen." Fierce now, with coloraturas and high notes. "I worked so hard for this, yes, for us both, diletto, carissimo, and you know how angry they get when we cancel. It's only us two, amore mio, he will sit and watch, never touch, oh, except perhaps the tiniest finger here or there." The high note: "We *have to*, or do you wish to sleep in the street tomorrow night?"

Ruccio was grinning at Ercolani: see, everyone wants me.

Ercolani nodded.

"Caro," la Carlù prompted, but halfheartedly. The scena's over and she's almost out of voice.

"Our romantic Rome," Anita sighed. "The city of love and money."

"Not love and money," Ercolani corrected. "Sex and power." His head leaned toward Ruccio—*strained*, I should say. His eyes were a fire on ice. "There is but one way to know a boy," he told Ruccio. "Inside him, feeling him, enjoying him. The one way, and all boys know this. Tonight? Yes? Now? Quanto costa la beatitudine?" How much will heaven run me?

"No one enjoys Ruccio," Ruccio replied, adding, "I am Ruccio," which seemed true but irrelevant. Maybe I was missing a Roman nuance some-where.

Well, lo Scenarista decided he had had enough *right then*, and bolted from the place; yet it was as if no one had noticed. Ercolani and la

Carlù were intent on Ruccio. Rita was whispering behind her fan to Anita.

"Shouldn't someone..." I began, but they all ignored me, so I went outside. I don't know if I liked lo Scenarista all that much; I just didn't think it right to let him tear off without at least making a stab at soothing his hurt. He was in the street, perhaps less looking for a cab than trying to get run down by one.

"Che casa lurida," he spat out. "What you must think of us now!"

"I liked it better than that sleazy mind-reading act in the restaurant. Why are you so upset?"

"Because I love him. Oh yes, *you* are aware! I make no pretense. You know his work? You know what savage honesty he brings to his art? He is a great, great man."

He had given up scanning the street and was working up a tirade. "You know how eager I am to write for him? He has never let anyone collaborate with him before—always it is his personal vision, his own script. I am the first. It is such honor! To admire him so, then to meet him and see how his mind is where the art comes from, yes, *so*. To love his work is to love *him*. I hate it but it comes from inside me, and how can I hate it then? It is noble to love greatness, no? It is glorious to work in his circle, to hear his momentous views, to join with him in his philosophical struggle! Everything he says, it is as if he can reimagine the world, you become so enriched . . ." He was almost in tears. "I am not content to be for tutta la mia vita the second assistant arranger for la Mostra. Oh, such a prestigious festival, but what is it? The politics. The corruption. I am embarrassing you."

"No."

"Sì."

"*No*, really. I have sympathy for you. I just think you're—"

"You admire him?"

"Oh, he's gifted, no question."

"It does not repel you, to see him hungry for that sordid terrone? Che robaccia!" What trash.

"Why should it repel me?" I said, annoyed because he thought of Vieri in the same way, and Vieri was sacred to me now. "If that's what he wants..."

"Would *you* want that?"

It was a little unnerving, everyone in Europe taking me for a homosexual when I was accustomed to passing for regular at home. Or maybe he meant that metaphorically. Not would I want that *sexually,* but... These circuitous rationalizations.

"I will tell you what *I* want," he charged on. "This would be someone I look up to, learn from. Not this slavering—so, ecco la diva!"

La Carlù had come out, with her arms crossed over her chest like a totem, to walk past us in a daze.

"She pimps for her lover, you saw that, no?" said lo Scenarista, looking after her.

"I thought you respected Ercolani's mooching around in the underworld. You saw it as his artistic mission."

"Son vinto," he said miserably. I am defeated.

Ercolani and Ruccio waltzed out about two seconds later, the one with an air of suppressed glee and the other suddenly high and happy.

"Well," I said, "here's our tormented genius and the bartered bride."

"Come, we'll drop you," Ercolani told me, with a proprietary arm around Ruccio's shoulder. Surely the volatile boy would shake it off—no, he suffered it gladly.

Yes, how much does heaven cost, I wondered, as Ercolani sped back to Via Torino and our temporary quarters. Ercolani and Ruccio were perfectly (and I thought surprisingly) silent and lo Scenarista made (do you believe this?) enthusiastically perfunctory conversation with me about the passing sights. I was doing that American-abroad thing, asking those uselessly pertinent questions of people with major work on their minds, and all three were certainly thrilled to be rid of me. Well, so was I of them. It was a relief to walk into the huge silence of the Princess's flat.

Good, they're in bed. Because I was all socialed up; all I wanted to do was play the *Sonnambula* records—the first time, I suddenly realized, that

I would hear Adriana sound truly glorious since I had come to Italy a year before.

You have to hunt for the stereo in a place like this—it turned out to be hidden in a drawer that pulled out of a great wooden something, probably a priceless Renaissance novelty. I kept the volume down, though I was about three quarters of a mile away from their bedroom. And I sat and listened.

Well, the singing was terrific, of course. I mean the security and the exploitation of color and the wheedling intermarriage of registers and the crazy coloratura—all the stuff you've always heard about the young Grafanas. But most special now was the amazingly plangent quality of the sad parts, not just the lyricism but the way Adriana suggested that this one heroine's doom was big enough to encompass all the world's sorrow, to take us all into her shadow. After all, in its story *La Sonnambula* is no more than a trivial bourgeois comedy about a Swiss village girl who is wrongly accused of infidelity, goes wild with grief, is exculpated, and weds her boy friend. It's not Aeschylus. Yet Adriana made such opulently plundered *music* of this grief that she built the piece into something worthy of the most sophisticated public. We hear the ravaging of beauty, yet she makes it beautiful. Touching. Unbearable. Awesome. I know opera buffs are supposed to like the fiery ladies, and Adriana certainly played her share. No Tosca stabbed Scarpia with greater relish, no Norma seemed quite so apt as the sovereign of a savage tribe. It's what they call a "phallic woman." But, remember, she was Violetta, Lucia, Manon, Luisa Miller: trusting women betrayed. And, like them, *La Sonnambula*'s Amina never gets mad at a man. But then she has no interior resources, no questing ego. Love is her whole world, and when love stings, she shatters. This is what Adriana, alone of her contemporaries, found and made us hear in this art.

I must admit, I skipped the opera's "other" scenes, jumping from Adriana to Adriana, and I was partway through "Ah! non credea mirarti," Amina's heartbroken solo just before the happy ending, when I heard a real Adriana humming lightly behind me. I turned to find her in a dressing gown, holding a gigantic glass of water (I guess everything in the Princess's flat is oversize) and looking absurdly carefree. She smiled and moved about the room in time to the music, gesturing as—who knows?—she might have done in the role on stage. Yet this was not the broken doll of the opera, the self-demolishing icon of bel canto. This was the Adriana you've seen in the newsreels, a bit abstracted but outgoing, ready to traipse down-stairs in a tasteful new outfit or to chide a poodle. She is cultured, well-balanced, considerate. That smile: credible. That look: bracing.

"Adrì," I called her. Yes, I dared.

"Sì, ce la *Sonnambula* della Scala che tu soni qui." You're playing the Scala *Sonnambula*. "Bernstein, della Torre, caro Cesare Valletti, Giuseppe Modesti...I was so happy then. I am so happy now."

"You've taken la Fleur again."

"I am the Princess. So elegant, so courteous. She knows no fear—imag-ine that. Imagine how wonderfully well she moves, like some magic of effortless sky blue. I moved quite badly when I began, but I have remade myself, no?"

Now she stopped dancing, put down the water glass, and looked at me fairly straight on.

"Did you enjoy the evening?" she asked, confidential, attuned, curious. The Adriana I most loved, not counting the one who sang. She even joined me on the couch, like a favorite cousin who wants to hear all about your ski trip.

"Yes, I enjoyed it very much," I told her. "Ercolani showed me his private Rome." Amore, segreto.

"You did not get into trouble?" Chiding her poodle.

"No, unfortunately not."

"Do not joke so, Mark," she said serenely. "Anything can happen with that . . ."

"'Tormented genius' is the term, I believe."

"I will make his movie," she said, stretching catlike, long and lean, life-enjoying. "It is too great a role to refuse. But don't get too close—that's my advice."

"How close did you get to Bernstein? To della Torre? Or to Valletti and Modesti, for all we know about them?"

"Don't be difficult, Mark. That was business. Music. One is polite, discreet."

"Ercolani's Rome," I began, but Adriana shushed me as applause broke out on the record—strangely sparse, perhaps the distracted salute of a crowd that had been moved out of its mind. Her eyes half-closed, Adriana murmured, "Com'essi m'amavano in quel'epoca!" How they loved me then.

"Europe is so different from America," I said. "The things I see here are so . . . well, I meet such . . . *free?* people. Anyway, I—"

"America was started by Europeans," she told me. "It is the same. Believe me, when you've seen a pharmacy in the Bronx, you've seen one in Athens. The opera house in Palermo is the opera house in Mexico City. The Nazis are the same no matter what city you're in. They invade, they kill the young men, they eat all the food."

"No, America is different," I said. "We broke away and defied the parents. We invented ourselves. We shape our own destiny. We are the authors of our lives. And you're not listening."

"Yes, I feel so alive after making love to Nik. You must love, Mark. Sì, some day some pretty girl will give you that certain *oh!* and then it's—"

"No, she won't."

"I *know,*" she laughed out, as if I were just being silly to resist. "Because I am floating in joy."

"Adriana, will you *please* listen to me?" With Nik's certification so recently won, it was hard to back down now and harder to let Adriana blackmail me with my colossal admiration for her singing. If you tell me what you are, I'll hate you. But it has to stop somewhere, no? It's stopping now.

"Adriana," I said, "I . . . What I am is . . . No. For so long you have labored under the . . ." Christ, why was it so easy with Nik? "Adriana, I am—"

"Hush, here's the cabaletta. *Oh,* that tempo. A little fast, but it worked so well. The notes," she said, as her music flooded the room. "Uhm, that wasn't easy," she chirped. "The color," she recalled, "hazy and autumn for such a young girl as Amina, to show how this calamity has aged her. Or that's what Leonard said. They always have a reason for how you phrase. I just phrase. . . . Oh, now the divisions. So tricky. I sang Amina often in the following seasons—oh, Edinburgh, Cologne, Milan again. But never again did I risk this particular fioritura." She could have been talking to an interviewer; I suppose she was. "Listen. There. Yes. Brava. Oh, that was a close one. Yes. The innocent. So ingenua." Unworldly. "She has no idea what is happening to her."

Then the curtain fell and the audience woke up and screamed for its life and Adriana playfully jumped up and said, "I must go back to Nik."

"Adriana, I'm a homosexual."

"Caro, what nonsense you talk," she said, wafting off down the hall. "Ercolani must have hypnotized you. Don't let his evil tricks mis—"

"No, Adriana, *listen.* I'm attracted to—"

"You *aren't,* I *cannot* be fooled," she trilled out, almost out of view. "Heaven has planned the way for us, and it is useless to defy this plan. I know what Mark can be." She was gone.

The cheering for her Amina was still sounding.

1 3

The
Collector

I didn't like Rome. It's an amazing place, I know, but the trip of (I had expected) two or three days began to drag out like a *Ring* narration, and, thus cut off from my work base at home, I had little to do but explore the city and send postcards to my parents. My mother collects them, actually, and brings out piles and piles to show to guests. Once, Mrs. Mondello tartly remarked, "This is like looking at slides of someone's vacation," and my mother, missing her point, replied, "Yes, isn't it fun?"

Well, I did have one errand. Through my correspondence with Adriana's fans I had organized a consortium prepared to trade most handsomely for the Venice *Adriana*, should we ever find it. A fan in Mexico City had contributed a very rare tape of Adriana's 1950 *Norma* there, a New Yorker offered Met broadcasts of *Roméo et Juliette* (with Jussi Bjoerling and Bidú Sayão) and Lily Pons's *Lakmé,* and a guy in Hamburg gave me Adriana's Berlin *Lucia* under von Karajan, with an all-Italian cast so rocking with Mediterranean heat that the Berliners encored the Sextet. The performance was a routine entry in the underground catalogue, the Hamburg man admitted, but he had it in sound superior to that of most copies.

I had all the reels with me and the address and phone number of yet another fan, one of such intense repute on the tape circuit that all three of my partners knew his name. They gave him mixed grades: he's difficult, but he has everything. He's eager to trade, but he makes you pay. He teases, he presses, he cheats. "Rapacious," the Hamburger called him. "He'd steal your underpants." But the New Yorker called him "the source" and said that if the Venice *Adriana* existed, he would have it.

He himself was coy about what he owned when we spoke, on the eve of the Rome trip. But the thing was so convenient: he lived in Rome, he loved to trade, and he was "looking forward" to my visit.

He dwelled far to the north of town, but the cabdriver had no trouble finding it, and after interminable bell ringing and four flights of stairs I entered the place where I at last had the chance to receive the Venice *Adriana*. My church, you might say.

The collector's name was Marco Fiala, but he turned out to be total American. Brooklyn. Around fifty, short and thick and lined, with spectacles hanging from a chain around his neck.

"My family moved here when I was sixteen," he explained. "They went back soon enough, but I . . . remained. La-di-du, I've seen it all. The war, you know?"

He had an airily gloating look and a bossy, wiry voice that one takes instant dislike to. He smelled bad, and his rumpled pants were stained around the crotch. I'm trying to be a thorough reporter.

"I have great things to trade," I told him. "I've really worked this out."

"I'm so sure you have," he said, showing me into his great den of records and tapes: a tunnel lined with shelves from the floor to well beyond one's reach, and every shelf brimming. In such an arcane, devoted atmosphere, the sunlight seemed to be sneaking through the windows, invading. It was a paradise of the damned.

"Feast your eyes," he urged. "There are many rare titles not easy to get in Italy." He purred. "But I have my contacts. Worldwide, you see."

"Yes, I can—"

"Twenty-nine cities answer to my needs," he told me. "It's a rich world, you know. The Simionato *Favorita? Which* Simionato *Favorita?* Vienna? Mantua? Mexico City? Naples '53, '56? 'How badly do you want it?'— that's what I ask anyone who hopes to trade. What would you most painfully part with? I'm not a public charity, you see. The Venice *Adriana*— do you know how elusive that performance is? And getting to Her Highness, where is your fabulous Adriana tonight?"

"She'll be singing at a reception for the . . . somebody Greek; to tell the truth, I never got the name straight. The ambassador to Italy? She's doing two *Carmen* arias. I played the dress rehearsal, in fact," I added, sending off a happy-go-me smirk that he did not acknowledge.

"You're so eager for her *Adriana,* yet you didn't bring her to meet me."

"Well, she doesn't—"

"I would have liked to meet her. And you didn't bring her, you see."

His fingers were doping out a dance, and his smile was embarrassingly forced. You know what Hugh would have called him? A column of spewing tosh.

"Look," I said, "Adriana doesn't even know or care about this performance. To her, opera is something you sing, not something you listen to. She thinks that once you do it, it's over."

"Silly her, I must say. If it isn't taped, it never happened. Tape is like blood to music—there is no life without it, you see."

"Well, of course there are recordings. Adriana's made a—"

"Oh, really! There are recordings? Let me show you . . ." He went to one of the shelves, running his index finger along a brace of typewritten labels till he found what he wanted. "Here," he said, though he didn't reach for it. "In this innocent white box, la-di-dee, is all that remains of

Giuseppina Cobelli, the greatest dramatic soprano of the twenties and thir-ties. La Gioconda, Sieglinde, a spectacular Eboli, and the greatest Isolde I've heard. Frida Leider was a *whine* compared with Cobelli."

"How come she's not more famous?"

"Because she was a stupid cow, you see, who recorded two arias. That's all, yes, you like it? That's her history. She was La Scala's queen of Wag-ner. *So?* Did she think that would last forever?" Punctuating his report with mock-mournful sniffs, chanting it out in a sing song style, he said, "She went deaf and retired and died in Salò after the war." That evil smile again. This is not going to be easy. "But here in this box is what she should have left behind—most of her Isolde, Act Two of her Gioconda, and her complete Eboli. I recorded them myself on 78s, disc by disc, right off the air, you see. Well, the sound's not perfect, and every so often the radio signal failed or there was the usual interference. Oh, and it was hair-raising trying to decide when to switch sides in Wagner. But I did it, you see. Nobody else did it, *I* did it. So why should I give it to anybody else, as certain people seem to think I should? What did Chicken Little say? '*I* grew the wheat and threshed it and baked it, and *I'm* going to eat the bread!' "

"Was it you who recorded the Venice *Adriana*?"

He sighed. "You *would* ask. No, I had to trade for that."

So he *did* have it.

"Yes, very often they would postpone a performance, or just broadcast one without any warning. You never know in Italy. I've missed a few that way."

"Well," I began, the brisk horse trader ready to deal; but he said, "Sit. I'll serenade you and get the tea."

"Oh, I don't want to trouble you." I was reaching for my briefcase. "Why don't we . . ."

He had paused; no, *frozen*. "You mean, you don't want to bother with me. You want to take your present and run. Good-bye, it's happy birthday to you. Is that it?"

"Well, I . . . I just don't want to . . ."

"Good." He switched on a machine. "I cued this up as a special treat for you. Sit, sit!" And out he went.

The tape clicked in, and on came party noises and a pianist warming up with a couple of flourishes. Then he slid into the lullaby opening of "Nessun dorma" and some horribly ancient tenor sang it in a degraded fiasco of a voice, his pianissimo an asthma and his high notes Sisyphean. There was one cute touch, when the (one presumes) party guests came in on the chorus part with dainty tact.

"Yes, the *tea!*" cried my host, as he returned, tray-bearing. He seemed merry now, perhaps by way of apology for being snippy before.

"Who *is* that?" I asked; the tenor had just launched an assult upon "Amor ti vieta."

As if prompting one in a quiz, he said, "Who does it sound like?"

"Frankenstein's Uncle Cy?"

"Hollalu, it's Merli!"

I just looked at him.

"*Francesco* Merli, the great Otello and Calaf of the 1930s. He's still alive, in Milan. I was at this party, you see—his seventieth birthday, if you must know—and you can't imagine how many of the guests' names ring through history. How you wish *you* were there."

He plonked sugar and milk into my tea without asking how I took it; but I hate tea anyway, so who cared?

"Yes," he went on. "Oh yes, there was Gina Cigna chatting away with Pia Tassinari. Oh, and just turn around, and you'd crash into—no! Enough, I'm changing the tape. You want something *galvanizing!*"

He took Merli off and put *Aida* on, and I was about to tune it out when I recognized Adriana's voice. I beamed.

"Mexico City, 1951," he said. "The high E flat at the end of the Triumphal Scene. No one had sung one since Tetrazzini, and no one *ever* sang one this big. Yes, it's coming . . . here . . . let's listen . . ."

Well, I guess if you want to hear Adriana do something nutsily extravagant, this was it—stunt opera, maybe. She soared up to this incredibly secure high note, and, okay, it's not flawless Verdian style but it sure is flawless excitement. The audience got so thrilled that some of them couldn't bear to wait for her to finish before they started screaming. Whose opera is this? I was wondering how Adriana felt in the first moments after she pulled it off: as if the whole world loved her?

"Could we have that again?" I asked.

"Don't enjoy yourself too much," he told me, tartly, taking the tape off.

That was so surprisingly petty that I just forged on with the social stuff. "Whom do you like today?" I said. "Among the young singers, I mean."

"I've no idea who's young today."

"Well, when you go to the opera."

"I never do. Not anymore. Never, never, never, *never*."

"But aren't you interested in—"

"There is no one to *be* interested in. Your Adriana is the last of the great ones. Or she *was*." He drew himself up, as they say, the preening little toad. "I heard Gigli's Chenier, Pampanini's Butterfly, Pasero's Boris." His mouth went moue. "What do I care for this new crop of bleaters and little sisters?"

"But if you love opera . . . I mean, it's a living thing. Organic, not historical. It's always—"

"Piff. My opera house is right here, as you see. All the great ones, from Caruso to Grafanas, are in this room. *All*, you hear? I have operas that no fancy-pants A&R man ever recorded. I have Caniglia and Gigli's *Traviata*, Flagstad's Brünnhilde, Pons's Lucia—the *young* Pons. I have performances so deliciously rare the singers themselves don't know they sang them. What do I need from an *opera house,* say?"

I just nodded.

"So what's she like?"

". . . what's . . ."

"Your Adriana. What's she *like,* do you mind? Oh, you don't seem to understand the question. Let me try some more. Is she as murderous as Medea, slicing up the world? Ooh, the screamy mother who kills?"

He sat there waiting for my answer.

"I identify her," I finally said, "much more with Amina."

"That Bellini twit." His fluttery hands. "Her boy friend rejects her, and suddenly it's Hiroshima in a Swiss village."

"No, that's just it. No pyrotechnics, just the deeply beating heart of—"

"You know what I would have told her?" he said, leaning toward me confidentially. " 'Get yourself another *boy.*' You know what I mean by that?"

Gales of his laughter.

But then I thought of something. "Have you ever seen her live?"

"In everything."

"Well, talk, please. Because I'm dying to—"

"She was *zoomingly* fat and awkward at first, you see. Before this Peter Pan phase. I saw her in a *Trovatore,* right here at the Costanzi, and they had obviously hired the costume from some great old trunk and then had to let it out *yard* by *yard.* This utter pig of a Grafanas who—"

"No," I said, so hating him, "not how she looked. What her style was like."

"*Oh.* Well. Her style, *hoo.* Yes, her style was quite . . ." He giggled. "Her *style,* well, my."

"I meant, how she carried herself. How she—"

"Carried herself? I told you, she was this stupid, clumsy—"

"No," I said, reminding myself to be cool. He's just our supplier. He doesn't matter. "I mean, what her acting looked like. How it matched the music. You can *hear* the vulnerability coming through, but—"

"Ohhhh." It dawns on him. "Well, I recall a twilly brilliant *Don Giovanni.* Milan, '55. Grafanas, Schwarzkopf, Noni, Valletti, Taddei, Lo Presti. The very first scene—Grafanas roars out in a white silk number trailing bits and pieces. This is after the weight loss, of course," he smirked out. "Otherwise—"

"Right."

"Then the Commendatore comes out for the duel, and Donna Anna runs back inside. But your Adriana contrived to exit with the dress kind of flaring out behind her, this sort of ethereally billowing . . . a Mozartean wave, you see."

I said, "I was wondering more about how she looked while she sang."

"Oh, I see." He brightened. "If you want to know *feelings,* there was that *Walküre*—back when she was still singing Wagner, and still a big tub of lard. Of course, that's how those old broads get through the heavy stuff. It's all physical. I was at a party when Furtwängler came down for the R.A.I. *Ring* in '53, and Martha Mödl walked in. *Well!* Let me tell you, she was no size four!"

I was wondering how this character got invited to so many parties when he so patently lacked social skills, so I missed the *Walküre* story—something about how Adriana fell to her knees while gazing raptly up at Wotan *just* as he launched the Farewell, right on the beat. That wasn't what I had in mind, either, and I said so.

"Well, *ha!* What have *you* seen her do?" he cried, all in a fuss.

"Just her Norma, last spring in Venice."

"Oh, I mean, *really* now!"

"Well, I never had access to her before."

"Her Norma isn't even a *souvenir* of what it used to be! It's grisly. She's trying to act her way through it!"

"No, it's still very moving and inspiring. Her voice is in decline, yes. That's well known. But *Norma* is an opera and you can't get through an opera without singing."

"The big moments," he maintained, "go *ha!* for nothing!"

"Wouldn't that depend on what you call 'big'?"

"That trickeldy high note at the end of Act Two, when she once filled the house with her *ruthless* joy!"

"It's gone. Okay. But to me a bigger moment is the way she cries out when she was about to kill her children for revenge on her husband and suddenly relents out of love for them. 'Son miei figli!' They're my *children*. And you see, through her delivery, what awesome power parents have over these little beings."

"What cheesy piffle."

"Don't you want to play some more music?" I asked, hoping to calm the scene down.

"No, let's get to business." The Collector rose, rubbing his hands together to simulate the relish of the transaction. (I'd never seen anyone do that before.) "Take out your wares."

I got my briefcase and retrieved the tapes, thinking of my colleagues in the consortium, waiting and hoping for me to come through. The guy in Mexico City had told me that he was finding it hard to sleep for the excitement, and our man in Hamburg promised me the bonus of a Ljuba Welitsch *Rondine* if I pulled it off.

"First," I said, slipping into first gear, "we have two choice Met bootlegs featuring not only the near great, the legendary, and the sacramental, but also the sole personality in all opera who could truly be called 'beloved,' Milton Cross, with his back-bench yet strangely omniscient commentary."

"Let's skip the sales talk," the Collector said, holding his hand out. "Give."

All right, sport, we'll play it your way, lean and mean. I passed him the tape boxes and watched his sour expression go through certain telling dilations as he read the labels. Adriana's Berlin *Lucia* brought forth a disappointed little frown. (Of course he would have had that one, so I said, "That's in unusually good sound." He made no answering remark.) The *Norma* gave him the slightest pause, though he instantly recovered his uninterested aplomb. But the Sayão-Bjoerling *Roméo* slowed him up a bit—he carefully read the label, as if his very concentration, rather than a simple business deal, were summoning up the noble, vanished past. And lo, at the Pons *Lakmé* (which the collector who contributed it assured me was celebrated as the sole existing Pons broadcast in which she actually lives up to her reputation as a world-class charmer) he almost, for the tiniest second, froze in terrified joy.

Then he dropped the boxes on the table, jarring the tea things. "Nice try," he said. "But what you have isn't as valuable as what you seek." He smiled wearily. "You have to deserve the prize to win the prize. Why don't I offer you something more suitable to your . . . your qualities?"

Yeah, that's what they told Adriana when she first came upon the scene. No La Scala for *you*. Weird voice. Fatso. Sings everything.

"I have a fresh copy of the Schwarzkopf-Karajan *Pelléas* you could have," the Collector blithely announced. "Even that may be a little crash-boom for this . . . for what you offer. Or maybe . . . just *maybe* now . . . I could let you have the Grafanas *Alceste*. Milan, '54. Yes, I see you're tempted."

"The day an opera buff is tempted by Gluck," I said, "Brigitte Bardot will make a Sonja Henie movie. I came for the Venice *Adriana,* and I'll take it or nothing."

"Sorry."

"Thanks for the tea," I said, grabbing my tapes.

He waited till I had them back in the briefcase. Then: "If only you could sweeten the pot."

For a millimicron of a second I considered going back to my partners to advance our offer—but to a man, they had warned me not to let it out that we were a team, that copies of the Venice *Adriana* were to travel to three others besides me. Once he knows that this rarest of all birds is about to fly out of his control, he'll never yield it up. They even coached me on the collector background and trading tactics, and made me handwrite all the box labels myself. We were so foxy.

"This is all I have," I said.

"You have Adriana herself."

"I have her grousing and not getting jokes and ignoring vital messages.

I want her at her height, in song. Great men aren't their breakfast conversation. Great men are what they do."

"Well, fo fa fee."

"Any place special I should go to find a cab around here?"

He said nothing, but his face read, All right, calm down, let's work it out.

"What?" I said.

"The Met titles are tasty, I admit. And the *Norma* I have . . . heard of. Still, there are other sources."

"If you had access to them, you'd have these tapes by now. You're the champ, aren't you?"

He accepted this accolade as Zsa Zsa Gabor might turn to regard a suitor's proffered diamond. Good, flattery, milk it.

"I came to you because everyone told me you're the source. The *source,* they said." Oh, what a peacock. All right, mi son corrupt, but it's for Adriana's art.

"Well," he confessed, grudgingly merry, "I have everything."

"Except Pons's *Lakmé.* And I understand that Bjoerling's high C at the end of—"

"I know about it, do you see? I know Bjoerling's high C and I will not be *rushed! I* will surely decide!"

I just stood there. Wear him down, wait him out, test his need: That's my application.

"Yes, Pons in that outstanding role," he said. "Sayão, to warm the heart. The Bjoerling, in one of his greatest roles—but were not all his roles perfectly chosen? What other singer so well understood . . ." How one's personal passion informs one's characterizations? But I was silent.

"No," he decided. "How can singers know what they sing?"

I waited, a blank, me.

"How would a Grafanas, say," he went on, so so so slyly, "deal with the collapse of her career and her love life as the heroine of Cilèa's opera must suffer it? Would she bring her autobiography into her music?"

"Of course not," I said, worrying about that.

"She'd have no choice. All art is autobiographical. Every role Grafanas sings brings her doom and terror. She collapses! She was great, and now she is *rags*! You can't bring her back on a tape, if that's what you're after. She's gone for real! She was dreams, and you must pay for your dreams!"

I said, "I think I should go now."

"Well, what are *your* dreams? You can tell me."

"These tapes for the Venice *Adriana*," I said, "or—"

"No. No, wait. Can't we discuss it?" He had put on a reassuring tone as he lured me down onto the couch. Well, he's got a nerve, after all his pouting and *ha!*s.

"Let's sweeten the pot," he again urged, starting to touch me.

"Don't do that," I said.

"Feedlee-du—"

"Hey!"

I jumped away.

"I beg your pardon, huh?" I said.

(Not that I'm so great, is the thing. These accidents occur if you're young; I know that now. I didn't know that then, and I was very taken aback, because it seemed to me that you had to be entitled in order to have a . . . an encounter. You have to deserve the prize, he said himself. You have to pay for your dreams.)

Anyway, I was on the run and out of there with my tapes, and he shouted, "Well, let's *trade,* at least, if that's what you *want!*" It was, so I stopped. He opened a drawer and pulled out a box—my box, the recording of Adriana's 1949 performance, at La Fenice, of Cilèa's *Adriana Lecouvreur*. He gave it to me. Then he ran to the Pons *Lakmé,* set it up on the reels, fast-forwarded, and picked up at the Lakmé-Mallika duet, "Sous le dômes épais." And he listened—no, rather, inhaled. We had chanced upon *his* version of a Venice *Adriana*: the music that soothes the soul. The treasure at the end of the quest.

The Collector went on spot-checking the *Lakmé* tape, finally reaching

the Bell Song and what you might call the Milton Cross Interpolation—
"That was singing E's with ease, I'd say!" How festive the old guy sounds,
as if opera were a party for life, the heaven where one need never be
forgiven for being oneself. Had Adriana ever sung Lakmé? No, just the
Bell Song.

Meanwhile. I'd been hanging around while the Collector did his sampling; I don't know why. Maybe I was proud to have delivered such imposing benison to the hungry, much as I disliked this man himself. Of
course, I was hungry, too, and I wondered how much that meant that we
had in common, he and I. Here's another problem I (eventually) discovered
as a homosexual: you worry about how much you're like certain other
homosexuals. You fear the mirror: it's all physical.

Anyway, the Collector looked at me as if he'd only just noticed that I
was still there, and he didn't rejoice. "You can go now," he told me, almost
gently.

Careening back hell-for-leather, in the Roman cab style, I thought, What
is collecting? You get great things—lovely music, great history, smarts,
and a glimpse of a kind of heaven. Call it redemption. But this is what
you don't get, I guess: a spring in your step. If this collector had everything,
why was he so angry and dissatisfied, jumping at everything one says and
so desperately needy?

Hell, I got what I wanted, so why dwell on it? I'll tell you why: people
like me start out knowing that we're different. It makes us aware of other
people, and of ourselves, in a heightened way. We have to "plan" ourselves
to keep everyone else from Guessing Who We Are. Then, even among
our own, we are still aware and planning: presenting a version of me. But
surely the Collector had no plan. He was like an alarm clock constantly
going off without being set. Yet what, really, was he collecting? Power?
Did he *enjoy* the music, or . . . No, I saw him *savoring* that Pons tape. Music
isn't power; music is music.

Or maybe I was rattled because the guy was so, uh, tempestuous. And,
quite aside from his uninviting demeanor, not one of God's fortunates. He

was the first person I'd met whom I could not imagine having sex. His style was so *off*. I liked to think that people like him were, you know, different from you and me, like the rich. They're not. Maybe I got too close to the mirror or something.

Nevertheless, I had found the Holy Grail and I couldn't wait to write my partners and bring them in on our find, so as I let myself into the Princess's apartment I felt a pang of frustration because I wouldn't have access to a tape machine till we returned to Venice. Tape playing, in 1962, was a little new-wave for a Roman palazzo.

I *think* I got halfway down the entrance hall before I noticed the clothes on the floor. Befuddled, I looked around the corner into the whatever-it-was room and saw the Princess languidly pacing the length of it like a statue on a private parade: nude, emotionless, settled. A powerful aroma of sex sat in the air—you could smell the sweat and the wild cries.

She noticed me.

"You're back," she said, smiling. "With the briefcase, the beautiful new tie, the wonder. L'Americano. Già, sii mondano." Play it cool, boy.

She was the most beautiful woman of the day—have I said that already? But I'd never before actually *seen* her as she was imagined to be: the absolute Aphrodite, all white and pink and round, perfectly fashioned to be amazingly tight at the center and blooming full above and below. In the years since then, I have learned a curious thing: that when men of my kind develop a culture unto themselves, they react more strongly to a particular type of man than to another. For instance, one man likes big virile galoots, another man likes amiable youthlings, someone else likes men of a certain race, E. M. Forster likes men in uniform, and so on. But it is meanwhile true that heterosexual men all incline to a sole order of beauty: and the Princess was the order's sovereign. It's all physical.

She was idly standing there, letting me glom her up; I suppose a woman of such absolute glamour would look upon modesty as hypocritical or inefficient. Anyway, Nik bumped in on us then; he, too, was nude, slick, and gleaming. The knight had a rose.

"Mark!" he said, looking as comically horrified as in his movies. "I thought you were Adrì. Già, cavolo," he added, philosophically, as he handed the Princess a towel.

"Let him know," she told his worried look. "Caro, I will not hide."

It made a lot of sense, actually. Of *course* Nik and the Princess would arrange for a fit: The most beautiful people tend to, don't they? Watching the Princess ever so lightly pass the cloth of the towel across her loins, about her neck, and along her breasts, I thought, How could Adriana have ever hoped to hold Nik? You have to be worthy of the prize.

I did the strangest thing at that moment, though it didn't feel so then: I opened my briefcase and held up the box of tape and told them both, "Look at this wondrous treasure I've found. It is more magnificent than you could imagine, something to last and last. It is utter music. I've been going crazy trying to find it, and today it is mine. I feel . . . complete, at least for now. Believe it or not."

Nik smiled, and the Princess, handing him the towel, asked me, "What music would have to be so magnificent? Beethoven? Mozart? Ah, you are sly, and we would never have suspected . . . Chausson?"

"No, it's Cilèa. Or, rather, it's . . . I guess you find it odd that I'm all excited by music instead of a . . . a date. You two have probably just known such marvelous ecstasy in here that the frescoes all melted off the walls, and here I am with a tape recording."

"Amore è fiamma," the Princess admitted. Love is a flame. "But there are other flames." The two of them standing together, so . . . well, symmetrical, the Princess considering my proposition and Nik patiently-nervously waiting her out. "I recall my father returning home after a performance of this opera of Verdi, *La Traviata,* and spending the entire night in tears. Something he had heard in the music, it seems. But love is easier than art, no? Easier to make, of course."

She was staring at me, waiting for me to agree.

"And art," she added, "is the more lasting. No?"

Nik signaled to her—a kind of Let's go—but she was concentrating on me.

"Can we enjoy both art *and* love?" she asked me.

"Why not?" I replied.

Nik gently took command of the Princess, and she allowed him to lead her down the halls, calling out an amused (hers) and resigned (his) "Buona notte" as they vanished.

I turned on the radio, found the reception for the Greek ambassador, and waited to hear Adriana sing the *Carmen* arias. This was typical of Italian radio—whole programs given over to socialized political events that consist almost wholly of makeweight speeches. (The countless religious shows were even worse, more committed yet more pointless.) The whole time, I just sat relishing and holding and feeling the Venice *Adriana,* till Adriana herself came on for the Habañera and the Card Song.

So she sang, and you had to salute her authority, her amazing ability to conjure up impeccable style out of nowhere. Adriana had sung the *Hoffmann* ladies, Massenet's Manon, and a number of Gluck's heroines, but all in Italian with companies genetically programmed for the Italian style. These two bits of *Carmen* marked her first real foray into French opera as the French sing it, and of course she came through wonderfully, so toss-it-off soigné in the Habañera and so intensely conscious of what it means to have a fate—to be tilted toward a destination that one is helpless to avoid—in the Card Song. And where had she picked up that idiomatic French? Marveling as I listened (and how well the two numbers suited her voice, so much better than the Normas and Toscas she was scheduling), I wondered why Adriana's Carmen could bring off the Habañera, a disquisition on the nature of love, with such delicacy when she herself was so overloaded on the subject; and why the Card Song seemed so ruthlessly vatic when Adriana lived from day to day as if everyone were free to choose. But then, everyone is, right?

After the two arias and the usual rigidly festive announcement from

Adriana about how happy she is to and so on, I turned off the program and put on Hugh's *Sonnambula* records. God, that music! While I was changing record sides, I heard, very gladly, the dim whoosh of the shower in another part of the forest. Good, I thought. Nik and the Princess will be cleaned off and calmed down and that's one thing that Adriana won't have to deal with today.

The phone rang—always jarring at that time, at least in Italy, where people tended to hold their aperçus and gossip till the next time they met you rather than unload them all day long, as folks do now, when the phone nags more than rings. In fact, to some people, in 1962, the phone meant trouble—something official, penalizing, catastrophic. And so it was here: Deodata had called to warn Adriana that that eternal mother of hers had collapsed and was in the hospital in critical condition.

"The redeemer," I told Deodata, in English, "is doomed to be herself unredeemed."

Of course, she had no idea what I was saying. I guess I was becoming weary of always having to remake my thoughts into other coin, and to make change for others, day in and out. I was growing weary of alien ways. I missed my people, my habitat, my born ways.

I began to see that I would have to start Adriana's biography in earnest, and develop it, and finish it. Or I would have to concede defeat and go home.

1 4

You Have to Be Worthy

"I will *kill* you if you don't tell me!" she was screaming.

"Adriana—"

"Kill or you *tell!* Who are you to stop my way, do you think? Who do you *dare?*"

I said nothing.

"Oh, *really?*" she demanded.

Nik said, "Adrì, it is between us, this, you please. Leave the boy alone."

"He *knows* and at least *he* is honest!" She turned upon me Medea's black headlights, peering, studying, scarring me. She is certain what has been going on. She wants informants now, witnesses who will make her worst dreams come true. "He knows and *he will tell!*"

"What will he think of you, Adrì, to see you this?" Nik is so understanding, so gentle; you'd never guess that he's about to dump her for the

Princess. And who can blame him, when she's so stingy with her appreciation? You start each day with her as if she'd never met you before; she won't let you build up an account of confidence. Lay out a hundred Sir Walter Raleigh cloaks under her feet, day after day—on the hundredth first day she'd cry, "Where's that stinker with the cloak?"

Adriana was stalking me around the room as I retreated. "You saw? *Tell!* He was? I *now* find *out*, you *tell!* Tell! Tell! Tell! *Tell* me, *tell!*"

I said, "I lose respect for you when you do this."

Well, that was a hot one, with her mouth as wide as in that famous photograph taken backstage in Chicago when a process server slipped past the security cordon to drop papers into her kimono as she stepped offstage after a Butterfly. She darted around the Princess's magnificent Baroque couch to get to me, but Nik intercepted her.

"He knows nothing, Adrì, and you make it worse, this. When you ask everyone, you *tell* everyone. Then why? You will—*no*, you *listen* now! You will hear from me, all. But this is not a time, when you are crazy mad. There is news from home for you, too."

"What home?" she cried, flashing and driving but riveted by him, his look and strength and utterly penetrating self-acceptance. What a package. What a thing to be loved by. What a way to be forgiven for what you are.

You're thinking, So where's the Princess during all this? Well, she's no fool and nowhere to be found. She probably has more than one apartment in a city this size.

"What home?" Adriana impatiently repeated.

"It's your mother," I said.

"That's not home to me," she spat out. "Casa Toscanini, Dorsoduro, Venezia—*that* is home," she went on, so glad to say so that she grew taller and surer with each syllable.

"She's in the hospital," I said. "Deodata called a few hours ago."

Accepting this inevitable derailment of her tantrum, she stood it for a few seconds, slapped her arms against her sides, let out a deep breath, and nodded. "What is it this time?" she asked.

"It's not clear," I said. "Possibly a stroke. Something . . . serious."

She nodded again.

"Come, Adrì," said Nik, starting to work her out of the room toward the hall. "We will talk."

I guess it's this Living at the Top thing, whereby you have to tolerate uproars with those you work with. They blow away; you start again. So I stood there quietly as they went down the hall.

Empty room. Calm. Me. I pulled out the *Purgatorio* volume of the Princess's molto elaborate edition of Dante's *Commedia* (with plates by Gustave Doré), which I had been dipping into at odd moments through our stay here. Once the Princess saw me reading away, smiled, and said "Già" in an amused way—See, the Americano is studious, respectful of national treasures. But, you know, it is fascinating to me that a lettered Italian can, if he chooses, steam through a work composed in the fourteenth century almost as he might read his newspaper. If one of us tries to read Dante's near contemporary Geoffrey Chaucer, we find a foreign language: English.

Anyway, listen. The way Dante lays it out, it is improbable for anyone to go right to heaven. You'd have to be a saint or Dante's girl friend. Basically, you either go to purgatory (if you repented your sins in time) or hell (if you didn't). But purgatory is almost as awful as hell; and you spend no little time there working out your penance. True, hell is dark, noisy, and smelly; and purgatory is at least a mountain in the uncharted southern seas that rises ever higher toward the light as one is graduated to paradise. Still, both places treat their inhabitants with ghastly torments because they enjoyed life too much. Dante's sufferers aren't for the most part murderers and rapists. They're intellectuals, sensualists, independent thinkers. The *Inferno*'s not unlike a fascist concentration camp—just as il Professore said—filled with nonconformists. The way it seems to work out is, if you had a sweet life, you'll pay for it but good.

The worst of it arrived in Canto 23 of the *Purgatorio,* in which Dante recognizes an old friend, Forese Donati, who for the sin of gluttony (which means that at some point in his life he attended a banquet) is ceaselessly famished and dehydrated in a prolific orchard. Speaking of this torture, Donati first calls it "pain," then retracts that word and substitutes for it "comfort": because we are supposed to view God's punishment as God's love, purifying us so that we may become yet more lovable. This hurts Me more than it does you.

Well, *cavolo!* Throughout his epic, Dante emphasizes the importance of free will yet asserts that we have been given it only to choose between submitting to the tyranny of the Father or resisting it. That is, we ourselves have no individuality, and no free will in any real sense. We are subject to the one free will in the universe—His. Obey the Father utterly and He will love. Disobey and He will destroy.

This is what, nowadays, they call a dysfunctional family.

I was musing on this, and wondering how lo Scenarista, an intelligent and sensitive guy, could have bought into this nonsense. And I was thinking how brisk and suave il Professore would be as he jumped into a debate with lo Scenarista on the question of whether the Father loves His children or simply insists upon controlling them. I thought of Vieri, and missed him, and wondered what his big secret was. And I considered Hugh, a pretty admirable chap, though I have to admit that in those days—in my green and naked youth—I thought men who liked to be forked were somewhat disreputable.

Adriana wandered in just then, in one of her la Fleur dazes, looking so sorry that an itemized, verbal apology would have been excruciating for both of us.

"They are calling Joan Sutherland 'the new Melba,' " she said, joining me on the couch. "All the German newspapers bill her as 'Der Englische Engel.' At la Scala, she is 'la Stupenda.' You have heard this.

"During one of my early seasons at Covent Garden, I sat in on a rehearsal of the next opera coming up. I was tired and wanted to go back to the hotel, but I don't miss any rehearsal—one learns so much. New music, interpretations, the producer's vision. It was some horrible new work, a world premiere. Some incomprehensible story and the mise-en-scène might have cost a dollar eighty. Ballet dancers and mythology and a bass who is a fish . . . I couldn't follow it."

She had been looking vague, with the face of a sheepishly nostalgic rambler, but here she tidied up—became, in fact, direct and intense.

"But there," she said, "miscast as the heroine, was a big, awkward soprano with a . . . well, I will call it a holy voice." She shrugged. "Yes, the English Angel. Then I remembered her from some years before, when she sang my maid in *Norma*. Such a voice, yes"—almost sadly, this. "So steady, all the registers beautifully married. Of course I knew she must replace me someday, as soon as she got out of this lousy modern stuff and sought out Bellini, Donizetti, Verdi. But has she replaced me already? My former maid?"

"It's wondrous singing," I said, "but it's lifeless."

"My mother used to write me these letters," she said, underlining what was to come with a ruefully amused smile. "About how Joan Sutherland was the greatest soprano alive. Always on pitch, high notes without strain, and such a big, *healthy* voice! Had she ever even *heard* Sutherland?" Adriana laughed quietly. "Those letters were my mother's death warrant. She signed them herself. E sia, I warn you! Let it *be* so, then! And yet . . . Yet I carry a grave sadness at having broken with her. I hate her, and I always will—but it is a sorrow to cut off someone who has done kindnesses for you in the past. She gave me piano lessons. She took me to the opera. She bought records—Galli-Curci, Melba. And Rosa Ponselle." She paused here. "Beautiful," she said. "The *Norma* and *Vestale* arias were enormous. As if from a throne. Then, in Greece, during the war, when I was first performing, she was proud, the mother, so proud, you see. How much of this goes into my book?"

"All of it."

She thought that over, laughed again, and said, "Let me tell you something. The first time I sang in Mexico City, I arranged to meet my mother in New York and travel south with her. We had been estranged even then, and it was an attempt to patch things up. Yet no sooner did she walk into the room than I was screaming at her. 'Stop criticizing my figure! Stop calling me names! *Stop telling me what to do!*' They speak of love-hate relationships, yes? This was a hate-hate relationship. I kept telling myself, She gave you music. And I gave her a mink coat, for the Mexico trip. Oh, she was so pleased—you know how conscious some women are of these status symbols? My mother, sì. Yet there she is, ordering everyone around, showing up at rehearsals, pushing and pushing in where she doesn't belong. I say, 'Mama, you are acting beyond your part,' *barely containing my temper*. Look at my eyes, you see how I felt?"

I looked and saw.

"Bene. She says, 'Who are you to tell me, you fat little nobody? *I* gave you everything and *I* will be in charge!' I say, 'I have roles to prepare, one night Puccini, another Bellini, and the *Trovatore* Leonora, which I have never sung before. I cannot be distracted by these antics of yours.' Oh, I can laugh now," she said, not laughing. "But she would not stop. At the dress rehearsal of *I Puritani,* she goes up to the bass . . . I don't know, some Mexican. My mother advises him on the way he treats a certain phrase, and he just opens his pants at her. She advises the conductor, the producer, the intendant, even my adored Peppino, the tenor of the decade. Everyone is complaining to me. And when at last Giulietta Simionato complains— Giulietta, who would sit quietly inside Mount Etna for twenty years before asking if they would please turn up the air-conditioning a little. Well, then I had to stop this advising, eh?"

"Wow. Was there a scene?"

"I drove her out of Mexico, so now you know. Uffa, that's it. But then. I get a letter from her, months later, when I am back in Italy. All of her letters had been typewritten on our neighbor's Remington, messy but formal. *This* letter was handwritten, and it said, 'The only thing in my life that I regret is having given birth to you.' "

She smiled and shrugged.

"You ask, was I hurt? I was *glad!* Because now I was free. Caro, what are these huge books you're reading, here in the Princess's palace?"

"*The Divine Comedy.*"

"It is enjoyable?"

"Well, it's . . . It shows how art can be not only redemptive but vindictive. Because here's this guy laying out his idea of the afterlife, with all his enemies tormented for eternity. It's pretty shocking. His Christianity is less a religion than a penal code, with everyone found guilty unless he's a beautiful little girl."

"It's all a beauty contest?"

"Why should Dante be different from the rest of us?"

"What's your religion?" she suddenly asked.

"Nothing. My parents are nonbelievers."

"Atheists?"

"They're not committed enough to be atheists. They regard religion as extraneous. As you might basketball or the hula hoop."

She was puzzled. "But doesn't il padrazzo Dante teach you of death and the Holy Father? Do you not fear judgment, caro?"

"What, Dante's?"

"That of heaven."

"Heaven is an invention. God is an invention. *My* Dante, Shakespeare, said, 'A man can die but once: we owe God a death.' But that's all. Nothing follows."

"But heaven," she insisted, "is all we can hope for after death." *Gently* insisted, I should add, under la Fleur's soporific guidance. Feisty just minutes ago, now she was fading quickly. "Don't you believe in the undying human soul?"

I believe in your recordings, is what I was thinking.

"We cannot leave anything behind," she was telling me, "so we . . . what's the English, hmm? *infaith* ourselves to God's holy trust."

"Is that why you haven't signed your will?"

After a moment, she said, quite dryly, "Now, why would you know about that?"

"Adriana, the newspapers write about everything you do *and* don't do. You have no secrets."

"Oh, I have a few. Some dandies."

"If you don't sign your will—which, I gather, leaves everything to a few friends, Deodata, and Nik—your mother and probably Ambarazzi's relations will get everything you own."

"Cretini!"

"So stop them!"

"Beh, I'm not planning to go so soon, and Mother will be dead. Anyway, it's enough to have a will. If you don't sign it, you live and live. Sign it and you die. And, I tell you, caro, I am not looking forward to the... immigration process. Getting into heaven will be easy compared with getting into La Scala, because God could not possibly be as vicious as Ghiringhelli was. Still... to meet the Father face-to-face. The Father..."

She was winding down, somnolent.

"Read me from Dante," she said. "No, not that one," as I grabbed the *Paradiso*. "Let's do it all the way," she said, pointing to the *Inferno*.

I plopped it open and it fell ready at Canto 32, in the Ninth Circle, that of traitors. One of Doré's plates helpfully depicted the sufferings of the doomed in icy Cocytus, including two shades locked together asymmetrically, so that the higher one gnawed the head of the lower. I showed it to Adriana.

"Lovely," she said. "Backstage at La Scala."

I began to read to her, and she stretched out, pulling her feet up and dropping her head back. I was distracted, because I kept wondering why she had verbalized a fear of being supplanted not by the Princess but by a singer. Joan Sutherland was then still on the rise; the Princess was the alarming challenge, the rival who would take from Adriana what she most prized *now*: love, not art.

By the end of the canto, I had arrived at the pair in the hole; and Dante, always the inquisitive tourist, asked the man who was biting his neighbor to explain his grievance:

Che sei tu a ragion di lui ti piangi,
sappiendo chi voi siete e la sua pecca,
nel mondo suso ancora io te ne cangi,
se quella con ch'io parlo non si secca.

Which is, roughly:

If you are right your foe so to revile,
Knowing who you are and his offense,
On earth above your accusations I'll compile,
Unless in time my tongue should grow too dense.

And I stopped there, partly because Adriana was asleep but also because I was struck by those last four lines. That wasn't Dante in hell. That was I in Arcadia: in Italy, to compile a book that would defend the infamous Adriana Grafanas by bringing the reader to understand her. And I shall, I was thinking; but, Adriana, you have to stop turning against your allies when you feel thwarted, or when your head aches, or when your lover slithers off. You have to be worthy of your unnaturally admirable art.

15

The Judgment of Parris

The Princess's party had everything: crudités, reporters, Adriana on wings of song, and Sophia Loren.

"Oh, she is classy, this," Nik told me, as we two entered—Adriana had determined to make a Late Entrance and was expected separately. "La Loren!" Nik exclaimed. "Assolutissima vedette!" The total star! "Bigger than opera, bigger than cinema. You know, Mark, the Italian movie star, she will usually sleep with the co-star. It makes a good picture, is sort of tradition, yes? But la Loren, *she* sleeps maybe with *nobody*. This is intellectual, I think, yes?"

"Nik," I said, laughing, "you're wonderful."

It was a blue-ribbon circus, that party, held in yet another astonishing palazzo and peopled by what I imagined to be the great, the near great, and the usual dolce vita apprentices. The Gossip was there, running rings around the Princess and darting over to some fanfare of a guest to voice a poisonous confidence, sotto voce, like a Restoration dowager. Mrs. Ruthless. The Duchess of Tellemoff. Fellini was there, or so it was insistently said; I never saw him. Hans Werner Henze, Lotte Lenya, and Elsa Morante were there. A coterie of musclemen, implausibly majestic in their size-fifty sport jackets, apparently represented Cinecittà, just then running through a cycle of threepence-colored sword-and-sandal epics—*Samson Versus Medusa, Hercules Conquers the Mongols, Super-Argo and the Queen of Evil*. Nik felt they were eyeing him, and it made him nervous.

"It is as like they would wish to key me, Mark, with those looks. You think so?"

"Perhaps they want to be keyed *by* you," I said.

He thought that over, shrugged, and said, "Meno male." Not so bad.

Also present was the Journalist, Edward "Doc" Parris, at the time a fixture of Roman life, a World War II veteran who had stayed on in Italy to become the foremost American reporter on political and cultural life in Western Europe and—for utterly mysterious reasons—Adriana's tireless foe. His was a unique assault, because it was not Adriana's singing that he decried: it was Adriana herself. Her professionalism, her clothes, her looks, her treatment of her colleagues. She would rage over his pieces in the Paris *Herald Tribune*—pieces she insisted she never read but somehow knew about.

Now, you should hear this about Parris, and it was said by many who couldn't have cared less about Adriana Grafanas: he lived to lie and he lied to live. He wasn't just uninformed—he was making it up. "Hating me is how they sell newspapers," Adriana would cry. "Oh, for another Suez crisis! They'd be too busy to bother Grafanas!"

It was Nik who spotted the Journalist—I'd never seen him before—and who introduced us, first warning me that it never hurt to pacify an enemy. "Adrì," he remarked as Parris began sauntering up to us, "she is always *inspiring* enemies. We will diplomacy them, yes?"

It's possible that Nik was mainly interested in buying a little assault insurance for himself. Certainly, Doc Parris turned out to be, for all his power, a cinch to woo: pompous, ignorant, and desperate for flattery.

So I hated him—and not just because of Adriana. I hate people who lecture at rather than converse with you. As Nik and I talked to him, I said something about "pop music," and Parris, trying to look like a bust of himself in some museum, started in on how the division between classical and popular music was "useless and obfuscative." (He spoke with a suspiciously magnificent southern accent, wherein all sentences end in about eight diphthongs and a question mark: "abfyuscateihyiivve?") Parris pursued this line, somehow uniting in a single phrase Ella Fitzgerald, Marcel Marceau, and Arturo Toscanini. Okay; but when he paused and I tried to reply, he ramrodded me with another eight sentences or so, and when he had to breathe I started to debate him, but he just paused for a moment and then talked right through me.

I turned to Nik. "You know how Italian film actresses sleep with their co-stars?" I said, improvising. "And how Sophia Loren will sleep only with her most prestigious directors? You *know* thees, Nik," I insisted, going into his accent, to his wary amusement, as the Journalist—absolutely silent, for once—pressed close to hear. "Well, they held a conference to decide who was the most important actress in Italian cinema. And the answer was Anna Magnani—because *she* will sleep only with Sophia Loren!"

I was making it up, of course, but Parris put a hand on my arm as if requisitioning a sheet of details. Sorry, I was already walking—smack into the Princess and the Gossip, unfortunately, the one bemused and the other working, regrouping, achieving.

"Confide in me," the Gossip urged. "How has our dear Adriana taken the news about her mother?"

I just stared at her. She turned to the Princess, cooing, "These stains of the family—never erased, try though one may!"

"You cannot say for certain," the Princess replied. "My own family is a very mixed group—emperors and perverts and artists. So who knows?"

"You, Princess?" cried the Gossip. "You, the sun that gilds even the eternal arctic night!"

"Poesia!" said the Princess, laughing. Nonsense.

"Yet so true, in its way," said the Gossip, recovering by taking stage, expanding. "I so often feel I was put on earth to extol beauty to the blind public. To give them eyes, don't you know? They ask, Why are you not married?, and I reply, I married the *world!* Oh! It's the Prince, I *must* say hello!"

So she went galumphing off; then Nik approached. He told me, "You are so reckless, Mark, to walk off on this Parris. Like me in movies, showing no regard for the anger of bad guys."

I shrugged. "He can't do anything to me."

"You do not respect his power?"

"I don't respect him, period"—but Nik and the Princess were picking up each other on their personal sonar, so I made myself scarce again. Strolling around, I saw Ercolani and Sophia Loren engaged in hot debate, as guests formed a watchful circle around them: a little theatre.

"Shtupido!" Loren was saying, in the Roman pronunciation. "You cannot have love in the cinema if you have art, and you cannot have art if you have love, you see? The film of art is war, il fascismo, calamity, identity, society. *Roma, Città Aperta. Miracolo a Milano. La Ciociara.* The film of love is sun, laughter, roses in the afternoon—"

"Lifeless, degraded, Americanized," said Ercolani. "It is true that le grand cinéma treats of catastrophe, tragedy—at least traditionally. But the Hollywood system did find the way to combine the love story and the important theme—as in the most typical of all Hollywood films, *Via Col Vento.*" Which I immediately reckoned to be *Gone with the Wind.* "As one watches, history and romance pass before us as if they were one, inseparable. But the modern European film has discovered ways to raise the love story to a higher socialist level, to discuss tragedy with a contemporary flavor of the people."

"Che cavolo," remarked Loren, with an upward thrust of her right hand, the fingers united to form a point.

"Ma sì. In my *House of Atreus*, I can be playful with the heroic, the epic, rigorous with the sentimental. All, in the end—all of life, dear lady—is about passion. It is a great life, or it is no life."

"Ma, certo, it is passion, it is *love!*" cried Loren; but there was the Journalist pulling up like a dirigible, ready to let out air.

"Waaal, I heah you speakin' a heroes, sir," said Parris to Ercolani in Italian so execrable that that alone got him everyone's attention; I preserve it in an approximation of his redneck English. "But theah's no heroes in your movies that *I* evah saw. Jus' violence an' cheap stunts."

There was a buzz of mild shock all around us. True, Ercolani was controversial, even notorious. His sexualization of violence had made him the Church's particular target, and many were those who abhorred his work. But it was disreputable of Parris to attack Ercolani so bluntly. It was, in a word, American of him: because Europeans do not believe that every citizen has a right to weigh in with a critique of art. One is supposed to command an expertise before passing judgment; otherwise, a night at the opera would be equivalent to a soccer match. All men aren't created equal, and the uninformed Parris had no business butting in on his betters.

"Why, yoah violence, sir," Parris went on, meanwhile glancing around to see how he was doing, "is the scandal a the Eyetalian movies."

"The violence in my films is mechanical," said Ercolani, quite suave about it. "It is a device of the story. The real violence in our lives is the corrupting evil of television."

"Waaal, if thet isn't the biggest load a doody piss, I jus' don' know!" the Journalist cried, gesturing to his listeners in an apparent attempt to encourage a ground swell of sympathy for his position. No one said anything. Anyway, his "doody piss" is my anglicization of his eccentric Italian coining, a misnomer so ignorant of how Romance languages function that I'm positive I was the only soul in the place who knew what he was trying to say. Was this jerk really the Paris *Tribune*'s man in Italy?

No matter; now Sophia Loren turned upon him the forces of her persona, charisma, and social conscience. She said, "And who fucked you, Genitals?"

General laughter to the nth degree.

"*Oh* yes," said Parris, pressing his disadvantage—for some reason, the famous, when losing, do not back off but, on the contrary, redouble. "It isn't television wheah you get yoah ideahs for violence, sir!"

"All models for violence are created on television," Ercolani patiently replied, as Loren moved a step or two and inclined her head to indicate solidarity with Ercolani, at least against Parris. "In ancient cultures, before television, acts such as murder, robbery, and rape were so rare that they mostly turned up in i miti—legends designed to justify the depraved fantasies of the subconscious mind. Television controls murder. Television controls all who watch it. It is impossible to speak of free will in an age of television. Because life becomes, so suddenly, *imitative*."

Ercolani, smoking, blew out a ring, and I nearly cheered.

"The question," he went on, "is not Is there violence? but Is there free will, a set of choices? One speaks of man's power to control his life."

"Yes," said Parris, "as mah next column will—"

"Please be quiet. We know that free will is enclosed upon all sides by society, by culture. How can we choose when surrounded by priests and demons of all kinds, each claiming absolute authority? Is there free will?"

Parris began—but everyone hushed him. Genius speaks.

"There is none," Ercolani stated. "Except for him who is without a culture. Without laws, family, patria. Someone new born of nothing. Someone pure, absolute!"

That's when Adriana glided in, flushed and content on la Fleur and bound in an Egyptian (I supposed) sheath with an elaborate black-and-gold stole. There was a great stirring throughout the room while Nik guided her to Loren for a diva meet, but they treated each other fondly. The whole party had taken a Luftpause to make witness (from somewhere or other I heard the Gossip in a punishing whisper), and all was still as

Nik led Adriana to other personages, till finally someone dropped a glass and everyone laughed nervously and chattered.

I was standing alone near some sinister chairs that a condottiere might have planned campaigns in when Adriana came up. "I have sinned," she said. "I must subdue my Furies and heed the teachings of Our Master." I presume the capitals—or did she mean Botticelli or someone? "I must . . . Mark, is she here?"

"The Princess? Of course, she's giving this party in your—"

"I will murder her on sight. Like Tosca, eh? Quick with the knife, when you expect a kiss! No . . . I have *sinned*, I must be grateful. I am struggling, you see? I will forgive, like Amina."

"The Princess asked if you would sing, so I suggested the *Carmen* arias."

"Certo—sing for my supper, then murder her."

"You're joking, of course."

"I'm muttering and unpredictable," she noted, in a rare flash of self-description. Mostly, all you heard from her was "Is the laundry ready?" or "Music is nothing but a task, for it is all there, right in the score, waiting to be carried out."

"Everyone's still looking at you," I told her. "Why are we whispering?"

"Come," she ordered, marching to the piano to look through the piles of music thereon.

"It will not be Carmen," she murmured, caressing her stole as she turned over music, investigated a song or two, listened to her inner voices.

I said, "It's funny to see you willing to sing at a party. A little informal for you, isn't it?"

"Humility," she said, reading through a snatch of song. Something by Mascagni. "Not what I need," she said, abandoning it.

"You're going to sight-read?"

"We must find just the right selection to honor the Princess. For I have sinned," she repeated, her tone tight and her features set.

I said, "Uh-oh."

"Adriana," said Nik, looming up behind us, concerned and gentling, or so he hoped. "You are wonderful at this party, beautiful as always you are, but so Greek, fiery. It is scary when a goddess makes appearances, having some plan in her mind. What happens then is terror to mortals."

Adriana paused, regretful in some profound way, as if she had just begun to repent of a sin she was determined to commit. Head down, she whispered, "Nik."

"There will be music, then?" asked the Prince, as he joined us bearing a ceramic apple in gold. "We are so privileged!"

"I married the *world!*" the Gossip was screaming somewhere.

"Ecco," the Prince told Nik, giving him the apple.

"Che cosa è questo?"

"The Judgment of Paris, of course. 'For the fairest.' The television will be present to film this famous presentation."

"Delizioso," muttered Adriana, hunting through the music.

"You," the Prince told Nik, "must award the apple to the most deserving of the beauties assembled here. Then—"

"Questo no," said Nik, calm but deeply disturbed. He stared at the Prince. "Vuoi gettarmi in un sacco?" he finally asked. Is this some trap? "To make many ladies jealous?" he went on, turning to me. "And for why?"

Nik pushed the apple back at the Prince, but that worthy retreated.

"I have done my duty," he said, fleeing. "It is in your hands now. Il giudizio s'avanza." The time of judgment is near.

"Yes, this one," said Adriana, running her hands over the leaves of a song. "'La Risposta della Civetta,' by Riccardo Zandonai." *The Coquette's Reply.* Handing it over, she warned me, "Prepare. I want this flawless."

"You look dangerous," I said.

"Adrì," Nik told her, with that brisk tone of a decision made in an emergency. "We go, this, yes? Please?"

"*Never,*" she declared, eyeing the Princess across the room as the dark, the despised, the defiled beholds the fair, the favored, the fancy. "I will sing." She could have been eight years old, telling her mother the future.

Nik looked at me for help; I was concentrating on the Zandonai.

"I will read over your shoulder," Adriana told me. "It is large writing, and I will press close and just *just* make it all out. You will play your best, and not too maestoso, please."

"This'll be a cinch," I replied. "I could get through this on my elbows."

"Adrì," Nik pleaded, placing the apple upon the piano.

"No."

"If you knew," he said. "How to avoid, when it comes, this. Trouble, anxieties. The smart one runs from this—you run *to*."

"I will sing," she smiled out. "I will have my say in this . . . this duel. I will sin. Let them talk, this room of courtiers and salesmen."

Nik moved off with a shrug—he was Socrates saying, I renounce this dialogue as a profitless matter—and the Journalist moved in. Behind came the voice of the Gossip. "I always knew I'd be a pawn in the international social game!" she crowed out.

"Are we to be favuhed with a ditty, ma'yam?" Parris asked Adriana. "Pahty singin's not in your line, I believe."

"Who are you and shut your snout," Adriana told him.

Parris laughed. "Introduce me," he said—to me, I guessed.

"Adriana, this is Pietro Mascagni."

She missed the joke, as usual. "You should be older," she told him, not truly taking him for Mascagni but not assuming he was anybody else, either.

"Doc Parris," he said, holding out his hand. She reached for it but, as the name registered, pulled back violently.

"They know me in Rome heyuh," he announced. "Known me for fifteen years and some odd. I'm guessin' you know me, too. Know mah articles and such."

"Do you speak Italian, Mr. Fifteen Years?"

"Ma'yam, I speak four languages, read another twenty or so, and—"

"Stick to Italian," she advised him. "Because your English is that of a redneck on a pig farm."

He went "Waaal," and laughed a good long time. One of those fake ones, stalling for a comeback. Then he noticed the apple. He picked it up, weighing it with a bounce or two. "This heyuh apple, so they say, is to go to the loveliest lady in the place tonight. Now, who do you think that'd be?"

"Why don't you go play in the Via Veneto?" I said.

"*You* are still studying the Zandonai," Adriana told me, imperatively but with lightness, "so as to deliver an immaculate rendition."

"Are you really going to sight-read this thing?" I asked. "Those *Carmen* arias are so in your voice now."

"Waaal, yes," said Parris. "They talk of Yer highness's musical expertise as a dagnab wonder of the world. Learnin' operas in three hours and whatnot. But where I come from, missy—me, Doc Parris of Denmark, Mississippi—a lovely lady is more than singin' talent."

Adriana was sipping her Pellegrino as if he weren't there. Exasperated, I looked for Nik to rescue her.

"A lovely lady, I say," the Journalist went on, full of reflection and pauses, as if dictating his next article to a secretary, "is jes' that: lovely. *Lovin',* as a maiden loves, or a daughter."

"Nik!" I called out, but he couldn't hear. "I'll get him," I promised, starting off.

"No, stay," Adriana commanded. "He is nothing. A parasite."

"Thet's so fahn for *you* to talk, I see," said the Journalist, putting down the apple with a look in his eyes. "After you almost kill yo-ah mother with ingratitude."

It was la Fleur, I imagined, that saved Parris's life: because Adriana gave that only a da Vinci Gioconda smile.

"Yes, I see you sure, lady," Parris snarled. "I know what you're made of, lady."

"Liberty," I put in. "Honesty. Genius, whether you like it or not."

"Waaal, bless my shoes! I'd uv said 'License!' and 'Depravity!'"

"Nik!" I shouted, and this time he heard.

"The *responsibility* of freedom!" cried the hectoring Parris. "The *anguh* of the egotist!"

Nik was there now, looking quizzically at Adriana; she only smiled. He looked at me, I pointed at the Journalist, and Nik, bless his shoes, bodied his way between Parris and the piano and by sheer blaze of manhood forced the egregious Parris into retreat.

"What is it," Nik asked Adriana, "that everywhere you go, it is someone on the attack? What do they want from you?"

"I can't wait to get home," I said.

"To the States?" he asked, surprised.

"Well, I meant . . . No, to 127 Rio Terrà dei Catecumeni. Home to Venice."

"Yes, of course, old fellow," he said, noting my confusion and patting my arm reassuringly. "I did not mean to . . . No."

"It's okay."

"He is hurt," said Adriana, of me, to Nik. "He feels that you have pushed him out of the house that you are never in in the first place." To me she added, going on in that strange depleted-yet-content manner induced by la Fleur, "It is good to learn something every so often, caro, and now I will make a lesson for you, yes? Home is best kept portable, as the snail's. Then you can take it away with you when the people in it become too hard on you, yes, caro? You become your own home."

She touched my cheek. Sadly.

"Adriana," said Nik, "this is nonsense, probably. Your own home? Your own *parents*, to be?"

She said nothing. She looked at Nik, still with that half-smile. She was coming down from la Fleur—unless she had rearmed when I wasn't looking. Nik pressed his cheek to hers—you know, despite what you've heard, he really loved her—and went back to the party.

"Greeks always pay their debts," she said, watching him snake back into the throng.

"You know," I said, "this Zandonai song is a little . . . well. It's just some

girl telling off her rival for their mutual boy friend in the meanest . . . oh."
She's going to tell off the Princess. Right.

"It's a clever tune with an easy range and I feel daring tonight."

"You're *really* going to sight-read? On television and all?"

"What television? As long as the music's not too far and not too close
for my eyes, I could sight-read all four parts of the Verdi Requiem si-
multaneously. It will make a cute snap for the papers tomorrow, no? True,
they'd much rather have me canceling a performance or setting fire to a
church, but we all have our off nights."

"That was a sharp question Nik just asked, you know? Why *do* they
start up with you?"

"They are beasts and I am the prey." She shook her head, mild resignation. "That is opera."

"No, it's larger than opera. Is it because you need it so much?"

"Need what?"

"Acceptance. It shows all over you—how incredibly fulfilling your success has been. Not just how badly you need it—how good it feels because
you are in fact getting it. Is that why your enemies are all small people?
The talentless? The jerks? Assholes? Is it because they see you glorying
in your artistic outlet, while they have nothing? *You* have what they *want.*
Isn't that it?" I said, roused by the thought. "That inner glow, or . . .
something that they can't reach. You reach it. They think, Why should
she have it?"

"Come," she said. "I sing."

And she then underwent—or, rather, *effected*—a transformation. Her
face went insouciant, know-it-all; her body lengthened, straightened. She
moved from behind to before the piano like a bold and silly schoolgirl
about to address a hostile pep rally. Adriana had gone into character: the
person the music was about.

I wondered if someone was to introduce her, but instantly everyone went
into listening mode, as if waiting all along for this very signal. Of course:
who could share a room with Adriana and not keep an eye on her? The

photographers rushed up to steal a few shots, then backed away as the television crew took over, with their equipment the size of war matériel and their great, flying cables. Nik, Ercolani, Madame Loren, dubious Parris, and the Princess and doting Prince were the point men, irregularly spaced at the front of the crowd. The Gossip pushed up from the back to support the Princess, and I saw the bodybuilders in a clump against the wall, trying to figure out what was going on.

"Dr. Riccardo Zandonai," Adriana called out, in that direly cordial voice and wearing her if-only-they-knew-how-much-I-hate-them smile. " 'La Risposta della Civetta.' " Walking around to stand at my right shoulder, she added, "Canzone," unnecessarily, I thought, though she made the most of it, tossing the word out with a bouquet of nuances—eagerness vexed by too much knowledge, fatigue, sarcasm, bite. Anything could happen. I didn't know whether she would say "Pronta, caro maestro" or "Hit it, kid."

She didn't have to say anything, actually. Normally a singer inveigles the pianist by getting into a "ready for art" pose; Adriana simply fixed the Princess with a look and I started playing. The song is as simple as a canzone can get, three strophes addressed by a young lady who has lost her boy friend to a competitor. She plots revenges—village ridicule, a slap? At the end, she settles on the worst punishment of all: she'll let her have him.

You might think that the great Norma of the age must be wasted on such lean revelry. But if Adriana lacked a sense of humor, her sense of irony was fine-tuned—and her gift for insinuation was very fetching. Of course, she acted the part of the partly self-righteous wench with vigor, addressing the lines right to the Princess and, with a rustic jerk of her head, indicating Nik as the cause of the quarrel. " 'NEW YORKER EXCELS,' " I thought wryly, as I whipped through the piano ritornello between the first and second verses. But a glance at the Princess told me she wasn't feeling honored, and Nik seemed really uncomfortable. Well, the words *are* insulting, I supposed, even defamatory if you take them literally, but surely the audience wasn't meant to. Except then Adriana started the second verse with a dryly contemptuous attack, virtually hurled at the Princess. The Gossip, looking from one to the other, began to whisper to her neighbors, in case they hadn't got it. Clearly, they had; even the Journalist was catching on. All this on television, too.

Nik's eyes sent a message to me: *Stop playing!* I guess I should have, perhaps faking a gallbladder attack. Adriana sang the third verse as an intense social assault upon the Princess—who took it calma, calma—and the room was buzzing under the music. By the third chorus, to the same words as in the first and second stanzas, Adriana had the lines down cold and so moved away from the piano toward the Princess, their eyes locking, the music a combat, and television eating it up. I suppose all the Italian nation saw Adriana capping the final chord with a rude gesture of her own invention, the right hand slowly scooping down, then shooting up with fingers splayed, all for the Princess, her alone, to her displeasure and dishonor.

The applause was delicate, a mixture of the chagrined but polite (Nik) and the deliciously scandalized (the Gossip). The Princess did almost nothing: a very slight, very mock bow to Adriana.

But it wasn't over. Adriana, with her exasperating habit of suddenly drawing a bead on something that she had till that moment been absolutely unaware of, stepped back to the piano, grabbed the apple, turned, and cried, "*Here* is the prize, for the most impressive of women." Advancing in fury, all la Fleur's consolations dissipated, Adriana went on, "But what impresses? Rank? Family? Beauty? Character?" She stared at the Princess as if awaiting an answer. Nik was shaking his head, the Gossip beside herself with evil joy. "Or is it those women who are boldest when they are most unnatural? Those whose pleasure is to betray? *Yes!* Oh—yes, so coolly they regard us, I *see*, I *see*! But they will blush for eternity for their crimes!"

And Adriana handed the apple to the Princess.

"Grazie," said the Princess, without meaning, without the slightest shad-ing.

But then *"Oh!"* the Gossip shouted. "She's gone too far, I'm here to say it," she continued, trying to cram herself into camera range.

The Princess held the apple in her outstretched hand. She was smiling at the seething Adriana. Otherwise, the room was erupting, as folks grouped and regrouped and the television stared at the two women. "Italia, ecco l'epoca moderna," said Loren, by way of a caption. This is modern life. Then the Journalist swaggered up, snatched the apple from the Prin-cess with a " 'Scuze me, pleyaz" (yes, in English) and held it before Ad-riana.

"Ah, *no*, this!" I heard Nik cry out.

"This heyuh apple goes to you, lady," Parris smirked out. Adriana was still staring at the Princess. "It's a kind of *black* apple to the stuck-up thang who insulted the President of Italy—the *father* of his *country?* Or am I completely off the track heyuh?" he called out to the assembly, the demagogue. "And all the airs she puts on? Why, they've reserved a special place in hell for you, lady. Yes, you are damned, *I'll* say."

At last Adriana turned from the Princess to look at him. Empty look. Roleless.

"Hellfire! Now, thet's the playus they put the worst of God's crimi-nals—the ones who *cayun't forgive theyselves!* They put the curse on they-*selves,* and I heyuhwith give you this apple—"

Adriana braced herself with her left foot forward and her right arm well back and smashed the Journalist in the face with such power that he flew high with a quirky turn and landed legs-up against the piano bench.

"Brava!" cried Loren.

"Ecco la mia maledizione!" Adriana cried—Here is my curse!—as she advanced upon him.

"No!" said Nik, holding her back.

"Sì!" she insisted, fighting him for freedom. Then, suddenly, she relented, or simply ran out of energy. "Who judges now?" she wondered.

The television camera pulling back, contemplating it all. A little theatre for the nation: the Princess looking soigné, Nik consoling Adriana, Adriana in a swoon, the broken apple lying under the piano, the Journalist struggling to his feet in a daze to the frantic popping of the paparazzi.

All are still in this worried pause, then the Gossip's voice rings out. "To the *phones!*" she screams.

16

Nel Mezzo del Cammin di Nostra Vita

It is a relief to announce that I spend this entire chapter in the garden of number 127, back in Venice—and maybe a relief as well to add that Adriana was in Paris singing Tosca. With Nik on family business in Greece, I was virtually on holiday, which I spent mainly reading Lord Byron's *Don Juan* in the soothing lull of the Venetian autumn, after the dizzying tourists' summer and before the unpredictable winter, during which Venice becomes a professional survivalist.

"I want a hero," Byron declares at the start of *Don Juan*'s first canto. *Yes!* Self-expression and liberty he sings: what inspiration after that constipated Dante! Yet the *Commedia* and *Don Juan* are strangely alike, as epic poems that present, by constant reference to people and events of the age and of history, a kind of encyclopedia of the known world. One might call *Don Juan* a *Commedia* for a post-Augustine civilization, in which the life-force replaces piety: Eros invades the City of God. But then, how can one compare two such different voices, Dante's misty-eyed clopping march to heaven and Byron's savagely pirouetting global ballet? The one is doggedly inspired, the other genius. Byron takes in not only all the world but all its aspiration, something Dante believes can occur only after you're dead—that is, after there is nothing to aspire to but the love of God. And yet: "What is the end of Fame?" Byron asks; and "What are the hopes of man?"

What is the end of Fame? Well, for starters, it gave Adriana some power. The police declined to prosecute her for the assault on Parris, for such cases generate only sympathy for the defendant; in Italy, women are perceived as innately concessive and pacifying and therefore incapable of assault except in extremis. For his part, the Journalist declined to make an issue of the matter, for he was hurt enough by the nation's having watched him goad Adriana into self-defense. (The telecast hit the screens at "the café hour," the slot just before dinner, when much of Italy slipped into the local to examine this novelty of television and see what was doing in the world beyond the limits of their neighborhood.) In fact, a number of newspaper columnists who had no reason to love Parris were using the episode to grind him into chili powder. They were willing to exalt even Adriana to get Parris. He must have been one of those hateful, stupid, arrogant people who can never figure out why nobody likes them.

I have to tell you something else that unites the *Commedia* and *Don Juan*: Byron is clearly aware of being Dante's successor. Otherwise, why does he at one point promise the reader the epic genre's typical descent into the underworld—just about the one thing that, in the end, Byron *doesn't* cram into his poem? It's as if he's isolating the very notion of a trip into the afterlife as impossible, a fantasy because all religion is fantasy. Byron actually mentions the *Commedia*, alluding, during the cannibalism of the shipwrecked company in Canto 2, to Canto 32 of the *Inferno*—the very episode that I read to Adriana in Rome:

And if Pedrillo's fate should shocking be,
Remember Ugolino condescends
To eat the head of his arch enemy,
The moment after he politely ends
His tale: if foes be food in hell, at sea
'Tis surely fair to dine upon our friends,
When shipwreck's short allowance grows too scanty,
Without being much more horrible than Dante.

Even Dante's opening lines are quoted, in a footnote—perhaps the most pregnant couplet in lit. Have I cited these lines already? Let me again:

Nel mezzo del cammin di nostra vita
Mi ritrovai per una selva oscura.
(Midway along this journey of our life,
I found myself confused in some dark wood.)

This Byron reduces, in the harem sequence in Canto 6, wherein the houri Dudù awakens from a nightmare and recounts it, to:

At length she said that, in a slumber sound,
She dream'd a dream of walking in a wood—
A "wood obscure," like that where Dante found
Himself in at the age where all grow good.

The last four words are surely meant to underline Dante's hypocrisy. Of course the middle-aged preach the standard cautions: with their youth over, they have little opportunity to sin. It is Vieri whom everyone longs for, not Doc Parris.

Or is that misleading? I wondered, sitting in my own *selva oscura,* Adriana's magic garden—and, perhaps, like Dante, at a crossroads of my own. How much power does one lose at maturity? Isn't that the age of command? Dante was forty-nine when he first distributed the *Commedia*: but Byron was thirty when he published *Don Juan*.

The crackling of pebbles startled me, and I turned to see Vieri approaching. We had not met since I had returned from Rome, and I was so glad to see him that I leaped up and shamelessly grabbed and held him.

"Sì, Mark," he said as we broke. "A fratù, amore, segreto, no?"

I was drinking him in, silent.

"No?" he repeated, holding me by the waist and waiting for my agreement.

"Sì, Vieri, bene, t'amo, che?"

"We sit, we talk? Mark, it is the older man Vieri of the motorboat and you will listen now. Serious, Mark, yes?"

"Yes."

"Oh, Mark, if only . . . But will you understand? Quand' il giovane svela una relazione, tutti ridono sotto i baffi." Everyone laughs when a kid like me says he's in love. "But you, Mark, will not laugh."

He sat there grinning at me in his very Italian white singlet and heavy shorts, his black hair falling into his eyes. An Etruscan prince, I thought.

"So. I guess you . . . you've got a crush on someone?" I asked.

"More than the crush, Mark. With crush, it is a walk around the Piazza in summertime. This is . . . gondola to Torcello, la regata, la festa." He leaned close and whispered, "Federica."

"What?"

"Sì, her *name* I tell you, Mark. Federica. So so so pretty, so sweet and shy with Vieri. I know it is amore, Mark."

I was startled, though I didn't show it. Somehow I had expected something different. Maybe something about me. Yes, I am that vain—or hopeful, wishy. I wanted to be terribly important to him. These ridiculous desires of ours. We must rise above them, ever so quickly.

"Federica?" I repeated.

"Sì." I vividly recall how he smiled then, as if the name itself could transmit to me the weight of his joy and manhood and ambition; and as if I must then, as another man and his friend, revel in it on his behalf, in disinterested love.

I said, "Could this be the girl you were kissing in Santa Maria Zobenigo when Adriana—"

"No, no, Mark! Federica is not a girl to kiss in the campo. She is prudent. Immacolata. Oh, but so *charming,* Mark!" He jumped up in his excitement. "Special, sì? Special for Vieri, who is coming all this way from the bassi napoletani to stay with the Professore and sometimes be drunk and break the television but he is avoiding the large trouble . . . just to meet Federica! Ecco la sorte di Vieri!" Destiny. "If you saw her, Mark! If *you* meet her."

He settled back into his chair, serious of intent.

"This is what I wish, Mark, why I am telling you. To recognize my smart American friend with Federica . . . Or 'recognize'?" He quizzically tapped his right forefinger against his temple.

" 'Introduce,' " I said.

"Sì. She will respect you, Mark, and this is respect for Vieri who beside this has no signs of importance."

I started to break in, but he stopped me. "No, listen, Mark. See what happens now to Vieri. First, it is the favoloso Ercolani movie, then it is a motorboat job, at the squero of Zorman'. Three afternoons every week. It is good, Mark, yes? I work. I learn. You see how Vieri starts."

"What," I began. No, go ahead. "What does il Professore say about Federica?"

"He will not know," Vieri replied, very simply.

"Because if you told him, wouldn't he . . ."

Vieri showed what I had come to know as Neapolitan handplay meaning, That act would lead to peril: miming the hangman's tightening of the noose and hauling up the rope.

"Yeah," I said.

After a pause, Vieri asked, "Mark, you are pleased for Vieri, yes? You like Vieri?"

"Of course I like you." A gesture seemed called for, something manly and tactile in the Italian style, but we bungled it and ended up shaking hands and laughing.

"Vieri," I said, "I think I know how . . . how full of life you must feel, how close to the source of something basic and rich and inspiring. You evade the . . . well, the roots that clutch and come into something wonderfully new and . . . and it's all yours."

"Sì, Mark, you understand so well I don't even know what you are saying."

I smiled. "Reading poetry makes me pompous, I guess."

Vieri rose and paced about the garden as he framed his words. "This is what I ask you, Mark," he said at last. "Will you help Vieri?"

"What do you need?"

"There must come a time when the Professore, he . . . come si dice 'sentire,' 'intuire'?"

" 'Sense.' "

"He *senses* that it is a new Vieri, thinking always, always of something, some*one*. Ma! It is Federica this boy thinks of. No, he *will*, Mark! He is saggio, furbo." A smart man. "He will learn of it just by *imagine!*"

Stooping to pick up a bit of gravel, he held it before himself at eye level, glaring at it as Adriana would at a critic. Playing il Professore, Vieri went on, "Oh, what thing is this? Amore? Segreto, I see! You hope to fool il Professore with betrayal and cheating? With your proud terrone brain, fit only for picking pockets of Japanese tourists on the ferry to Sorrento? Il Professore, he says, Who is this girl that is your mystery? Do you want to be now thrown out onto the street? Does that serve you now, amore?"

He tossed the stone up, then kicked it soccer-style into the courtyard.

"Yes, but what do you want from me?" I asked.

"How to not this *happen*, Mark?"

"Well, if you're certain he'll...divine what's going on, maybe you should be honest about it. Jump ahead of him."

"Come *clean* and *sing*? In ten minutes, Vieri is living on the Zattere."

"How about if *I* tell him?"

"Oh no, Mark, he still—"

"It's called 'breaking it gently.' Instead of exciting his jealousy, we impress his sense of reality. A fine young man—that's you—naturally must bond with a fine young woman. That's Federica. With his intrepid old-world grace, il Professore can't get angry at *me*, and you aren't around at the moment. We give him a chance to consider it rationally. And he quickly realizes that of *course* it had to happen. It's fair and it's right. It's the chain of life."

"But *when* you tell, Mark?"

"Not immediately. I'll catch him at *just* the moment, and—"

"Oh, Mark," he cried, all still and seeing it. "That *must* be right. You always know what Vieri likes!"

"I know my customer," I was saying as he charged up and planted a heavy kiss on my lips. I grabbed the sides of him and responded, deep and all the way and thinking, Don't be in love with him! But when he broke the kiss I held on, my hands casing the sides of his torso as he bobbed and weaved like a boxer. I was trying to catch him, net him. Of course I couldn't, not possibly; and how can you wish for the impossible? Yet there is this lurking hope that someone redemptive—someone, I should say, not necessarily gifted or brilliant but very, very beautiful—will drop everything and love you. Then you'd feel beautiful, too.

Maybe you'd say, If he's in love with Federica, how could he kiss you? But Italian men are always kissing one another. It's like bringing a box of candy to a party. It's like their language's inability to distinguish "I like you" from "I love you." Maybe it's because their culture understands that certain men can love each other without sizing each other up for Eton or Harrow style.

Hugh.

(Whom I thought of a lot.)

Vieri.

(Strictly for dreams; we all need them.)

Nik.

("What a guy!" was how they put it then. Enough said.)

My Don Juans, if you will—and each entirely different from Byron's, who is a surprisingly passive hero, done to more than doing.

The Seventh Canto starts

> *O Love! O Glory! what are ye who fly*
> *Around us ever, rarely to alight?*

Now that sounds more like Adriana than like any man I know of—that embattled choice between happiness and opera. To a man, love *is* glory. To a woman, love is life—except for Adriana, who, almost alone of women of her epoch, really did have the choice to be in love for what she was or in fame for what she did. That gives her a *lot* of story. It explains why we push close, not only to hear but to comprehend her.

And that is why I felt not just swindled but ruined when I played the Collector's tape of the Venice *Adriana*.

I swear to you, I'd not been back in the house a full minute before I loaded the reel into Adriana's Wollensack and pushed PLAY. Adriana, weak on la Fleur, travel, and fatigue de scandale, went straight to bed under Deodata's care, and I was just unplugging my tie when the music reached the heroine's entrance. I remember looking into the living room mirror just then and spotting a big grin on my face—because how often do we get our magic wish? Then the heroine uttered her first lines, and it was not Adriana's voice. I kept listening and puzzling over it. Was bad microphone placement misguising her? Then the first aria started, the first real singing in the role . . . and no go. This was not Adriana Grafanas.

Calmo, I thought, running FAST FORWARD. Somebody had spliced in a bit of some other performance to fill in a transmission washout. (Though it seemed odd that the Collector hadn't warned me.) I made three spot-checks—still no Adriana. Okay. Second reel. Act 3. Speed up to her entrance, hit PLAY . . . No. It wasn't Adriana.

So I . . . *ran* . . . to the phone and called the Collector in Rome, and I recognized his voice in the "Pronto" with which Italians start phone conversations. But as soon as I identified myself, he hung up. I kept calling him, but he let it ring. Nor did he respond, eventually, to my telegram. Damn, I thought. *He set me up!*

After an emergency round robin with my trading partners—none of whom was, like me, incredulous at the sheer brazen cool of the swindle—I had the tape copied and sent to them. It was my Hamburg colleague who identified the performance—Mafalda Favero, Elena Nicolai, Luigi Infantino, and Sergio Bardari; Palermo, 1951. He took it least hard of us all, saying perhaps we simply weren't meant to have the Venice *Adriana*.

Meant by whom? Who decides such things if not we ourselves? The Mexican fan heartened me, insisting that we intensify the search, and although I'd exhausted every imaginable point of access by then, I resolved to keep at it.

But mostly what I was doing was reading *Don Juan* in the garden and receiving envoys like a pasha. Not long after Vieri left, il Professore popped in to welcome me back from Rome.

"So noisy, dangerous, angry," he said. "The *eternal* city?" After a split second of reflection, he added, in a delicious shudder, "La xe buta, Roma." Ugly place. "How relieved you must be to return to la Serenissima, the city of choices."

"Choices?" I asked, smiling.

"Ah, your Lord Byron," he noted, examining my book as he appreciatively waved the attentive Deodata away. No refreshments necessary. "One of Venice's great amateurs, you know. He swam the Grand Canal and studied Armenian with the brothers of San Lazzaro—the last little island one passes on the boat ride to the Lido. A poignant spot, yet strangely glamorous. How I envy you, reading Lord Byron in the original. An all too delightful character," he enthusiastically added, speaking of the remote past, like all Venetians, as if he had been there at the time. "Yet he was refused an audience with Egberto the Defenestrated, a Byzantine grandee passing through Venice on a curious pilgrimage to Baden-Baden, though no doubt he had his reasons. For the pilgrimage, I mean, not for snubbing your Lord Byron."

"My Lord Byron? He was English."

"It's close enough. What's in a country? It's *language* that bonds us. Have you seen Vieri yet?"

"Yes, just now."

Il Professore produced a slyly weary smile. "The young man seems in his finest fettle of late. He is never drunk and entirely avoids the rough crowd of intimates he had collected. He is so unnaturally well behaved that one is irresistibly convinced that he is getting into his most ambitious mischief of all."

He paused. He toyed with the Byron. He gave me an opening, did I care to speak.

"How I envy you your youth," he finally said, shutting the book. "So much freedom. So much to look ahead to in the city of choices. But Madonna? She is away?"

"*Tosca,* in Paris. Her debut there."

"Ah. They will worship her. The Parisians have an eye for style, they say. Let Venice sink, but Lutèce will have her fashion. And your English lessons with Vieri—they continue, I hope, now that you are with us again?"

"Certainly."

"Favoloso—as Vieri says. To tell no lie, he is getting smarter and more beautiful by the day. The heart bursts to look at him. Are there many like Vieri where you come from?"

"In the States? No, there's . . . We have other kinds of . . ."

"Highly impressive young men?"

"Yes. They take a different form in America. Chad, Dave, Mike. But their effect can be quite similar to Vieri's."

"Someday you must tell me your tale," said il Professore, getting up. "Your people have a strangely magnetic power. Vieri is quite besotted. He will answer only to the name 'Rhett Butler.' Is this an echo of your history? An Indian, perhaps, dressed in animal skins?"

"No, Rhett Butler is a fictional character. A hero—well, not a hero *exactly*, but a great romantic symbol."

"Ah," il Professore agreed as he left. "Those are the best kind. Arrivederci."

Hugh was in town, producing a recording at the Fenice; he came over for dinner and to listen in with me to a radio relay of Adriana's Tosca. Patiently, he let me go on at length about my visit with the Collector and the immense subsequent disappointment when he really wanted to hear about the Princess's party and Adriana's reaction to everything.

"How *is* she?" he finally got in.

"My life's dream has been chopped into messes and you don't even—"

"Of course, lad, of course. Torrents of sympathy, I assure you. Only . . . what's that ever so intoxicating Hollywood line about not asking for the moon when we have the stars? You Americans always want to get a corner on *every*thing. Conquerors you are. As a race. A bit greedy, I daresay."

"How she is," I said, "is suffering. Nik's leaving her, her voice is getting even with her for not being Joan Sutherland, and she's on some goofy drug that the Princess—"

"Will it mar her performance tonight?"

"Ironically not. She gains in power when she loses love, I've noticed."

"*Fas*cinating."

"Anyway, it's the daunting roles that galvanize her. That's why she keeps doing Normas and Medeas and Toscas. She could glide through Mimìs and Santuzzas, but she thinks them unworthy."

"She likes a struggle?"

"She hates a struggle. She just can't avoid a struggle."

"Gad. She sings about herself, then, doesn't she? About her battle to be perceived as *what* she in fact *is*—the most able singer of the day. Oh, she'll go out as Norma, won't she? Not because she'd like to. Because she has to."

We listened to the *Tosca* broadcast like contentious aficionados, muttering and olé-ing almost line by line. "Don't care for that note," quoth Hugh; "Watch the conductor," I advised the errant tenor; "Fresh from a jumble sale," Hugh remarked of the breathless Scarpia. "That's Adrì," I said, when a high note spread like spill from a Liberian tanker.

Okay. But it was decent *Tosca* and great Grafanas, wayward in certain details but eloquent overall. What a piece—aren't the best artists at their best in it, always? Adriana matched her qualities to those of her character: I am sensual yet pious, formidable but powerless. As always, she made "Vissi d'arte" the central statement of the evening, the O Love! O Glory! of an artist's autobiography. Paris went mad. But the one high spot for me came at the very end of the show, when Scarpia's henchmen converge upon Tosca on the roof of the fortress where her lover has just been killed and she leaps to her death. At the moment of the leap, you could hear the audience gasp—there were even a few stifled screams. I looked questioningly at Hugh.

"Oh, haven't you ever seen her do it?" he asked. "It's a shock. She doesn't edge up to the jumping spot and check to see if the mattress is ready and such. She just runs up to the parapet and flings herself blindly into space. Gives one a turn, the first time."

"Wow."

It was a triumph unalloyed, to judge by the cheers. Then Hugh and I tasted brandy in the moonlit garden, till he said, "Tell me, laddie, are we going to have it off tonight?"

"Sure."

"What an American answer. So direct and unconcerned."

"I'm going to Greece tomorrow."

"On holiday?"

"Business. I've got two interviews for this biography of Adriana."

"With whom, laddie?"

I smiled. "The roots."

17

The Teacher

Gilda da Coservo was a celebrity forgotten but for one thing. She had been a lyric soprano specializing in the coloratura repertory—Lucia, Rosina, Amina, Dinorah, Norina, Zerlina, Despina, Adina, Linda, and Oscar, possibly her only part that didn't end in a short 'a' vowel. She was born in 1892, made her debut at age sixteen at the San Carlo in Naples, and quickly became nicely popular along the international Italian circuit—London, Buenos Aires, Madrid, New York. When World War II broke out, she was in Athens, teaching at the Conservatory.

The one thing was her pupil: Adriana. The younger soprano's flight into fame naturally cast some subsidiary pixie dust upon her maestra, and, in a nicer way, Gilda da Coservo became popular all over again. She was the name that Adriana dragged behind her, something not unlike a second mother, or the tin can tied to the honeymoon car.

"Sì, è tanta cara," Adriana would say when I mentioned her. She's so dear. Then Adriana would immediately change the subject.

I wrote to Gilda da Coservo about my book, and she wired back that she'd be happy to talk to me. But listen, why had she remained in Greece, a land without a strong professional opera base and with, to a Latin, a daunting language? Could she be one of those dazed individuals whose dime runs a nickel short? Why interview someone whose judgment is so poor? I kept recalling Adriana's explanation of why her mother moved from the United States to a Europe on the brink of conflagration: "She's an idiot!"

Anyway, there I was in Greece, getting around mainly through numbers and pointing, because nobody but *nobody* spoke a word of English. After polyglot Italy, this was a useful reminder that there is a lot more world out there than we may imagine. I managed to reach Madame da Coservo's at the appointed hour, though no Madame was to be seen.

"Sit," ordered the maid, in Italian, as I entered a drawing room dominated by a grand piano and decorated with maybe a thousand photographs of—I quickly determined—Gilda da Coservo in costume as Lucia, Rosina, Amina, and so on; Gilda da Coservo in mufti on boats, entering palazzos, pleading with a poodle; Gilda da Coservo with colleagues (including Toscanini), fascist officials (including Mussolini), tony admirers, and even plain old dust-in-the-street fans.

"No, *sit!*" cried the maid, because I was strolling through the room. "The music *after* you sit!"

"The music?"

"Down!" she insisted. I sat, she wound up an ancient phonograph and applied the arm, and through the 78's scratching came . . . well, it must have been Gilda da Coservo, in Dinorah's Shadow Song. The maid and I sat there for three minutes listening—or, rather, I listened and the maid fidgeted and rolled her eyes and consulted a pocket watch at fifteen-second intervals. When the music ended, she jumped up, shut off the machine, and said, "Clap."

"What?"

The maid was clapping and nodding imperatively at me, and Gilda da Coservo came in, bowing as if to a theatre audience—a few gracious inclines from the waist and then a gala dip to the floor, her eyes, as she came up, rising to case the top gallery.

"Clap!" the maid urged me. "The diva is near and true."

So I clapped a little, and the diva threw back her right arm and half closed her eyes to favor her claque with a pose. Or so I reckoned.

"Miei cari," she doved out. "O, i miei amanti." She sat across from me on a low couch, saying, "I always called my fans 'my lovers,' yes—because to me, singing is sensual. It is the act of love."

The diva was absurdly overdressed: brocaded, scarved, fringed, and cameo'ed. She looked like an abduction from the seraglio. The maid, who had vanished, now reappeared with a tray of medicines.

"Not now, you evil thing!" the diva protested. "I'm giving this lovely interview, as you can see!"

"It's quite time for your elixirs, all the same," the maid calmly replied, doing something with a spoon. Looking straight at me, and not even making a pretense of lowering her voice, she said, "Poor soul, she's falling apart while we sit here."

"What shall we speak of?" the diva asked me brightly. "My debut season, and the lovely, lovely audiences? The great Antonio Pini-Corsi was so moved by my Margherita that he fell to the floor in a strange heap." She turned to the maid. "Or no?"

"Open wide," said the maid, brandishing a pill.

Downing it and recovering with the help of a small bottle of Pellegrino water, the diva went on, "Or my beautiful seasons at La Scala, the very temple of song."

"This was during a flu epidemic and they were short-handed," the maid put in. "Or they wouldn't have let you sweep the stage, much less—"

"Actually," I broke in, "as I said in my letter, I want to talk about your relationship with Adriana Grafanas."

"She is like a daughter to me, and what a proud mother I must be! La Regina della Scala, they call her! Of course, in my day—"

"It is well that you have come in the morning, sir," the maid told me while helping the diva to the Pellegrino. "By evening, the medicines have weakened and no end of disgusting noises and smells are coming out of Madame."

She mimed fanning herself.

"In my day," the restored diva went on, "there was far, far too much talent at La Scala for there to be a queen. We were a bevy of princesses. Emma Carelli, Armida Parsi-Pettinella, dainty Rosina Storchio, and that awesome Ester Mazzoleni. Who was the Norma of the age?"

"Who?" I asked.

"Ester Mazzoleni! Who was, and I say it, the only and absolute soprano of the time who dared the Cherubini *Medea,* which drove other sopranos to madness and death?"

"Who?"

"Ester Mazzoleni!"

"Tell me about your first meeting with Adriana. How did she strike you?"

"Oh, *never!* I thought. So fat and shy, always the eyes on the ground so she shall not see the rough laughter of boys. She was hurt, she was feelings, when she came to me. Well, poor thing, she was not what they wanted. But she was clever. I saw it at once. An excellent pianist. And *devoted!* She used to arrive hours early and sit outside listening to the other students' lessons. I thought to myself, She hasn't much to work with—the figure of a cow, the many fears, the strange timbre. Maestro Sesto Contramin, her mentor in Italy—he called it 'una grande vociaccia.'" A big, ugly noise. "Nothing to work with, but ferocious determination. What are you doing, please?"

This was addressed to the maid, who had taken out a white lace handkerchief and was twirling it about. By way of reply, the maid stared keenly at the diva's bodice, dabbed at her right breast with the lace, then examined something she had picked up. "A bit of halvah," she confided to me.

"She was *destined* for opera," the diva went on, "and I was destined to bring her into the world of song. Scales! Technique! Placement! The thrill! The portamento! So many students become impatient. They want to sing arias the first day. Not Adriana. *Foundation!* That's what she wanted. She had to build a voice out of nothing, and she knew it. She had no love, but she had her work."

"No love at all? She didn't go out with—"

"Who would have her? Besides, as I often told her, sex and music don't go together."

"Too bad," said the maid. "If they did, you'd have been an international sensation."

"I *was!*"

"Time for the second selection," cried the maid, jumping up to ready another 78 on the phonograph.

"What will it be, Lisette?" the diva asked with a girlish thrill.

"You'll see when you get it" was the maid's tart response, as she searched through a pile of records stashed in the phonograph cabinet. "The beauty of song," the maid went on, thoughtfully. "All song belongs to God," she murmured. She located the disc she wanted and put it on, saying, "Every sin may be expiated, not necessarily by the sinner." Back on the couch, a distant expression on her face, she said, "Let's attend."

It was the diva again, this time in a song of some kind, to piano accompaniment. Unlike the diva's opera repertory, this was uninflected music, pure melody—and very expressively sung, I should add. The two women looked dreamy, listening.

"What is that?" I asked, at the end.

The maid shrugged.

"No," I insisted. "You were very intent on finding that particular—"

"All music is equal," she replied.

"Well, it's beautiful. Adriana should put together a recital's worth of songs like that and—"

"Never," the diva declared. "A wonderful idea, but when did Adriana take advice? The slightest suggestion, and she was like a dragon defending its hoard. Like a stubborn child with its head down, charging at all the adults. It is her version of the act of love, I suppose. 'I will sing Norma,' she told me. I said, 'Oh yes? You don't have a Norma voice.' The *look* on her face! I *will,* like a man in rut! Everywhere she goes, I *will!* None shall stop my way in music! Ghiringhelli tried to close La Scala to her. I *will!* You *won't!* Impasse! Then she sings Luisa Miller at Florence so magnificently that Ghiringhelli has no choice. All Italy has heard her Verdi now on the radio, and she is in danger of becoming too important for Ghiringhelli. He must reach for her. The cosmos is giant, but the number of people who instruct one's little corner of the stage is small. Ghiringhelli's stage is now under Adriana's power, and he must submit to the destiny that she creates. I *will!* I *will!* And everyone submits! Serve the tea, Lisette."

"Serve it yourself."

"She cries, I *will!* And it was good. That is Adriana's way."

"Have you seen her lately?" I asked. "Spoken to her?"

"But she has turned her back on music! It's all movie stars and Riviera cruises! It won't take much of that to dissipate her abilities. It was a *manufactured* voice, remember. Without vigilance, the production crumbles. The talent? Absolute. But the physical material was always in question."

"All song belongs to God," the maid primly reminded us.

"The Father," agreed the diva. "Adriana is most religious, of course. She lives with the warning charms that have haunted us since the original sin."

"After death," the maid speculated, "she will return as a harsh wind."

"As a retribution?"

"As a diatribe."

"She hasn't long," said the diva. "At this rate. She has sacrificed every-thing for music."

"Sold her soul," the maid put in.

"She is Greek. An unforgiving people."

"She is American," I said.

"Puff!" replied the diva, throwing up her hands in exasperation.

"The music owns you," said the maid, caressing the diva's hands with the handkerchief. "It can leave without warning."

"If neglected," the diva sighed. "If taken for granted. Yes. I *will*. Always at war. Rebellious. The Father. Yes."

"But have you two spoken at all?" I asked again.

"After her Manon in Milan. Or no . . . Maria Stuarda?"

"That was three years ago," I said. A real shadow song.

"Once she was a hopeless little ignota per nulla." Absolutely nothing. "And now? Regina della Scala? Del *mondo!*" Queen of the *world!*

"I *will!*" the maid echoed.

"To master our time on earth," the diva stated, with some pensive hesitation, "we must be strong in spiritual values. To conquer? What is it, in the end? We must seek harmony with the world of God. The sun. The serene or angry sky. The water. The green."

"The love of the tree," said the maid.

"In this land, Adriana's land, many *many* strive to learn what is this harmony. There are three harmonies. Yes, the harmony of family. Now, yes, the harmony of marriage. But then, yes, the harmony of dreams. Some live in the harmony of family: these are men. Some live in the harmony of marriage: these are women. And some live in the harmony of dreams: these are the cursed, who will never know peace."

"Repentance is infinite," said the maid, stroking the diva's hair.

"It is a false harmony, this one of dreams. It is arrogance, independence. It is rejection of the Father." She moaned. "Draw closer. Don't fear."

"Thank you for your time," I said, getting up and leaving, real fast.

18

The Brother

"Did you meet with the teacher of song, this?"

"I did."

"She had many stories to tell? The young Adriana? Athens in the war? Did you find out, old fellow?"

"Not really, Nik. She was sort of a loon."

"And now the brother?"

"Yeah."

Over the phone, Nik's laughter sounded oddly comforting.

"Soon we will be back in Venice, Mark. It is autumn season, of fresh and lovely winds. We play calcio in the street, the ball hops into the canal, and all these boys of Dorsoduro jump into water to save it back. It is sweet time, this. When comes winter, it is plenty of time to be the sorrowful Mark. So you cheer up, yes?"

"Okay."

"The brother, he will surely tell stories. A young Adriana, it is fine to think of. Delicate, unsure, yet still demanding and Greek."

"Where will we meet, Nik?"

We were taking the plane back to Italy together; and we set that up. I must have been doleful still, for Nik said, "Come *on,* Mark! Be like Hollywood!"

"I want it finished," I said.

"What finished?"

I was thinking of the ski trip we took—my family, I mean—to Mount Poseidon, and how my father talked this young couple into going downhill *backward* in front of us with the girl as lookout so the boy could hold a camera and shoot us. The skiing family Trigger. I was thinking of Central Park in the summer, just walking around and enjoying the world. I was thinking of Christmas.

"I'm an American on a mountain called Europe," I told Nik, "and I need to get back to base camp."

"Ciao, Mark."

Adriana's brother, George, opened the door to an almost madly huge apartment, with the gaping spaces and lofty ceilings that are rare in the crowded New World. Two little boys and a girl—in cowboy hats, aiming cap pistols at one another, then letting them off in the air—ran past me while a woman, obviously their mother, came out to fuss at and pamper them. George introduced her as Marta; she seemed to speak neither English nor Italian, because I tried both. She was very pretty, very thin, very active.

"Gus, Eleni, Nikos," she called suavely, corraling them out of the room with a parting smile.

"Children," said George, explaining.

As we settled down in his study—he was a psychiatrist—I complained about my failure to get anything solid out of the many interviews I'd held.

"No one knows her," I said.

"They know what she's shown them," he said, comfortable in his armchair, soft in his speech. He grinned a lot for a psychiatrist. "She presents different Adrianas to different people, you see. Always has. Of course, she needed to, to survive. She was one thing at home, another at school. Or one thing to the Nazis and another to the patriots."

"She never talks about her youth."

"Not to outsiders. To me, she speaks of nothing else."

"To . . . you? I thought you and she . . ."

"Never spoke?" he nodded. "Yes, that's the popular view, fostered by the press. The . . . what? . . . hostile daughter. The unloving sister. They seem to like her that way. But most people need to maintain their earliest emotional ties. There are many kinds of love. And first love . . . well—"

"I beg you to pardon my incredulity," I said. "But I've been living with Adriana for fifteen months now, and I don't ever recall hearing that you had telephoned."

"I don't. Dee Anna likes to control that herself. *She* decides, you see. She'll call from anywhere—Milan, the States, Mexico City. She has rehearsed, dined, studied her scores. It is late. The hotel room is empty of diversion. She calls."

"Dee Anna is Adriana, obviously. But . . . how?"

"That goes way back. When we were kids. There was a children's talent contest on the radio, and one little girl sang an opera selection. Puccini, I think. A little bit of a number, perhaps cut down. But she was young and it was opera, and my sister was fascinated. For days and days, she would speak of this one girl. What did she look like? How was she dressed? Her name was Dee Anna, you see, and my sister developed a concept of this girl, all fleshed out as an ideal of herself. I hazard a guess that it is an ideal that she has never renounced. Tell me, what does she look like now? I see only newspaper photographs."

"She's glorious. Audrey Hepburn as Hedda Gabler. Tell me about her. Things I couldn't know."

"She likes Bing Crosby, Errol Flynn, ice cream, 'Night and Day'—"

"You're kidding."

"Well, she did. Ice cream was her passion. Not anymore?"

"She subsists on steak tartare and fruit. And, lately, a kind of tranquilizer called la Fleur. Do you know of it?"

He shook his head.

"Though," I went on, "it doesn't just tranquilize her. It also makes her...crooked. Different. Wild, sometimes, but sometimes hideously quiet."

"I wonder if science is giving up the struggle to free our minds of self-destructive impulses *naturally*, through verbal therapy. The prescription of experimental drugs can soothe symptoms but does nothing to heal the disease."

"Does Adriana have a disease? Psychologically?"

"No, she has a mother."

"Good, *you* said it."

"Will you take coffee with me?"

"Sure."

He buzzed something on the desk, said something in Greek, and presently a manservant brought in a tray with all the fixings, from the java pot to those crazy unsweetened biscuits that Europeans dote on. Me, I missed saltines and Cheez-its. Meanwhile, we had been idling on near empty, talking of the newest French movies, rock and roll, the Kennedys. Then, suited up, we hit the field.

"My mother, you understand now, is a very driven and angry woman. Our neighbors simply thought her a nag. Looking back, I'd call her a person frustrated by the limitations of her culture. She should have been a movie star, but she was a housewife. And that gave her nothing to chew on. Work with. So she honed her frustration into a weapon and beat everyone with it. My father was absolutely baffled. He kept retreating from her. Late nights out, affairs with young women. He was a Lothario, like many Greek men. Married but free."

Stirring sugar into his cup, he frowned very momentarily, then, with a shrug, said, "Children are very, very vulnerable in this kind of situation. So many restrictions are placed on them from so many different directions—their parents, their coevals, religion, schoolwork. When you add an angry mother to the mixture . . ."

"How did you handle it?"

"Greek families adore male children. Boys are viewed as innately faultless. Wondrous. It's awful, really. My mother spoiled me and tortured Dee Anna."

"How?"

"In every way a mother can. Well . . . No, in one way only, by depriving her of the slightest shred of self-respect. It was a little like a losing politician berating his opponent's record, but of course much less graceful. My sister couldn't put a foot right, and my mother was always there, on top of her, criticizing her, getting her. She actually said as much. I'll *get* you! My mother's war cry."

"She encouraged Adriana's singing, right?"

"She made her sing. My mother does not encourage. My mother bullies and humiliates and gets you."

"She hasn't gotten Adriana now for over a decade."

"Well, you can alienate even the tenderest heart. Steadily. Act by act. Over the long haul, you see."

"Surely Adriana is not . . . well, not *tender*."

"Everybody starts out tender," he said, gently. "Then life happens."

"Is Adriana religious?"

"Not in the least."

"Did she ever date boys when you were teenagers?"

"All the time."

"Hmm."

"This contradicts what you know of her, I imagine. But great personalities *are* contradictory. They're so rich, we can surround no more than pieces of them. Each onlooker selects a different piece, it would seem.

Marilyn Monroe, for instance—who *was* that, really? No one knows. Oh, I won't say that my sister never sets foot in a church or that she never knew a season of chastity. But she told me, not all that long ago, that she had never been in love."

"She is now."

"Yes, this actor." After a sip of coffee, he said, "Please tell me about him."

"Oh, he's another of your Greek Lotharios," I said. "I have every reason to believe Adriana will lose him while she makes this House of Atreus movie with Giampaolo Ercolani. Nik is not your one-woman man. But then, is Adriana a one-man woman?"

"Yes, but not this man."

Startled, I almost stuttered. "What . . . what do you mean?"

"Describe him. Nik."

"He's a heart-wrencher. Just . . . just everything. Very handsome and manly and he has it all."

"Let me hear some details. How does he laugh?"

"Easily. Not a big theatrical laugh, but a small, intimate laugh, just for the two of you. He isn't a life-of-the-party show-off, is what I mean. He hears you. He's nice. He's giving. He's elusive. The kind of man you're afraid to trust but *have* to trust, because if you don't you're going to miss out on something."

"On what?"

"On . . . life? He's got energy and he can lift you up and take you riding."

"But he can vanish for a time? Go off and come back without explanation?"

"Yes."

"But you forgive him, because if you demand an explanation he will vanish forever?"

"*Yes.*"

"Perhaps, also, he is a great admirer of women, yet can enjoy the company of men. He is, let us say, sexy with men. Flirtatious? Yet it's not a tease. It's his way of communicating this energy."

"Yes!"

He nodded. "Of course," he said. "It's my father."

I took that in in silence.

"Of course," he repeated.

"But surely Adriana's father figure was Ambarazzi. Her ex-husband."

"Not at all, actually. There was no emotional transference, as we put it in my line of work. Ambarazzi was important, certainly. He was a man of respect who courted Dee Anna when, to all men of her own age, she was invisible. You have to understand, my sister had had a difficult adolescence, but not an impossible one. As I say, there were boys, joking, kissing. She was chubby and unhappy, but she was pitching. Her first years as a woman, however, were a despair. She came to opera dismally heavy in a country that delivers stern judgments on the physical appearance of women. No—I see your impatience and loyalty, but listen. Her looks are . . . not right for Italian opera. And what do Italians listen for in opera? Sweetness of voice and manner. This my sister never could have. All these hurdles, you see. Suddenly, a businessman adores her as a woman and offers to help her get started in music."

"She used him, you're saying?"

"He helped her and she was painfully grateful, is how I read it."

"Did she love him?"

"How could she not love a man who guided her to her first feelings of self-esteem?"

"Has she ever told you . . . This is going to be awkward . . ."

"You must understand something about my sister. She is unique in many ways. Even her neuroses are virtually her singular inventions. But she shares many needs with the rest of us, and one of those is to be wholly honest with one person whom she can trust and who already knows all of her secrets anyway."

"And who but her brother . . ."

"Exactly."

"Okay. Has she ever told you if the marriage to Ambarazzi was erotic?"

"Italian men do not enter into platonic marriages under any circumstances. It was certainly sexual, though probably, for Dee Anna, not truly erotic. I imagine the sex ended considerably earlier than the marriage did."

"How did she feel about him then? At the end?"

"She despised him."

"What about the gratitude?"

"Emotional attachments undergo development, like everything else in the world. When they met, he had power and she was nothing. Some years later, she had power and he was excrescent. She had lost respect for him, you see. That can be fatal in any relationship. My sister has high standards. Well, all Italians do. They are obsessed with showing what they call bella figura. Good style."

"You think of her as Italian? A Greek girl raised in New York?"

"I think of her as my sister. She thinks of herself as Italian. It was part of her transformation. You know, what most hurt her about the way the press handled those scandals of hers was that the Italians were the roughest of all—and she swore to me that it was because they saw her as a foreigner. Italy is the least racist country in Europe, but it has some xenophobic tendencies. Especially when you become the dominating star at the state theatre."

"So, all this time, you and she were speaking."

"We were never not speaking, at any time."

"Well, I'm . . . I'm amazed," I said, getting up to try walking off my wonder. "You think you know someone and . . . Why are you laughing?"

"If you want to know someone in a meaningful way, it will take more than fifteen months, even up close."

"Are you saying I shouldn't write the book?"

"No, you must write it. My sister needs a defender. A translator. You have her imprimatur, you know, or I wouldn't be speaking to you at all.

Besides." He paused, then: "I don't think you would want to write a book that really understood her."

"Why not?"

"It would have too much mother in it, and too little music."

"What are these puppets doing?" I asked, noticing hand-in-head models of a princess, a knight, a crafty dragon, and a merry walrus. "Do you use these on your patients?"

"They put on plays for me."

"You're kidding."

"The children do, you see, and the . . . young at heart."

"I suppose it becomes horribly revealing," I said, trying on the princess. "They think they're just schmeiing around with toys, and instead they're emptying their guts out."

The princess looked around the room and, in something like Adriana's dreamy la Fleur voice, said, "At balls, I dance with distinguished men, artists and thinkers. Zeffirelli is one, Lord Harewood another. World-famous designers vie for a commission. Statesmen do me honor. They are mostly older men, surprisingly vigorous and charming. Young men have that lovely vitality, but their seniors show an authority that must not be flouted."

Her brother—thoughtful, amused—nodded slightly as I hesitated. Go on, he meant.

"The love of fathers is important," she continued. "Everywhere we turn, society demands it of us. We must love the head of the nation, our president. Also the Holy Father. We must because nature instills it in us, and if nature fail, culture requires at least the enactment of a suitable piety. In earlier times, women who denied the father were called witches and lavishly punished by way of cautionary message to all daughters. But what do we receive in return? Why did not my father intercede on my behalf when my mother's destructive wrath grew most penetrating?"

"In Greek households," the brother told me, "it is considered unmanly for the father to concern himself with the rearing of children. Especially daughters."

I had meanwhile slipped the knight puppet onto my other hand, and the princess addressed him thus: "Could you not have defied the code of behavior out of love for me? Did not Christ in His infinite love defy the codes? Is He to be an example for daughters only, namo yet to fathers?"

In the voice of John Wayne, the knight replied, "I did not see your pain."

"You saw it surely, and were silent."

"I thought it came to be thus with all families, that the mother is wicked."

"You saw other families with beautiful mothers, and were silent. Lo, how did it end between us?"

"The mother took my children from me. It was my punishment."

Now the dragon spoke, on the brother's right hand. "Nay," said he, as the mother, "it was your test, the test of fathers. You should have stopped me. As I walked up the gangplank, I looked for you in vain."

"You were reckless, spiteful, unbearable. I was relieved when you departed."

"You sacrificed your children to win your freedom."

There was a tense pause. The princess turned to the knight. "Is it true?" she asked.

There was silence.

"Tell her!" the dragon ordered. "Tell your daughter what is true!"

"I was silent," the knight admitted.

"And your daughter was heartbroken." The dragon turned to the princess. "Tell him how only the mother could give you what you needed."

"Not love," said the princess.

"Respect!" the dragon thundered. "Power! The beauty of fame! The awe of genius!"

"Can one live without love?"

"*I* did! The question is, Can one live without greatness?"

"You did."

"I gave you to the world," the dragon insisted. "*That* was my greatness!" She took a conclusive bow, and the brother's hand let her go limp.

Freeing my hands as well, I said, "I hope this isn't a rude question, but are you cut off from your mother, like Adriana?"

"No. But I have had to limit her access, in the better interest. The more she's around, the more she infuriates. And, you see—this is so odd, really—she *knows* that. She pushes even as she trembles to push. She cannot stop herself."

"She *can,* surely. She simply refuses to. Pushing, to her, is too delicious." He smiled, attending to his coffee.

"When you talk," I went on, "does she avoid the subject of Adriana?"

"Dee Anna is her only subject."

"It's all complaints?"

"It's all dreams. They were dress-shopping buddies on the Rue Faubourg-Saint-Honoré. They alternated as Norma in Aix-en-Provence. They were on television. On a steamer. On a tear."

"Here's the sixty-four-thousand-dollar question: Was this war of theirs *fated*? Because you seem to believe in . . . well, having no choice to—"

"Nothing is fated," he said. "Everything is *tilted*. We are all aimed, more or less strongly, in a direction. This is what we mean by neurosis. We are . . . *led*. Yes—led to protect an imperfectly integrated ego structure by committing acts that may vary from the slightly foolish to the ambitiously self-destructive. Some dwell within this pattern all their lives. Some others gradually come to recognize and then defeat it. We can resist the tilt, if we want to badly enough. If we want to move out of the destructive pattern into a healthier one."

"A tilt?"

"It's a bit like the conception of original sin. After all, what is original sin but the sensation of having offended the father without knowing why?"

"Gosh," I said, floored.

"Well, isn't that the story you're proposing to write? The tale of a woman who can't figure out what she did wrong, yet is blamed for being what she is by all the world?"

"I'm quiet," I told him. "I'm thinking. Who's the walrus, by the way?" I added, pointing to the puppet we hadn't used.

"It's you," said the brother. "Patient with her tiffs, loving, filled with admiration. All this she has told me, you see. But you, too, will deny her."

"Never."

"She will give you no choice. It is Dee Anna's way to infuriate. To push you to the limit, like her mother. It is my sister's tilt."

"But . . . Gosh. No. Deny her?"

"She will, I know. Trust me," he said, his voice still soft but commanding. "She has surprises that appall even herself."

19

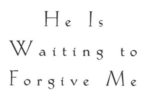

He Is
Waiting to
Forgive Me

Athens to Venice wasn't a long plane trip, and Nik and I flew in the early afternoon; nevertheless, I found a chance to collapse into a nap of exhaustion in order to rest my head on his shoulder. It's odd, in this avidly erotic age of today (1998), to think back to a time when such mild contact could feel exhilarating. I want a hero.

As we prepared for the descent to Marco Polo Airport, Nik told me that he was going to end it with Adriana, and that she seemed already to know it and not mind.

"At first it was such this crisis, Mark," he said, as a steward came down the aisle, checking for seat-belt scoffers. "The party in Rome and bad headlines. It is not good, this anger always so quick to come, as if left from some other thing and never finished. Always coming. It is sometimes true of great people, no? Whatever happens, Hitler is screaming."

"Yeah, but quiet people don't have adventures."

Pulling something out of his wallet, Nik handed it to me—a snapshot of a woman.

"What do you think, eh?"

"Gorgeous. Who is she?"

"Suzy. American movie star. We meet in Rome. Mark—*instant*. Two minds are one." He smiled. "Oh, if I could tell you."

"Suzy who? She doesn't look familiar."

"Beh, she is what they call 'starlet.' On the rise, like me, Mark. She knows everyone in Hollywood. Think, Mark, is this not very good for Nik? You mention director, producer—she is first names with him!"

"Uh-oh. Sounds like a Hollywood phony to me, Nik."

"Che significa ciò? 'Phony' is a false thing, no?"

"A load of people in show business claim to be intimate with people they've never met. It's the identifying mark of the loser."

"You think this girl is loser, Mark?" he said, studying the photo. "So beautiful, this?"

"Nik. Hollywood is full of women that beautiful. They can't all be stars. Some of them just fuck producers, and some of them have tiny careers in tiny roles. Why don't you get friendly with someone who's already made it?"

"Yes, who, Mark?"

As we dipped, the plane leaned over the lagoon, giving us a beautiful view of the city of choices, which seemed a big silly fish looking to the west.

"I always liked Leslie Caron," I said. "Did you see *Fanny*?" Actually, I always liked Leslie Caron's *Fanny* co-star Horst Buchholz, as like unto Vieri as Hollywood was offering at the time; but this was about Nik, not me. "She's European, too," I added, "so you'll understand each other."

"I understand Americans, Mark. I am Hollywood Nik!"

"Take it from an American, Nik—only we natives can comprehend the native culture."

"Campanilismo, eh?" he warned me. Provincialism.

"No, that's just it, Nik. I've seen the world, now. Son mondano, io."

"Beh. What have you seen? Some Veneza, a bit of Roma, three days in Xellas. You slowly read through most of an article in the Gazzettino, you learn who it is said 'ciao' to and who it is 'arrivederci,' you order an ombra in the café. Suddenly, you are mondano?"

Okay, I just put my head on his shoulder again and sat like that till it was time to disembark. I don't ask for much.

All was quiet at number 127, for Adriana was still giving Paris her Tosca. So Nik moved out at leisure. When he left, I asked for an address, in case I wanted to—no, he signaled me with a gesture. That would be . . . indiscreet. We shook hands, then embraced; he whispered, "Be good to her. Forgive, yes?"

"I'm too forgiving," I said as we broke. "It's my worst quality."

He laughed, grabbed his bags, and was gone.

I have to say that Adriana took it with a valiant stoicism, la Fleuring herself from morn to bed but, nevertheless, being very adult about it. (That means your life is over but you just go Huh.)

Her real problem lay with Ercolani, because some Paris movie house had been running one of his films, a version of the life, work, and consequences of John the Baptist that was quite controversial in its day. So Adriana had marched in and seen it and gone totally unhappy.

"Bestemmia!" she kept crying when she returned. Blasphemy!

"If you had *been* there, Mark!" she cried, unpacking but mostly stalking through the house in an uproar of offended horror. "A saint's life with whores and nudity! The scene is Calvary—so holy a place, I blush even to mention it. And what does this director do but fill the screen with the trash of the Roman streets, grinning like . . . I don't know, those cities in the desert that were so sinful God destroyed them.'

"Sodom and Gomorrah," I said, quietly.

"Yes!" She turned to me in her peregrinations about the house, as much pleading with me for support as lecturing me on the woeful case of Adriana Grafanas, trapped in a contract with hell. "Yes, they are grinning like Sodomites!"

"You mean 'grinning like homosexuals,' don't you?" I asked.

An arrogant hand swept the air. "Whatever they are. And I am to shoot a film with this . . . Who *did* this to me? Deodata, quick!" she called out. "A bowl of broth, perhaps stale bread and rotten figs, so I may repent having signed this lousy cinema contract. And all to please Nik! How stupid I was, no?" She smiled. "I thought, He wants movies, I'll be a diva of movies, what could be easier? Deodata!"

"Subito, Siora!" Deodata called from downstairs. "But we've no figs."

"Just the broth, please, and two boiled eggs!"

Adriana stood stock-still, stared into a mirror, turned to me. "Oh, Mark. How am I to face a camera? In music, you have the composer, who tells you everything you need to know right there in the score. But the camera—"

"You have the director composing the movie around you, which is better than Bellini or Verdi, who are long gone and who in any case composed around other singers."

That stopped her, but only momentarily. "Well, look at you, the philosopher of cinema. Oh, this calamity! Never have I so needed a double!"

"A double?"

"A substitute. As when you are not contracted to do the last *Maria Stuarda* in Edinburgh, and they beg you to sing it but you are so exhausted, so they bring in little Renata Scotto, who has an immense triumph, and does she ever thank you for this opportunity?"

"She didn't owe you anything. You weren't willing to sing, and she was. She deserved the triumph."

Adriana gave me a look, but she was too busy monologuing to chew me out.

" 'No one can double Grafanas,' they used to tell me," she went on, almost muttering now. "So where was la Scotto when I had to give up the *Norma* in Rome?"

"Italian cinema," I told her, "is the greatest in the world today. The most vital, the most ingenious, the most honest. And Ercolani is one of its masters. Somehow or other, you figured that out, or you wouldn't have signed the contract. So you've nothing to complain about. And I have to tell you, not for the first time, that I am getting fed up with your attacks on . . . Sodom and Gomorrah. You're talking about real people. Yes, Ercolani is one of them. So is Amforto della Torre, and Leonard Bernstein, and Franco Zeffirelli, and David Webster, and I think maybe Gilda da Coservo, and a lot of other people in the arts. This may never have occurred to you, but you haven't known a lot of heterosexuals, and you may owe a lot of what you are to—"

"Deodata! The broth! I'm coming down!"

"Sì, Siora!"

Adriana scrambled down the stairs to the dining room, but I went right after her.

"Not another word," she warned me, in her steely mode. "I've been under too much strain. There was Paris, and Nik—"

"You're always under a strain. The strain of I won't listen."

"Not! Another!—"

"No. No, this time, no. No!"

"Mark—"

"No, you will *hear*."

"Deodata!"

"She can't save you."

"I'm sitting for my broth, and that is *all* that happens *now!*"

"Don't waste that Medea mask on me, lady." I said, standing opposite her as she fiddled, fuming, with the pepper mill. "And I tell you this— you'd better stop attacking people whose . . . taste, yes, is different from yours. Because if all the . . . oh, right, the *Sodomites* suddenly vanished, who knows why, you'd be without collaborators, without a theatre, and without much of your audience. And without, not that this matters, me."

She was staring at me in amazement. I turned, brushed past Deodata

and her tray, and sped out into the Venetian afternoon: through the garden
and courtyard and down the street and around the corner eastward along
the Zattere to the Punta della Dogana, where Dorsoduro comes to a triangular cap overlooking the great Basin of San Marco. I had noticed, now
and again, that men seemed to lurk around here for no discernible purpose.
Nervous older men. Shrugging younger men.

"I don't know what I was after" is the operable cliché here. But I
knew: someone with Vieri's power and Hugh's availability. That wouldn't
fairly describe the smiling, somewhat ratty fellow I encountered. At my
glance not of commitment, merely of appraisal, he left the wall he had
been holding up and asked, in Venetian dialect and with dishearteningly
false courtesy, if he could "assist the signore." Was the signore lost? Did
he need a guide? The city is so old, the signore so young. Did the signore
perhaps need a companion? A few moments of consolation, it may be, for
a disappointment in the ways of love? In which case, he would be delighted to accompany the signore to a secluded spot for a laughably nom-
inal fee.

The guy was missing a tooth and hadn't done a lot of bathing that day,
but he rubbed my neck as he spoke to me and promised me an excellent
time.

"Ma che vòa el signore?" he asked. What are you looking for? "La
chiavata?" Fucking. "El brindisi?" Blowing. "Seu foresto?" You're a foreigner?

"I've nowhere to take you," I said.

"In Venice is many places," he replied, clapping me on the shoulder
and leading me along the Giudecca Canal. "Secret love places, signore. We
will come upon un sacco." A hideaway.

"One you've used before?"

"Oh, every corner of Venice has been used before, signore, for every
kind of thing. You are so nice, I think. Do you favor la chiavata or el
brindisi? We must know, so to think about what it will be, so enjoying
the thought. Yes?"

"I'd like to key you," I said, as he guided me along the walk. "Or, as a friend of mine puts it, fork you."

"The signore foresto has a friend from the south it seems. Perhaps many friends of this kind." He laughed, and we passed on for some time in silence. At last, he said, "In the south, it may be that the signore will do this. But the boys of Venice do not receive the pleasure, signore. To give is heaven's blessing, it is said. *I* will give, and the signore will pay. How much will he pay?"

"On second thought," I said, halting, "I'm going home."

"The signore is with me."

"Let go of me!"

"The signore will pay, or I will be forced to call the police. But no. We have made friends, sì, signore? Sì. We will turn right down here. Do not struggle, signore. Our secret love . . ."

"Zormano, *aiuto!*" *Help!* I shouted, running ahead of my, uh, associate down the canal to the squero that Vieri hung out in: for we were indeed on the Rio San Trovaso, just across the water from Zormano's ridiculous Swiss chalet of a place, and to my intense relief Zormano bellowed out a "Cozza?" in reply, and even made an appearance (albeit casually, incuriously). Better, Vieri himself came out and immediately raced around to the bridge at the Zattere as my date began to back away down the canal toward the Accademia and escape. He couldn't resist letting pass a few insults at Vieri. "Pandolo!" he called out. And "Simioto!" Vieri kept coming, and my pickup started to run. "Oh, bela zoveneta!" was his gleeful parting shot at Vieri, delivered in an evil melody. Then he was off like cannon fire.

"Mark, what are you *why* with this strange fellow all a sudden?" Vieri incredulously, breathlessly asked, as Zormano placidly went back inside his shop. "Is this classy act, I wonder? Who was that rogue?"

Despite my recent fear, I was laughing.

"Well, it is so funny that Vieri has to run to save you, Mark. I see. First aiuto. Then wc arc laughing."

"No, I . . . I'm really grateful," I said, touching his shoulder, about all I felt I could get away with at that point. "What was he calling you?"

Vieri made a fist and pushed it to the right, then to the left, his traditional Who-cares-what-*he*-thinks? gesture. "These foolish Venetian names. 'Monkey,' 'idiot,' I don't know. Even 'pretty girl,' he calls me. Why are you out getting into trouble on the Zattere, anyway? What, then, you are looking for a friend as when Vieri was in Rome? The Piazza di Spagna kind of friend? Sì, Mark?"

I was embarrassed, and looked away.

"Give, Mark."

"My money and my life."

"No, I mean 'Come on,' " He laughed out, mock-swatting me. "You tell Vieri, please."

"I'm . . . All right. Piazza di Spagna, sì."

Mild disapproval from Vieri's shaking head. "The Inglese, he is not in town?"

"Hugh? No, he left three . . . Why do you ask?"

"But he is your . . . your doppio, sì?" Your double. It doesn't exactly mean "partner," but maybe this was underworld slang. "You are not displeased that Vieri knows, eh?"

"Well, how *do* you know?"

"A fratù, Mark," he said, his forefinger tapping my shoulder. "This is Vieri. You and I understand us. I see in the eyes. In the smiles."

"I thought Hugh and I had been absolutely discreet."

"What this word means?"

" 'Undetectable.' 'Subtle.' 'Surreptitious.' *What* eyes and smiles?"

He grinned. "Oh, Mark, everyone thinks he is so segreto, and all the time everyone can tell about him."

"Huh."

"I even know who is the woman and who the—No, what are you getting this angry for, or I throw you into the canal! Cattivo, you stop!" He'd called me a bad guy. "Sure, I know *he* is woman."

"But how do you know?"

"He is too wide here—" Vieri slapped his hips. "And that always means he would be forked. Basta, Mark. I must help Zorman'."

He put an arm around my waist and drew me the few paces back to the Zattere. "Try to get home without more trouble, sì?" he said. "We have exciting movie in four days. The train to Pisa. Staying in hotels where men in uniforms bow to you. 'Servizio, signore?' Trying not to look so young when paparazzi arrive. Avoiding telephone when family back in Napoli asks for money."

"Sì," I agreed.

"Sì," he warned.

I blew him a kiss and headed for home and

Now what?

She was right where I'd left her, at the dining room table, staring down a cup of tea.

She took a deep breath.

"So," she said. "But listen to me first. Why must you be always gnashing your teeth at me for my opinions? Have I not the right to express myself in my own house? And please don't skulk around in the doorway, come and sit at the table like an adult and you can have dinner. Deodata! Il figliuolo prodigo è di ritorno! La cena, subito!"

"Sì, siora."

I sat with her, greatly resenting her austerely fussy tone, Tallulah Bankhead as a schoolmarm.

"I confide to you my fears about Ercolani," she went on. "Such fears of moving from the world I know to a world I am helpless in. Cinema, tricks of lighting, a whole new set of critics to attack me. Suddenly, you are lecturing me. My employee, n'est-ce pas? This must be seen as an awkward situation."

"I," I decided to announce to her, "am Sodom and Gomorrah. I keep telling you this and—"

"What nonsense, Mark!"

"Vieri? The boy in the courtyard with il Professore? I'm in love with him. And Nik—I want him the same way you do. And Hugh and I—"

"*Mark!* C'est affreux, ça!" That's appalling!

"This is what you do every time," I said, as Deodata set a place for me and topped it with a bowl of soup. "You scream me into silence. I can't go on letting you neutralize my . . . the what I am. I can't let you express disgust for me just because I like men. It's not that big a deal."

"Then why do you make such a noise about it?"

"It's an amazing and ungovernable wonder that is in me, and I love it. Of *course* I make a noise. But it should be nothing to you, like . . . like a stamp collection. I love it, you don't care about it, and that's how we get along. Because when you say atrocious things about stamp collectors, you're saying them about me."

"Oh, I am to approve of this . . . this—"

"You are not permitted to have an opinion. It is none of your operasing-ing business."

"And my book? I suppose you will fill it with praise for these other Sodomites?"

"Who are you, Jeremiah? And what would Jeremiah have made of *you*, lady?"

"If I had spoken like this to my seniors, there would have been—"

"Adriana, you *have* no seniors! Nor do I! Nor does anyone! Whom do you mean, anyway, 'seniors'? Your mother?"

"Eat your soup."

"Listen, everyone's equal, right? Right. So everyone's desires are equal. Your plague is that people are always judging you unfairly—so why do you do it to others? Why don't you save judgment for those who move against you, and lavish your tolerance upon those who support you? You're like Dante, consigning people you don't care for to torment. Why don't you be like Lord Byron, and laugh at the world?"

"Poets!" she cried. "What have they to do with anything real?"

"Ercolani is a poet. He has to do with your debut in film, and *that's* real."

Looking at me across the table, she was struggling, uncertain, suspicious, and—rare for her—game.

"Will you help me, Mark?"

"Sure. But stop judging me."

"*God* judges."

"There is no God. You don't presume there were One any more than I do."

"Mark, such *horror!*"

"This is a swindle, this fake piety. It's what conventional people do when their neighbors are watching. You're the most unconventional woman in the world, so why do you care what Mr. Jones thinks?"

"The Father is always listening," she told me, in a reverie. "Let the mother die, but the Father will communicate."

"Yeah? What's he saying?"

Shaking herself out of her dream, she said, "He is waiting to forgive me. There is some act I must commit, some . . . anointing thing . . ."

"Ercolani's movie?" I said, as Deodata brought in the pasta. "Is that it?"

"How does one know?" Adriana replied, finally smiling.

20

The Place of
Miracles

"It is about the world of nature," lo Scenarista told us, meeting our train in Pisa a few days later. "The film so brilliantly poses our civilized neurasthenia against mankind's most primitive instincts."

Adriana gave me a look.

"Where's Ercolani?" I asked, as assistants grappled with our luggage.

"He is inspiring the crew, developing their sense of instinct and intuition. The maestro wants the cameras to pick up scents as dogs would."

"C'est dégoulas" was Adriana's comment; she often went into French when offended. Disgusting she called it.

"If you'll follow me, I'll lead you to your accommodations. There is some problem, because the hotel suffered a small fire, a water damage, and now there are not enough single rooms. It shall be worked out with the greatest of care, of course."

Before Adriana could register diva fury, lo Scenarista assured her that a veritable star's suite had been arranged for her at another hotel.

"Did Vieri get here? Orestes?" I said.

Why Pisa? you wonder. It was Ercolani's plan that *The House of Atreus* would start amid the most primitive settings, continue in a quasi-civilized atmosphere, and finish in the codified splendor of Renaissance architecture: from barbarians to Social Democrats. Ercolani's idea, of course, was that Nothing Changes, that some all-basic error sets into motion many successive errors, till all society is corrupt. Most of the early sequences in the narrative had been filmed in the wilder parts of Turkey and even Yemen (one of the few places in the world, one can say, that had till now been visited solely by fanatics and pilgrims).

There were a few reporters and fans as we Pisa-ed in, but basically it was a smooth autumn day in Tuscany, and lo Scenarista and his followers left me at my hotel, where, so he informed me, I was to share a room with with Ercolani's Agamemnon.

"It is Dave Ryatt," lo Scenarista exultantly told me. "The American cowboy star."

"It is who?"

"*Oh* yes, he is so big in Italy now, as a hero of western films. *Three Bullets for Tobias. Tobias Against the Dalton Gang. Tobias Meets the Queen of Sheba*. They are not of the first quality, but very popular. Signor Wyatt plays Tobias as comically amoral, the gunslinger who wins despite the odds. The Maestro had him in mind to present the mythic Greek warrior as his contemporary counterpart, the lawless avatar of your American west."

Adriana, probably eager to get to her hotel, hate her rooms, and walk out on the movie, was getting very Norma, so I urged lo Scenarista to speed along with her, and I checked myself in.

Dave Ryatt was in the room when I got there, and I haven't felt so uncomfortable alone with a man since . . . well, I've never felt that uncomfortable with anybody. Edgily amiable, inquisitive, and full of himself,

Dave Ryatt was one of those people who seem most thorny when they are most extending themselves.

It's strange, though: I already knew him. He was one of the American bodybuilders who flooded Italy in the wake of Steve Reeves's international success as Hercules. Reeves's hit inspired not only a cycle of pre-Christian superhero epics but also a cycle of Italian cowboy movies, in which the protagonist brought the Atlas look into the culture of sagebrush, dance halls, and villains in string ties. I remembered seeing one of these Tobias movies before I left the States for Venice, with my old high-school friend John Eagren. John had said it would be this big goof, but he went notably still when Tobias was stripped by Apaches and more or less tortured; and also during a scene in which Tobias paid a dime for a bath and, in the tub, overheard two guys (in neighboring tubs, and they weren't too bad, either) plotting a bank robbery.

So. Here he was, Dave Ryatt, shockingly American. Shocking to me, I realized. Because I'd been too long among the elegant, the subtle, the long-established, I had forgotten what *my* people were like: unrehearsed, innovative, sloppy. Everything Dave Ryatt preferred was "ape" or "tough," and everything else was "nothing doing." These mundane terms! Yet, endlessly repeated, while they lost their meaning as information, they grew in power as expressions of an autonomous self. Ape. Tough. They were barriers that this cowboy had set up for protection, defiance—the opposite of poetry, wherein the speaker strives to connect with the ear by his invention and vision. Hell, it was the opposite of language, which is meant for communication, not resistance. He was pretty darn good-looking, but I don't like heavily built men.

What I like was Vieri, who dropped in on us, wholly agog at his room, his roommate (a distinguished English Shakespearean cast as Atreus), the hotel, and the adventure of being in a new place. The Cowboy didn't know what to make of Vieri, clearly. He didn't so much listen to as stare at my young friend as he spoke, as if puzzling something out on a purely visual level.

"You in this movie?" the Cowboy asked Vieri at one point.

"Sì."

"Like, who are you?"

Vieri looked at me. "Ma che ha lui? Chi *sono*, Mark?"

I said, "He means, Who do you play in the movie? Your role."

Vieri looked at Dave. "I, Vieri, will be to play Orestes in this movie. Star part. And who you play, please?"

"Guy called Agamemnon. Hero type, like Tobias."

Vieri looked at me again. I explained, "Dave plays the lead in a series about Tobias the Cowboy."

"You're Italian, right?" Dave asked Vieri—rhetorically, I think. "You should know Tobias. He's like the biggest star in Italian movies here."

"I only see American movies," said Vieri, a thing of impulse and a child of song. (That's Byron again.) "Come, Mark, we esplore Pisa, yes? We see how much this famous tower is leaning today!"

"Gonna scare up chicks?" the Cowboy asked. "Italian signorine go hog for movie actors. It's all in the recognize."

Vieri was looking at him.

"Come on," I told Vieri.

"Hold up while I shower," said Dave, throwing off his clothes—not that he wore much in the first place. He kept house in his undershorts. "We could work up a sextet," he added, strutting into the bathroom. "Three of us throwing the chicks all at the same time, you get? Each of us next to the other, la signorine go *hog* for that, don't know which way to look."

The sound of the shower came on.

"Andiamo, Mark," Vieri whispered, and out we went.

After Venice, Pisa was Bridgeport, but it may be said that almost anything you do with someone you really like is good sport. Vieri and I closed the evening by bringing a bottle of lacrima christi up to Vieri's room, where the old Shakespearean regaled us with backstage anecdotes of Gielgud, Olivier, and Sybil Thorndike.

The Cowboy was asleep when I tiptoed in, well after midnight, and I wondered how much noise I could get away with.

The thing is, I like to have a bath before I go to sleep. I guess it's left over from childhood—what kid bathes in the morning?—but it does feel good to slip into bed all crisp and fresh. So, much as I wanted the Cowboy unconscious, I risked rousing him to enjoy a good wetting before turning in.

Maybe the running water stirred him after all, or maybe this would have happened anyway: a few minutes after I closed my eyes, I heard a rustling on the Cowboy's side of the room. He was out of bed and walking around, and in the darkness, not daring to move, I opened one eye to monitor developments.

I saw well, for the Cowboy had pulled back the window curtain to look out upon the street, and moonlight filtered into the room. The Cowboy was nude and restless. He came over to my bed and stood for a long moment, and though he surely noticed that my eye was open and locked on him, he said nothing to me. He went back to his bed, sat on it, exhaled, lay down, got up again.

Now he spoke: "Oh, man, I'm horny. You guys ducked out on me and prob'ly hit home runs, too, but I'm not complaining. Stuck in this nothing-doing town where the girls don't understand you most the time. Rome, everybody's parla ingleezi. Yeah, I'll say you guys scored real pretty, huh?"

Then silence.

"All the fellows warned me not to do this movie," he finally went on. "They said, Look, you know Rome, you have the fixings, the car, the know-how. Get laid every night. I work hard on my looks, I get noticed. They all like Tobias. They like his smile when he's killing folks. He's ape all the way through. Heavy in the shoulders, tight little navel, big buttons on my chest, it's scary. I was some little Sunday-school boy in Ohio, now I'm the Cowboy of Italy. On the street, they call to me. 'Ciao, Tobias!' I show them the smile, they expect that. They like me."

Silence.

"I know you guys scored, double-dip right to home plate. Oh, I'm so hot and ready. They say the president has to fuck a new girl every day or he goes nuts. Kennedy? Like some old god they sacrifice virgins to. A lay a day. Pulling on it *does not do* it for this guy, has to be that all-the-way fit. Oh, but I wasn't always like this. I was some kid. Nice American kid. But they didn't especially like me. Now they do, because when your outside changes, your insides change along."

Silence.

Then he said, "Sleep tight, Mark," climbed back into bed, and went to sleep.

Not all that long after, when my alarm went off, the Cowboy was already up and gone. Well, he had makeup and costume to get to; I had only to show up and "assist" Adriana.

Ercolani had chosen this day to shoot the Banquet of Thyestes, the film's big set piece, in which literally every principal was to appear. Moreover, Ercolani had elected to film the scene in the Piazza dei Miracoli, Pisa's main square, at an immense—no, and even "colossal" doesn't describe it: at an all but intercontinental banquet table, sparsely populated along its sides by groupings of guests but dominated by, at the bottom end, Atreus (who is serving his brother Thyestes the body parts of Thyestes's slaughtered children), and, at the head, Thyestes. Along the table's perimeter their predecessors (Tantalos, Pelops) and successors (Pelopeia, Aegisthos, Agamemnon, Menelaus, Orestes) in the cursed House of Atreus were to stalk, parade, wander. (Pelopeia giggled.)

"What a heavenly day to be making unholy art in Pisa," said the old Shakespearean, coming up to me sipping a bottle of Africola. "Especially after those ghastly weeks in Yemen. My boy, have you *seen* that place? Of course, you haven't. You have the wisdom of the young. Never go there. Promise me? The one ineluctable impression one retains, having visited, is, with places like Yemen on the earth, no wonder there are immigrants. But tell me, is it true that Ercolani fills his films with his bits of rough? His rent boys? What a recipe for stirring up a fallen romance:

Give me two more months of love and I'll put you in a movie! And that *glorious* boy last night! Forgive my impertinence, but are you two . . . No, say nothing and let me *spot* you out. But so handsome, that young chap. He takes a draft of his glass, looks up at you with his hair falling in his eyes, and . . . Well, what's a bloke to do? So impish, yet so manly. One sees in him perhaps a personality that is, in the best sense, uncivilized. Pure. He is not a presentation of elements. He *is* what he *is*. His manners, his emotions, his sex feelings—all one. But, tell me, *where* did he learn his English?"

"I taught him."

"Ah, they're calling us to the set."

It was that typical Italian thing wherein executives and assistants of various departments are all directing and coaching at once—loudly— which is one reason why Italian directors shoot their films silent for later dubbing. Ercolani himself was in conference with his technicians by the single camera as his many-coated actors assembled—here a Hollywood movie queen replica, there an international tycoon, now a Harvard liberal U.S. president, then a white southern singer of rhythm and blues: the VIPs of Now were the guests at Thyestes's banquet.

"It is called 'celebrity,' " lo Scenarista informed me, as the players were given their instructions by Ercolani and his several experts. Don't look into the light. Keep the costume straight. Know whom you loathe.

"Celebrity," lo Scenarista repeated. "Television, Oscar movies, gold re-cordings. This American idea of always to outsell your colleagues. It is the panorama of the modern gods of American entertainment, which colonizes the world. They are the witnesses of this sinister feast, *oh* yes."

Like an aficionado at a bullfight, he looked on ecstatically as Ercolani began to walk everyone through his paces. Adriana had not appeared, but there was plenty yet for Ercolani to do with everyone else. He had a choreographer work with Vieri—"Right, left, back to the side, arm, yes, look, freeze"—and drilled Agamemnon and Menelaus in close-arm ma-neuvers.

Vieri looked utterly tempting in a charcoal gray suit and a green Alpine hat studded with ski-run pins.

"Mark," he said, pulling me away from lo Scenarista during a free moment, "I must tell you of this breakfast that I have with the Dottore Ercolani this morning. Oh, Mark, he is complicated! Everything comes out at once. History, artistic subjects, the political, many things, from all directions. But he is honest, he say that he likes boys like me. You know, I am not willing, Mark. Not forked. He admire that and wish to know me, how whatever I would permit. But, Mark— Oh, also there is Luisetta, who is playing my sister Elettra and is always near me saying sweet things just like il Dottore Ercolani and she is so . . . What is that word you like, Mark? Vaga? No, ingannata?"

" 'Beguiling.' "

"Sì! Ma here she is, still coming with strong intentions, and she will *beguile* me, Mark. Should Vieri be tempted?"

"Everyone's crazy for you. You should know that by now."

"But what I do about il Dottore?"

"Vieri, vieni qua!" cried a lovely blonde in some designer toga: Luisetta, obviously. "They are about to turn the film!"

"Pronto, subito," Vieri called out to her, with hand gestures indicating Be soothed, but stop nagging me. "Mark, how much Vieri have to give to il Dottore to be always in the movie? Not he be mad?"

"He's too serious about his work to—"

"Vieri!" Luisetta cried, repeatedly banging her hands against her hips.

"Only this," I said. "If you give in, he'll take. If you resist—politely— he'll accept that."

Vieri kissed me, right on the lips, all'italiana. Then he ran to Luisetta, took her hand, and ran back with her to the set.

"Si," lo Scenarista told me as he sidled up. "È grande scena che si palesa." Here comes the big moment. "It is the banquet of the cannibal, of the incestuous one, of the curse that never dies. Oh, see!" he added, as the

Cowboy came into view. "Here is a most crucial actor, the Agamemnon. He is important to the Maestro's conception. Towering, as you see. Well-planted, formidable. You notice the shoulders. Of course, the Maestro has visualized him as a most denuded hero, an illustration of the terror of the great man. His power and beauty. Do you not agree that he is . . . bene . . ."

"A stud?"

"But what does that mean?"

"Amato, amante, amore," I said. "Casanova, only sexy."

"Or no, more the Michelangelo Moses in Rome," lo Scenarista countered, pensively regarding the Cowboy, who was throwing off a few push-ups (one-handed) while waiting for the shoot. "He is art," lo Scenarista added in an awed undertone. You could tell: Ercolani had decided to run the Cowboy right through the movie in next to nothing but nude. Jumping up from the push-ups, the Cowboy caught my eye and shrugged. Smiled. Very handsome guy, I had to admit.

"Does Ercolani like him?" I asked lo Scenarista. "I mean, as a boy friend?"

Too distracted to blush, lo Scenarista kept watching the Cowboy while saying, "He is not of the archetype that il Maestro favors."

"What archetype is he? Why is he in this movie? He's so modern, like . . . like Fellini having caffè on the Via Veneto."

"La monezza," lo Scenarista muttered, as the Cowboy leaped up to grab a rod overhead on the director's crane-shot chair and try a few chin-ups. "La malavita." The underworld, he meant. "Sì," as he recovered himself, forced his gaze away from the life-force that he feared. "Il Maestro will show lubricity, the ambition that deceives, demented hungers!"

"Where is the priestess?" asked Ercolani, coolly rearing up out of no-where. "Bene, she is la diva, but it is time to work."

The epic was falling into place, with about fifty bodies dressed, coached, and eager; and the techies of the various departments declared themselves prepared. Ercolani extended an arm to me: So where is she?

And *just* then Adriana made her entrance in a sedan chair. Really. Borne, yet, by what appeared to be Nubian slaves.

"Yes," said Ercolani, affirming this extraordinary presentation. "I have always seen in her the barbarian, Eastern, a figure of the ancient world who tries and fails to live as a bourgeoise. The past is strict with her, so she insists on dwelling entirely within the present. She is the woman without a father."

"Mark!" Adriana was shouting, as the black guys lowered her sedan chair. Actually, they were extras helping out with a prop; Adriana had apparently mistaken them for her chauffeurs. Well, so ran the story in the Italian press that evening.

"See!" Ercolani cried, with a rare smile. "The heathen queen of myth and newspapers!"

He was virtually backing away from her as she approached, maybe preparing a shot. The Thyestes was already in the sedan chair, ready to be filmed arriving at his cannibal banquet; and Ercolani had Adriana pace along the side of the endless table with Vieri, Luisetta, and another very pretty young girl. Chrysothemis, I presumed.

"What about my costume, my toilette?" Adriana demanded, but Ercolani violently shook his head. His actors worked without shellac. "How you are costumed," he informed her, signaling all the while to the lighting crew, "is how you are."

Adriana made unhappy noises.

"Your hands on them as you walk," Ercolani directed, "very like a mother." Possibly he was unaware of how Adriana would construe this direction. "And the children: loving, helpless, all confused, looking up at the mother. Yes … Yes … The other characters walking, too. Around, around, yes … Stillness at the table, the guests all staring at Thyestes. Atreus leaning forward, hands on the table." (The Atreus, our Shakespearean, complied, trying different faces till Ercolani shouted, "That one!" and he froze it.) "Thyestes is motionless, eyes closed, pensieroso, quasi stile concitato." Thoughtful, almost agitated. "No one moves at the table. Others are walking, walking."

Ercolani studied the view, moved into the scene to stare at the table of warring brothers and jet-set guests, paced in front of the other principals strolling the outskirts. A hovering crowd of Pisans and tourists took their own photographs; Ercolani ignored them. He could be recklessly appetitive in his personal life, but when he worked he was absolutely professional.

"Agamemnon," he ordered, "no expression, no plan, just walking. He looks at no one . . . Clytemnestra looks from Thyestes to Atreus and back."

But Adriana, unused to taking direction on the fly—spoiled, probably, by the genuflecting conferences that della Torre or Zeffirelli would hold during rehearsals, as much to soothe her nerves as to enlighten her—stopped walking to listen. I couldn't hear their talk, but then she raised her voice impatiently. "But *why* am I looking? Why am I even *in* this scene, since I am not alive at the time? And why am I dressed in *street clothes* at a *banquet?*"

More talks followed, in lower tones, and at length Adriana shrugged and made a face and started walking again, the kids with her, reaching for her, wondering at her, as she glared at Thyestes and Atreus.

"Sì. Sì," Ercolani urged her. "The fathers. They are the reasons why."

Quick as a dart, Adriana turned to look at him with alarm, but he held his hand up to her—reassuringly or instilling discipline, who knows?

"The fathers, destroyers," he reminded her, his tone low but insistent and his arm sweeping the view for emphasis. "See, he eats his own children."

Then he quickly abandoned the scene, nodding, when he got out of camera range, to an assistant, who called out, "Si gira!"*Action!* And Thyestes was served his stew.

I have to hand it to Ercolani: he really did prepare a splendid pageant. Adriana, for all her nervous noises, was clearly his idol, beautifully worshiped. It was, nevertheless, an exhausting shoot. Everyone was demolished; Adriana had to be sent back to her hotel in the sedan chair. I promised to follow presently, and paused only to arrange for dinner with Vieri at a trattoria whose posted menu had fascinated him with its astonishing variety of pizza toppings. "Did you see me, Mark? I was Greek Orestes! Which pizza will you choose, Mark? Alla Parigi? Alla New York?"

I laughed and grabbed him; he shook me off, then hugged me, rubbing my cheek with his. How could I not be in love, I ask you?

Adriana, meanwhile, was less exhausted than anxious. She worried that "this sordid film" would wreck her career.

Your career's already wrecked. Your voice is shot, you cancel everything, and you're a monster.

I didn't say that. I did what my job called upon me to do: hearten her, unplug her theories of conspiracies against her, and apprise her of the next day's shooting schedule.

Sitting at the dressing table, she let out a long exhaust of pseudo-despair and asked me, "What's Nik doing now?"

"I've no idea," I said.

"I let it get to me—*that's* what I can't forgive. I let something matter."

"Adriana, everything matters. What do you—Oh, not that drug again!"

"Taci, Mark, I need it more than ever," she said, gulping down three at once. "How do you think I survived Nik's betrayal? It tastes like sugar candy now."

"You're living on that stuff."

The hotel phone announced Ercolani downstairs, ready to make the traditional first-day visit by the director to the star, a rule in Italy's film as in opera and theatre.

"*Now* what?" Adriana wondered, though she was pluming herself. God, this vanity stuff!

Now what, at first, comprised the expected pleasantries, room service providing those weird Italian drinks that are neither wine nor whiskey and which no one seems to like but everyone ingests at certain times of day or upon Occasions.

Soon enough, Ercolani got to business, signaled by a very firm setting down of his drink on the coffee table. Madama seemed upset this afternoon, particularly when discussing the role of Clytemnestra in the regeneration of the curse of the House of Atreus.

"But what blame would you lay on this woman?" Adriana cried, immediately upset, though there was probably enough la Fleur in her to gentle a Crusade at the gates of a ghetto. "You tell me she kills her husband out of revenge because he murdered their daughter so the warships could sail to Troy. You say this woman is innocent? What *innocent* woman kills her husband?"

"His was the more despicable crime," said Ercolani, imperturbable as Adriana paced and crashed through her suite—sitting room, dressing room, bedroom, bathroom. Now you see her; now you don't. "He slaughtered the guiltless," Ercolani concluded. "She slaughtered the guilty."

"To be a wife to a man," Adriana insisted, heaving back into our presence, "is to unite your life with his at all cost." A mirror. She looks. A stray hair. She corrects it. A woman's way. "To be antagonistic to the husband is an outrage. If you refuse to undertake a wife's responsibilities, you have no reason to marry. I am as hard as a German about this, I assure you. And—this is worse!—to bear children without wanting to nurture them? It is criminal."

The phone rang.

"Per cortesia, Mark," she said, and I picked it up. It was Adriana's brother.

"I thought you never called," I said, strangely overjoyed at his voice.

"It's an emergency," he said. "My mother."

"Not . . ."

"No, but . . . well, not yet. It looks bad. I'm flying to New York tomorrow. Now, don't put Dee Anna on yet. Tell me first, how is she? I'll toss out the adjectives, and you select. Ready? One, receptive. Two, Unsteady. Three—"

"Who is it, Mark?" Adriana asked.

"Hang on," I told him. Okay. "It's your brother. Can you handle any more trouble, or—"

She had strode up, taken over the receiver, and begun rattling at him in Greek. Ercolani simply sat where he was, waiting, no opinion. Adriana listened to her brother, spoke, listened. Then, in English, she shouted, "Then let her die! What is that to me?"

She slammed the phone down and turned to us, hot with fury. She cracked into a chair and hated out a smile. "Where would Dante put me for that, I hope?" she asked.

When Vieri and I got back to the hotel after dinner, he was so tired that I had to help him to bed, complete with a final lingering hug during which he let me run my hand up and down his back; the Shakespearean was already asleep.

The Cowboy, however, was still up, lying facedown on his bed, going over the script.

"Hey, man," he greeted me. "Can't make head or tail of this story, you know? Like, why doesn't Agamemnon ever say anything?"

"He's the strong, silent type."

"You going to take another bath tonight? That your beat-off time? You like the water for that, huh?"

"I just like to feel clean," I said, docking my shoes and loosening my shirt.

"Hey. Yeah." He got up, adjusted the hang of his genitals in his shorts, and came over to me. "Listen, guy. Would you by possibly know anything about the girl playing . . . you know, one of my daughters? The blonde? Cute as anything, with hard buttons right through her silk thing, you can see them head-on. I know she's young, but this is Italy."

I said nothing.

"Know who I mean?" he asked.

"Elettra. She's Luisetta Something. A local girl."

"Oh, Luisetta. See, I was wondering if she's doing it with that friend of yours. That Italian kid. They look tight as spies."

I said nothing again.

"What I mean," he went on, "are they having parties together? Because how much does he tell you? And how would he be about doing a share date? Where each guy brings someone, and then we all switch? Because this town is so low, man. Can't get a hold on anyone. Who're you scoring?"

You won't believe this, but he then pulled off his shorts, sat on his bed, and began to work himself even as he talked, right before me. I was flabbergasted.

"Man, I so dearly want to do the dip, you know? You like to do the dip, Mark?"

I watched him for a while. I asked what the dip was.

"C'mon, man. *You* know. The dip? Sure, it goes in, it's the ... Man, don't you see?"

He was still working away; I asked him to stop.

"Can't give it up now, bo. Gotta get there. Man, I've been away for too many minutes. Oh, thumper, keep it up now...."

I turned from him, thought it over, and decided to head outside and walk till he was asleep. But he jumped up and stopped me at the door, his cock on high and his expression hurt.

"Don't be sore!" he cried, pulling me back. "Hell, I didn't want to offend you, did I? No? C'mon?"

"Then stop doing that in front of me."

"Shucks, we're both guys. Two guys'll work it off while they talk things over. What's the harm?"

"It's rude to me," I said.

"It's rude to Mark," he echoed, trying to understand that notion. He grinned. "You don't like me, s'that it?"

"No, I don't."

"What is it? How I come around and get into everything? Guy arrives out of nowhere, no parents, no basis, suddenly he's the king cowboy of . . . everything you fear . . . or maybe—"

"I don't like that gum chewing," I said.

"Well . . . huh?"

"It's your right to look like a dreary idiot, if you so choose. But have you ever seen anyone intelligent chewing gum?"

"Who *sees* anyone chewing gum?" he asked—still holding me, I should add.

"You don't notice it," I said, "because it's essential to you. Sailors don't notice tattoos. Pianists don't notice black keys."

"Tobias always chews gum. It's his trademark."

"How about letting me go?"

"Sure." He did, grabbed me again, then laughed. "Just joking," he said. "Sure."

I sat on my bed, so he sat on his, facing me off.

"Who're you screwing on the set?" he asked. "You like the dip or cunt-style?"

"The dip," I said, wondering what that was.

"Yeah. Oh, I love it, too. Pop 'em first. Heat 'em up so nice?"

You're boxing above your weight, I told myself, but I hung in there. "I don't always pop them," I said. "It depends."

"You got to. Most girls are so scared of the dip, you have to reassure them. Ease 'em in." He smiled, very broadly. "Shucks, do I *love* that part! Finger in, so sliding. And the purring sounds they make. Two fingers in, you fiddle them together, it's concerto-style, and they go *ape* for that, popping . . ."

He wasn't talking to me. He was deep in some ritual for one alone that must nevertheless be attested to, witnessed, like an Oscar-baiting scene in some movie. The actor doesn't need *you* there, but you have to hear him out all the same.

"You love the dip, sure," the cowboy went on, brightly, turning to me. "But what about the double-dip?"

"Best of all," I said.

"On their backs, where they belong, hissing how they love it. You? Stuffing 'em with love. Her? Creaming you tight. Double-dip, there's nothing like it."

He came over to my bed and sat next to me.

"How do you prefer it, Mark? Shove it in, or the sweet entry, getting all nested and loving? Do you kiss them? Do you like them afraid? That Luisetta, now—"

"She likes the double-dip. She's afraid."

"Shit, I *knew* it! Why didn't I make the play? Guess the best man won, huh?" He eyed me with some skepticism. "Yeah. Was I mentioned?"

"Mentioned?"

"She say anything about me? She like me?"

"Well . . ."

"I'll take the truth!" he said.

"She doesn't mention you."

"No hard feelings, Mark." He offered his hand. "Shake?" We did. "Besides," he theorized, "you could always pass her on to me when you find the next one. There always is, you know. No one's permanent."

"Adriana is," I said. "She's the greatest opera singer who will ever live. That's permanent."

"So Luisetta likes double-dip . . ."

"She likes a handsome man like you," I offered impulsively. "With your big construction and your madly sensual ways, you'd have her on her back in no time."

"Yeah?" he asked, wanting to buy it yet wary of me.

"Indubitably. She told me she dotes on a Rocky Mountain guy."

He paused and said, "The what?"

"Clearly, she likes a powerful American man—bold, confident, determined." I kept my voice low and willing, like his; he put an arm around my waist to bring us closer, to see us into agreement.

"I love the dip, Mark," he whispered, now rubbing my neck. "You love the dip. Right?"

"Right."

"Feel good?"

". . . well . . ."

"It's testing that tightness." His head nodding, we're ear to ear, "Mark, it's body to body."

I said, "It's deep. Slow. Fraught."

"It's sex," he said.

"There are dangers, yet we forge ahead," I got out, moving his hand off my neck. But he put it right back, importunate, relentless.

"Can't we talk of it?" he pleaded.

"Except I'm not Luisetta."

"Just wanta—"

The phone rang, I jumped at it, and Adriana cried, "Mark, it is catastrophe, get over here at once!"

"I come, my lord," I said.

Holstering the phone, I told the cowboy, "Darn, it's my boss."

"Yeah, you just don't like me, no matter what."

"Listen," I said, jumping into my mature-and-responsible clothes. The suit that Adriana had bought me. "It's not that."

"Just want to be nice to you. You think I'm a slob, is that it? That's what the fellows warned me about, you know. Said it's one of those fancy-dan movies, everyone'll be judging me down. That how it is, Mark? Maybe you think you're better than me, huh?"

I was scolding up my shoelaces, racing around, worried. What catastrophe?

"I just wanted to have a man-to-man with you," the Cowboy was saying, standing still as I moved around him. "Because we're the only Americans in the whole place, you know. We should be pals and stick together."

"Adriana is American, too."

"Clytemnestra? She's some Greek opera star," he replied. "Hey, can't you look at me when we're talking?"

Once more, the phone rang, and the Cowboy, carefully waiting for the third ring, grabbed it with a "Yeah, hello" lazily dwindled into two syllables: "Yealo." He handed me the receiver. "For you, buddy," he said.

It's Adriana again, I thought. She's going crazy with father-mother-daughter fantasies. She's a Clytemnestra who wishes she were Electra. Forget la Fleur—she'll overdose on the House of Atreus.

In fact, the phone call was from the German tape collector, keen with a lead on the Venice *Adriana*.

"Are we still at it?" I asked him. "I thought we had decided to give up the quest and maybe let it come our way by chance."

He was polite, insistent, and confident. I was wrong, he said. I must not let our Roman disaster discourage me. What had we lost? Pennies' worth of magnetic tape, no more.

"It's a dream," I told him. "Everything's a dream. Adriana's career is a dream. My book about her is a dream. Sex—"

"My dear fellow opera fan"—"Operliebhaber" is the German word, much more telling, suggesting a romantic intensity—"with us now is a sure thing. A man in Pisa is Antonio Dorozábal. A Spaniard. I have spoken with him, and he *has* the Venice *Adriana*. No. He has *parts* of it. He will make to us a present. No trade. I offered him—"

"Why don't you like me, huh?" the Cowboy was nagging just behind me. "I like you."

"Quick," I told the German. "Give me the info."

I snatched it down on my pad, rang off, and ran for the door.

"Not yet, Mark," said the Cowboy, taking hold of me. "Just tell me about Luisetta, okay? Just a few cute little details, while you're being top cat and running around on high-toned errands. Like, does she start to move with it when you pop her? Or is she sulking, the way some of them won't admit they want it, but you know they do. Right? Just admit that much, Mark, and tell me about her secret taste while you're at it, getting these important phone calls. I've seen her smiling at you and your Italian actor friend, never even been in a film, has he?"

I tried to shake loose, but he had me locked up tight.

"Dave," I began, faking patience.

"Why should I let you go if you're holding out on me, see?"

"Why should I like you if you bully me?"

"C'mon, Mark, I just want to hear a little something from you. A little friendliness is all," his voice avidly gentle. "Asking for so little from you," his arms tightening around me. I suddenly realized that he was going to put his mouth on mine, and I was panicked; though at the same time I wasn't. And he did kiss me, full on the mouth, deep and slow and heavy tongue. He was a jerk and I shouldn't have enjoyed it, but I guess you don't have to admire, in the artistic and intellectual and moral senses, everybody you touch. When we broke, I said, "You're very, very handsome, but you have to stop smirking like a sixth-grader who just blew up a urinal."

Well, that bewildered him, and in the confusion I made my getaway and hurried to Adriana's hotel.

She was utterly incoherent. Mothers, critics, the Scala public, that wonderful intendant in Mexico City, her loving Pippo (di Stefano), some louche nonsense about Ebe Stignani's cousin from Pozzuoli, the London fans, the New York fans, the Paris fans, Ghiringhelli, della Torre, that Contramin taking all the credit that rightfully belonged to *her*, and fathers—all came bounding out in an exhausted tirade that gradually took shape and theme. Ercolani, it seems, was the problem.

"Oh, that *miserable* director! If *only* I'd been warned before *leaguing* myself with his cinema di bestemmia!"

Then—just before I froze up on her—she added, "Mark, yes, I beg forgiveness, you are right, it is a low thing to . . . oh, what is the word? . . . disestimate people? . . . for what they are. Sì. But now—"

"*You* beg forgiveness?"

"Bernstein," she said. "Zeffirelli. Della Torre."

"You *accept* what I said?"

"Mark, I will not argue. Oh, look, the full horn of fruit the hotel has graciously provided. Which will we taste? A pear? These plump grapes?"

I waited.

"Yes," she went on. "We're sampling the fruit and calm, calm. Only . . . Could we convince il maestro di regia Ercolani that he must not . . . How is one to phrase this? . . . He must not hate Agamemnon and love Clytemnestra."

"Adriana, the story's thousands of years old. It's beyond revision."

"Clytemnestra is in the wrong."

"Agamemnon killed their daughter."

"You don't know what Clytemnestra is like!" she raged. "*I* know! *You* don't! You don't know who I . . . am . . . ?"

"*You* don't know who you are," I said, backing away from her, as everyone did, I gather, sooner or later. But then I felt so guilty, I tried to lighten and please her. "You don't even know," I said, in a complete change of tone, "about the pieces of the Venice *Adriana* that I am just about to—"

"Don't waste your time, Mark. Either it is there or it is not, no? If it is not there, you will never have it. Finito! If it is there, it will come to you—trust me on that. If you need it that bad it will *find its way!*"

She gave me that ironic smile, that loaded look, as if she knew where this tape of my dreams was and would not tell, or as if she was just about to give it to me.

I said, "The Cowboy who is playing your husband looks at Luisetta and says, I want it now! And that's how I feel about this long-lost performance of yours."

"Don't be ridiculous, Mark. The American actor? That overgrown muscleman with the lovely eyes? Luisetta non vuole, because he is always behaving in a way of the slums. He is trash."

"Why am I here?" I asked her—a startling question, I figured, but it didn't stop her for a moment.

"To save me," she replied.

I paused. "From?"

"If I could, I swear to you, I would pack and go. The Rome walkout? The Edinburgh walkout? I wouldn't be *walking*, I'd *flee!* But the producer would rob me in court, you know how they love publicity and revenge! You see, Mark ... we could, couldn't we? ... so gently ask Ercolani to change Clytemnestra from a hero to a criminal? He is so *enthusiastic* about her!"

"She's a remarkable person."

"She is a hater, and this is the way I must play her. This is the honesty that I bring to my work, surely, Mark. This woman wants to kill everyone she's related to, and everyone she isn't!"

"I feel that way myself sometimes," I say.

She actually smiles. "You never do," she tells me. "That's what makes you so sweet. Go, Mark. Seek out your tape. Who's next, some Pisan?"

"In fact, would it kill you if I tried calling him right now? It was a little awkward in my room just before."

She waved at the phone with a resigned look: the *things* you put up with from servants!

As I crossed the room, I said, "By the way, how's your—" "Mother," I was about to say. No, jerk, dumb question.

"She's dying and I don't care," Adriana replied, very flatly. "Tell the reporters, let the world curse me."

The Pisan collector—well, the émigré Spaniard collector—had an odd phone manner, with long pauses after you spoke, though I suppose he might have been having trouble with my Italian. I asked, When? and he responded, Anytime.

"Now?" I hoped.

"V'attendo qui." I'll be waiting.

"Ha!" I said in a triumphant manner, turning back to Adriana, who was inspecting a grape. "*Now* we'll see."

"Have a good time," she replied ironically.

At the door, I stopped. "Adriana," I asked, "*is* there a tape?"

She ate the grape. "I told you once. With my things in the warehouse on the Zattere. It's possible."

How I stirred, but she held up a hand. She said, "Would you so truly and deathlessly love me if you had that music? *I* had that music. I *was* that music. What love did it give *me*? Music is love, I suppose. Yes. Is it sufficient? But it does not feel sufficient. All the music in the world cannot bind a wound, Mark. Can't one be loved just for the love of it, or must one earn love? But if it is earned, is it love? No, it is applause. Ambarazzi was applause, Bernstein was applause. Della Torre—applause. But Nik. What was that, you ask?"

Tears were running down her cheeks.

"Why this need of love? Why can we not live on applause? Why are we hollow? What was in the plan of le bon Dieu that we cannot abide on food, sleep, and applause?"

She sank onto the couch—slowly, as if on stage.

"Music and Nik," she said. "That was to be my diet. Fool that I am. Beautiful Nik. Do you not think so? No, don't answer that, what am I thinking of?"

"He *is* beautiful," I agreed.

"Perhaps it was best that he left before I came to resent and attack and at last to hate him, as my mother hated my father. I will *not* turn into her!"

She jumped to her feet.

"Defend me from this trouble and I will give you whatever you want! Protect me from these producer geniuses!"

"Yes," I said. "For the tape?"

"Done!" she cried, advancing upon me. "Though why it should matter

I cannot imagine. When the curtain falls, it's over, sì? It *happened*. That's opera, Mark. That's life. Something very temporary. It happens...by chance."

"Lives like yours don't happen by chance," I said, taking off.

The Pisan collector was quite a change from our Roman friend: youngish, affable, and far more interested in the song itself than in the singers. His enthusiastic conversation led, again and again, to unfamiliar operas he had discovered, not—as with so many fans—to the opera stars he loved or loved to despise.

This was unusual enough for me to remark to him upon it; he laughed and told me of a recent trip to the record store with a fellow devotee. In the used bin was Ferruccio Busoni's *Arlecchino,* a bit of neoclassical drollery from the Glyndebourne Festival, cast with quite able but not personally luminous singers.

"I jumped at it," said the Pisan, after another of those strange little pauses I'd heard on the phone. "This wonderful revival of the commedia dell'arte by Italy's second most intellectual composer. There was no tape, ever, and suddenly this record."

"Who's the first?"

"Dallapiccola, certainly. The Italians feel first and then consider, so there is no third. At that, Busoni was only half Italian—his mother was forestiera, from north of the Alps, so that's where he got it, one supposes. I don't know Dallapiccola's story. No, but *even so* . . . I have my hands on this album and I am overjoyed. This rare, rare thing, right here in Pisa. My friend—bene, I don't know him all that well—he says, 'Who are the singers, to send you into this rapture?' I show him the record jacket, and his expression changes as he reads. No Tebaldi, Grafanas, del Monaco. He looks at me now as if he had come upon me eating slops in the gutter on my hands and knees. He says, 'I always wondered who bought those.' "

"Some friend."

"No, he has his qualities. But come, you wish to know about the Grafanas *Adriana*."

For a moment, I could say nothing. Couldn't focus, couldn't move. It *is?* It really *is?*

"This legendary performance," he said, moving through the room to the tape recorder, clearly cued up and ready. "Yes. It is, of course, one of the lost classics. I hope your friend in Hamburg warned you that it is only selections. Ay! there is no last act at all, when she would be at her foremost in the part, rivaled only by la santa Olivero. I do so apologize," he added, as if he himself had engineered this blunder of music history. "I must remark, all the so, on how much music she finds in this piece of idiocy. But now I should have asked first if you like it." He pressed a button.

"It's my favorite opera."

"Ay."

We joined the music right at her entrance aria, "Io son l'umile ancella." The Pisan smiled, his head tilted, as I cried, "There she is! So it *does* exist!"

We listened. "Yes," I could not resist uttering here and there, triumphantly.

"Ecco," he shrugged.

"Oh, *right*," I cried. "Hear, now. Yes! She gives it such intensity, yet..."

"This is what is called, in my country, 'gracia.' Not just 'grace'—much, much more. Something..." He paused to let the music through. "Something totally pure, yet expansive. It is unique, yet it contains all the world."

"Awesome," I said, as she reached the last phrase of the ascending octaves. "The truth of life itself is not so honest." I was crying, so help me. "I have found it. Well, *applaud*, you cretins!"

They did, with fervor, but the tape suddenly jumped to a later scene, then jumped again.

"It's very much a sampling, I'm afraid," the Pisan told me, reversing the tape. "But, as you hear, it is airwave rather than in-the-theatre sound, so it must have been broadcast—which means that any number of people might have taken it down complete. Surely it can be found."

He handed me the box, already refusing any offer of recompense.

"No," he said. "I love to give someone a thing he really wants. Because then someone will do the same for me. No?"

"Yes."

We shook hands.

"Go with God's blessing," he said at the door.

I called my German partner the minute I got back to my room, the Cowboy looking on dispassionately from his bed. In the excitement, I had forgotten about him.

"You were really crowing there," the Cowboy said, as I hung up. "Must have got something of the highest value, hey? The true ape?"

"A tape recording, actually," I told him.

"For what of?"

After a moment, I said, "You know, you have a way of doing everything wrong. You want to be friendly and take an interest in what someone's up to, but the words come out hostile and challenging. You brag. You attack. You make people nervous."

"Shoot, how wrong you are, 'cause I'm Tobias, who does none of these things you mention. I'm a great man, you know." Getting up to cross the room, he asked, "Now, what's the recording you're so happy about?"

"This tape," I said, pointing.

"What, in the box there?"

"Don't you ever wear clothes?"

"Man, you just won't ever cut me a slice, will you? You getting everything you want, me getting the nothing doing, and you're gonna call me names on top. All I want is *talk* to you, huh? What do you have to be so rude about? It's like...man...like someone put out a *word* about me? Everybody gets the word and they won't play with me now. Bad boy on the block, and what'd I do?"

He stood near me as I got my jacket and tie off.

"Okay," he said. "You want to hear about what was my best date in history?"

"No."

"What no? Can't I just talk to you?"

"Why me?" I asked, sitting on the bed, facing him.

"You're the one here."

"Can I ask you something?"

"Fire when ready, Gridley," he replied, sitting beside me with his copious smile.

(I know you're thinking, What are you complaining about, with this hunk on your trail? I just don't like big, pushy men.)

I said, "What made you build up your body like that? What was the plan?"

"So I'd look good. Why'd you even ask?"

"But plenty of guys are considered great-looking who aren't muscle-men."

"Who?'

"Robert Wagner. Anthony Perkins. Pat Boone. Paul Newman. Elvis Presley."

"All famous guys. Well, maybe I go, I'm not famous, so I need an angle. I'll be very body, super-extra. Worked, didn't it? Why you think they made me Tobias, in the long run? Italian movie producers, they like their heroes hero-size. You don't see them hiring Pat Boone, do you? Skimpy guys? Didn't you tell me Luisetta likes her boys Rocky Mountain–type, despite I notice that she's running around with that little boy friend of yours? Let's put it this way. There's this girl, Dolores Walkey. Back in L.A., this is. So, now, Dolores, she is a girl who knows what she needs. None of that hesitating stuff they think is so cute, so you practically have to rope them like a calf in a rodeo. She says right up what she likes, and that's muscle. Hangs out in gym parking lots, seven, eight of an evening. All smiles, leaning against a car, big gorgeous stuff up in front and down behind. Grab hold and you are *never* gonna let go. Redhead, too." He winked. "Guess you know about them."

"No, I don't believe I do."

"Can I whisper to you?"

Holding me by the sides of my torso, he leaned so close that his tongue was in my ear.

"Screamers, every lovely one of them," he said, his head very much lingering next to mine even after he spoke, and his hands very much moving up and down. I'm being seduced by Tobias.

"You know what else?" he whispers on, his right hand flat atop my head, resting there. "With redheads like Dolores, too much ain't ever enough. A date with Dolores, that's from here to eternity. And there's always her crafty surprises. Like one day, she says, first thing, *she's* gonna pop *me*. I go, Hold on. Forget it. She's not budging. 'F I want to dip her, I got to be popped. Fuck that! But she says, Hey, it really makes a guy fucktious when he's popped first. She says, Hey, come on. She'll love me up with a tongue trip and all. Well, I don't know, but she's so total! I mean? And anything's worth it if you get laid, is my policy. So she puts me down on the bed, mouth all over me so ape—you like that, Mark? Just lying there and letting her?"

"Fine."

He gave my shoulders a push. "What *fine?* You like it or not?"

I started to get up, so he said, "Okay, okay," pulling me back down. "Fine's the word, so sure. Anyhowsle, when Dolores sees I'm all done on one side, she gets me over, does me some more, and now I'm on my belly and it's pop time. This is so serious, Mark. Right? Right. She starts in slow, just hardly. You're thinking, All this attention for me."

"That's exactly what I'm thinking right—"

"You're so wrong to talk at this point of it, Mark, I just don't know how to tell you," he got out, real quick, his right hand gripping the back of my neck and his left shaking a schoolteacher's no-no finger at me. "It's something sacred here, don't you see that?"

And blast me if I didn't reach over and pull him to me and hold him. My friends, if you're young and full of the dickens, the most decisive thing isn't affection or fantasy. The most decisive thing is opportunity.

"Well, ain't you the sweetheart, at long last," he said. "We're just two horny guys, and it's perfect sense. Like getting popped by Dolores. That's true love, a camera type of thing. There can be such excitement when it happens. Makes me so hard, Mark. Especially when they go to the double-pop, which is, as I have already made clear, two fingers sawing away in you, and what a feeling, like flying through suns. Double-pop leads to double-dip. That's what *I* say, Mark, and what do *you* say?"

"I say that I've been known to get quite giddy when popped."

"Yeah," he said, "I know you're goofing me. You goof with that cute boy friend of yours? Are you nice to him, like I want you to be with me? You shouldn't hold back on me now, Mark."

I stroked his hair, a rich black concoction, easy, clean, and free: American.

"I won't hold back on you," I told him, as his mouth came up to mine. Sure.

"Go on," he urged, between kisses. "That's right." And "More." He got creative with "Nice taste of you." He growled out what I eventually learned was the perennial libidinous "Yeah." He worked me over to the bed, pulling off my clothes (I helped), and we kissed some more and then I seized the lead and licked along the lines of his muscles to see what was there. All that big. But maybe I was just missing home; and he was home.

Yet I was apprehensive, too, because like many a newcomer I figured the bigger guy gets to take charge, and I had assigned myself a quota for getting forked: zero for life. But it turns out that bigness itself doesn't certify the top man. It has to do with character, avidity, taste, virtuosity, vocation, habit—anything but weight.

Because now the Cowboy slithered up out of my reach with a punk grin, went to his dresser, pulled out a tiny jar of something, tossed it to me, and threw himself back on the bed facedown and legs wide to murmur, "Load me up, Mark, and go kind of heavy, okay?"

This Viking is like Hugh? was all I could think. Ye gods, what I didn't know then! Straddling him, I started massaging his arms and shoulders and slicking up his ears with my tongue while he spat out erotic pleas-antries. "Pop me," he urged, and I did, moving down his body to between his legs, drunk on power. "Oh, sure, that's pop," he let out, "but go to two fingers and do the fiddle.... Yes, Mark ... buddy of mine ... now this," as he got on all fours, "and feel me up while you do that to me really got the ... the touch and that's so ..." Then he let out a howl of joy so delightedly initiating that I promptly snapped open the jar and worked the jelly inside him. "Like that?" I asked, getting into his swing; but he said, "Don't talk, just do it," so I tipped in, then grabbed his shoulders to pull him onto me.

"Make me squirm," he said. "I've been so hungry all this time. Got to be so famous and charming, so how come it seems nobody likes me? What'd I do wrong, or something, you know? Yeah, Mark, you're my buddy, so ape like that now." His steady growling as I pumped him. This vast, conceited man, so needy all of a sudden. Façades, self-inventions, amore, segreto, forgiving oneself in the chain of life. This. Sex. Strength. I have already said that young gay men always fall in love, however tem-porarily, with the men they top; as if, like primitive tribesmen, they were warriors collecting the souls of those they had o'ermastered. But I was not in love with the Cowboy. I was in love with Vieri's look and Adriana's song, and if I could only unite and package the two, I'd own the world.

"Marky," Dave called me, with a conniving smile, as he turned to watch me do. *"Harder, more, go!"*

21

Original Sin

"What if she's impossible and screaming?" I said.

"Then I must to soothe her, tell her stories, give her skin rub, loosening. Sì, Mark?"

"Say she's caught you with another woman."

"But she is l'unica, amor e madre. She knows there is no substitute for what she is. She *knows*, Mark."

"*I* know: say she—"

"No, it doesn't matter these questions," Vieri told me. "Federica is loving, perfect, always forgiving."

"She sounds great, then."

"I can't wait that you see her. Oh, look who is."

It was lo Scenarista, to whom Vieri had taken what was for him an astonishingly antagonistic attitude. He actually walked away.

"I feel so well this day," lo Scenarista announced. "And I have learned this new American word. 'Kooky.' Vuole dire 'pazzo.' "

"No, not 'crazy,' actually," I told him. "It means more like 'eccentric.' Or even 'individualistic.' Really, 'unconventional.' Affectionately, it means 'inventive.' Reprovingly, it means, 'I dislike your strongly inflected sense of liberty.' "

"Prego, would you call Signore Ryatt 'kooky'?"

"No, he's very regular. Well . . . maybe—"

"I wonder, mornings, if there is not . . . the passionate look? He is so . . . so large to regard. Does he ever . . ."

"What? Want to get naked with men?"

So of course lo Scenarista blushed and clammed up. These guys hunt and giggle and nudge and wonder, and when you say, Oh, is this what you want?, they run away.

"I could have contempt for you," I told him, very mildly, without sting, "and it would be entirely your fault."

"This American," he went on, undeterred, as, indeed, cowboy Dave came strutting up to the set in—on my oath—nothing but a leather Tarzan cache-sexe hung so low you could read auguries in his public hair. "This Dave," lo Scenarista insisted, "is il Maestro's coup of casting. To pull the world-famous Tobias into Greek tragedy."

"What do you want to learn about him?" I asked. "You know he's worthy, because you've been staring at him nonstop since we all got here. You want the details? The noises he makes when he's keyed?"

Angered, lo Scenarista observed, "You whip me thus."

"I tell you the truth thus," I answered. "If you want it, reach for it. If it's torment, pass it by. If you're worried, decide."

Ercolani was bustling around, positioning Vieri, the Cowboy, Adriana, Luisetta, and the Aegisthos, yet another beautiful Italian boy discovered who knew where. For a moment, I considered becoming an Italian film director, to live for love as well as art. (It can be done, see?) But what a madhouse! It was assistants and shouting, portals and columns, back in the Place of Miracles, for the murder of Agamemnon—in which, once again, the entire cast would take part.

"The terror," lo Scenarista finally replied. "It is about terror."

"Of what?"

"I don't know."

"That's how stupid you are," I said. "It's your terror of nothing. You invent your own terror."

Taken by surprise, he said, "You are discourteous, Signor Trigger."

"I'm disgusted with you people who would and yet pretend that you won't. I thought Europeans were smarter than Americans. Maybe more open about the details of life, I thought. Ercolani certainly is. What do you think makes his movies so great? Dishonesty? Masquerade?"

At that moment, Ercolani was staging the very moment of the murder—not in Agamemnon's bath, as traditionally, but in public, as if it were to be a state occasion, accompanied by the wailing arabesque of a lovely, somewhat Oriental slave (Cassandra?). In fact, Ercolani had the singer intoning ad lib throughout the rehearsal. As always now, I was impressed by the difference between the Machiavellian Noël Coward that Ercolani seemed in life and the brisk, sage professional assolutissimo he turned into when shooting. Anyone can be gifted. It takes genius to be efficient.

"What did you come here for?" lo Scenarista hissed at me. "This civilization, built up in two millennia of war and oppression and uprisings of the popolani and the revelations of such men of truth as Dante, Leonardo, Giambattista Vico, and Verdi, is not your finishing school, oh no! And the proud Tobias is not keyed, I am so sure! How do you dare to—"

"Oh, wake up, Gianetta. People are full of surprises. I keyed Tobias myself. Last night. He loves it, take my word."

Ercolani had Agamemnon spread-eagled against a wall, Clytemnestra standing before him, a great brutal knife lying on the earth between them, with Elettra and Orestes also flat against the wall, flanking Agamemnon. The cinematographer seemed to be concerned that the knife blade's reflection of the sun would vex the film. "È troppo brillante," he kept saying.

Too intense—though intensity, of course, is what we want from art. Ercolani tried a different grouping, with Aegisthos stalking Agamemnon with the knife, Clytemnestra trying to wrest it from him.

"You did not key Tobias, I tell you, signore," lo Scenarista insisted. "Tobias is a model of the man who feels himself to be complete and always dominating."

"Tobias got forked, and Tobias loved it."

Tearing his gaze from the doings on the set in the Place of Miracles, lo Scenarista cried, "But you are *nothing!* You cannot deserve Tobias this way!"

"Oh?" I smiled. "What way *do* I deserve Tobias?"

"Nothing for you!" he solemnly declared. "Nothing of such beauty and power! We speak of the elect, of the gods!"

"You jerk," I told him.

Whereupon there came a crash as Adriana—apparently—threw the knife at the wall and started screaming.

"She does *not* feel regret!" Adriana maintained, of Clytemnestra. "She feels *vicious!*"

"She loves," Ercolani replied.

"She *destroys*. Mark!"

"Because of helpless need, not—"

"Because of evil! Evil people do evil things! Mark, you are paid to assist me, so why—*No!*" This was addressed to the Cowboy, who had attempted to calm her. "I do not care for this dismal paisan to . . . At last, Mark, you choose to stroll onto the job!"

In fact, I had hurried over at the sound of my name, lo Scenarista dogging me at a distance. "What?" I asked.

"Hi, Marky," said the Cowboy, with a grin, at which Vieri looked quizzical.

"Please, Mark, *tell* il Maestro how I feel about the characterization . . . and all others are keeping quiet, I believe," she added sharply, shooting a discouraging look at Luisetta, who had been giggling and whispering to the Aegisthos.

I could tell at once that Ercolani had no desire to discuss characterization or anything else with an assistant, an American, and in any case someone outside the inner lock of his vision. But I quickly said to him, sotto voce and no doubt garbling my Italian, "La donna fears the person of anger and frustration. She refuses to . . . duplicate the . . . model."

Adriana, not listening, was pacing wildly around us, every step a blow on the bass drum. Ercolani, gazing from Adriana to the others, was gauging his choices. Luisetta was leaning on Vieri, humming some tune. The Cowboy was chatting with lo Scenarista.

I had never in my life been in the presence of so many near-naked males except in the locker room in high school. The Cowboy, as throughout the movie, was almost all skin. Vieri wore long white cotton pants, the Aegisthos purple gym shorts. The women, however, were bundled up, Luisetta in Attic Technicolor and Adriana in robes of lurid dark red, like flame.

"You are trying to turn her into her mother," I went on to Ercolani, who allowed me to draw him a bit away from the others. "But inside her is a driving need to be as unlike her mother as possible."

"Ma perchè?"

"I . . . because she . . . wants a different destiny?"

"Oh, this film!" Adriana cried, passing us in her travels. "A take-attendance of the cronaca nera!" The black book, the names of the underworld. "This way to destroy life . . ."

Alarmed at her dazed look, I blurted out, "Life is a dream. Only God is real. We are his fantasies. We are not here." Of course I was being a raving hypocrite, but I felt that she could use this.

She did not appear to be listening, in the end. She continued to wander around in a self-absorbed rage.

Vieri and Luisetta, laughing, ran off a few paces to talk.

The Aegisthos started complaining. "Perchè non va? Quando si gira, *daimo!*" Why aren't we shooting, huh?

Ercolani called the lunch break.

Vieri immediately flew off with Luisetta, and the Cowboy, watching them with narrowed eyes, allowed lo Scenarista to pay him shy court.

Tugging at the waistband of his shorts, the Aegisthos made himself scarce.

Ercolani, pensively considering Adriana as the others made their lunch plans and drifted off, said to me, "She is thrashing, like a captured beast."

"That's what I mean," I told him, leading him a step or two away. "You've got her virtually under siege in this role. Everything in her forces her in one direction—that's release, escape. But you're trying to pull her in another direction—that's despair, surrender, doom."

"Sì," he whispered, like a doctor consulting on a particularly lavish procedure. "She is entirely instinctive in art, never calculated. It is her greatest distinction."

"Right. So can we—"

"She cannot save herself," he went on, not listening to me. "*Konyechna!*" This last bit, Russian for "Of course," burst forth as a dawn of amazed understanding. "Like all in this maledicted family, she hustles onward as if driven. She is not vindictive, but possessed."

Lo Scenarista and the Cowboy strolled off together.

"Mark!" Adriana cried, worrying the grass behind us. "I cannot bear this indecision!"

Ercolani turned to regard her as if taking in a masterpiece. He *examined* her.

"It is entirely wrong, the cinema," she went on. "They will say I am washed up in the theatre. 'She has lost the music, so she goes to the movies.'"

"It is as if some power were running her," Ercolani remarked. "Some-one she herself ignores, or cannot allow herself to know."

"I should never have left the theatre!" Adriana observed, ranting at us from a certain distance—say, that of an orchestra pit; so that, had she been on a stage, we would be in the front row. "Sì, tornero!" she cried, looking at heaven as if seeking out a supportive Vision. Yes, I'll go back! "Nel trionfal sorriso dell'Arte io voglio inebriarmi ancor!" I will bask once more in the fulfilling smile of Art!

"Divina," Ercolani breathed out. "Not of this world."

Turning pale as she tottered, Adriana called out, "Mark!" Ercolani and I dashed forward to catch her.

"No, it is nothing, surely," she immediately told us. "Too much of the lurid Tuscany sun."

She touched her heart.

"Are you hurt?" I asked, in English.

"From the first day."

"No," I said, thinking that la Fleur was finally presenting its bill. "Are you suffering pain now? Perhaps where your hand now rests?"

"Sì, il core."

"Adriana, I found your tape," I said, feeling her, coaxing gently, as if trying to revive a stricken butterfly. "It's only highlights. But it is you."

"That awful opera," she smiled out. "All those words and noises." She was panting. "Who was the tenor, Raimondi?"

"Yes."

"Il mio caro dolce Giannino. When I was very young, life was a terror. But in Italy, when I was just young, life was such adventure. Each new role. Verdi, Bellini, Donizetti, and that Wagner. Giannino, Giulietta, Pippo, of course, and Saturno, Elena, Mirto—such a musician! La Stignani, amazing Tito, Miriam, clever Tatiana, gala Fedora, always ready for a party, versatile 'Seppino . . . il Taddei, naturalmente, in *Aida* the most titanic of fathers . . ."

Even in our arms, she managed to stagger.

"Un medico," Ercolani breathed out, and two assistants started running for a doctor.

"Onta su me," Adriana whispered. Shame on me.

"No," I said. "No."

"Never in all my life did I delay or perjure a rehearsal." She was back in English, her mother tongue.

"All'erta!" Ercolani barked out at some other assistants. "Forza, su!" Quick! Now they ran off, too.

"But I must delineate this Clytemnestra through my unique abilities," she told Ercolani, almost conversationally. "I must see her as she must be."

"Bene, sia," he said. You get your way.

"It is better as I see her. Sì, Mark?"

Flustered, I quoted Byron:

What, after *all*, are *all* things—but a Show?

"I will rise," Adriana suddenly said, with conviction; we other two helped her up. Vertical, Adriana tried a smile and looked almost whole: ready, willing, and able to work.

"We must talk of the murder of Agamemnon," she told Ercolani. "We must consider the nature of guilt. All mankind is born guilty."

"Some of mankind is born into a culture that leads them toward guilty acts," Ercolani countered, ever the political philosopher, smooth, even in tone, but so delighted by Adriana's recovery that he winked at me.

"No one is born guilty," I put in. "People commit guilty acts."

Adriana looked unhappily away. "All of this our life is expiation," she cried, almost pleading.

"All of life is a hopeless quest," said Ercolani. "A quest for beauty, which is, by very definition, a selfish lie."

"All of life is choices," I told Adriana. "Surely you know that better than anyone. 'NEW YORKER EXCELS,'" I added, to hearten her. "New Yorker decides to create the greatest opera career ever known. New Yorker dares. New Yorker wins. *That* is life."

Then there came the sound of prancing hooves, and we three looked up to find a phalanx of reporters advancing upon us, bearing—upright, in reading position—newspapers with headlines telling of the death of Adriana's mother in the street: È MORTA NELLA STRADA LA MADRE DELLA GRAFANAS.

The reporters were grinning and chanting, "*You* did it! *You* did it! *You* did it!"—all right, I admit it, no. That's the version that Ercolani might have filmed. Still, a few of them had indeed unfurled papers, and they were all yelling at Adriana, not just What's your reaction? but How could you do this?: as if she were not only the result of a calamity but as well the matrix of it.

For a moment, Adriana stood frozen in their headlights; then she began backing away, wearing that drained la Fleur look.

"Don't let them get to her," I told Ercolani; but now she was running from them, right to the wall. Bad planning, I thought—but in fact she had gone for the knife. Her grasp was tentative, or at least pensive, and she was staring at it, not at the enemy. Tosca? Still, a knife is a knife, and the relentless defile of reporters halted.

"Madama Grafanas," one called out, "what makes you so angry?"

Another: "What preserves you during these times of trial?"

A third: "What do you most regret?"

Staring at them, she started to wobble, dropped the knife, murmured, "The love of the father," and fainted flop-dead on the earth.

"Presto," urged Ercolani, picking her up. Let's move quickly.

"My place is closest," I said, as the reporters swarmed over us, shouting insane questions as we hastened along in a really furious silence, Ercolani puffing with the effort of transporting Adriana. I spelled him at one point, and at last we made it to the hotel lobby, where the reporters had to back off by the gentiluomo code of the Italian press: no one can rush the front door, no matter how hot the story. Ercolani went to the front desk while I sat Adriana in a chair. She was conscious now, and before the elevator arrived she became not only quick but abusive. She chewed us both out for sins at best arguable and at least imaginary, but she agreed, at Ercolani's insistence, to rest in my room.

"A doctor has been summoned," he said.

"Ridiculous," she muttered. "Security on the set was all that we needed."

There was silence till we got to my room. "Yes, I will rest," Adriana said. We entered to find the Cowboy and lo Scenarista doing the double-dip in the Cowboy's bed.

This time the Cowboy was on top. I admire a versatile talent.

"Dio mio," cried lo Scenarista, legs high.

The Cowboy turned, saw us, and grinned down at lo Scenarista. "Now the world knows," he growled out. "Hey there, Marky," he added, pumping away. "Yeah, we're on our way here, as you see."

I was so shocked I couldn't move; Ercolani bustled past me with Adriana and made her lie down on my bed. Made her: because she clearly wanted to bustle, too. She peered at lo Scenarista and the Cowboy. "What life is there?" she asked, in English.

"True life, lady," said the Cowboy, pumping away. "But, Daddy, that's *so* sweet!" he added, in a breathless shout.

Lo Scenarista tried to pull out of the whole thing, but the Cowboy grabbed his shoulders and held him in place, moving heavily.

"Ships, making port," the Cowboy cried. "Yes, now. Oh, what a song!"

Ercolani had Adriana on my bed, feeling her forehead. He glanced over at the doings and raised an ironic eyebrow at me. Nothing is forbidden, he seemed to say, but there is a reasonable place, a fit time.

" 'What are all things,' " I said, " 'but a Show?' "

Trying to free himself from shame, lo Scenarista flailed so that he and the Cowboy went crashing off the bed to the floor. *"Yippee!"* the Cowboy cried, abruptly jumping up to show us his life-hard, clutching root. "Folks, wherefore come you?" he asked, as always grinning at me.

"Get him out," Adriana murmured. "I see him. I know him."

"Get me out? I live here, lady," the Cowboy told her. "Say, you see me now?"

Supine though she was, Adriana let off a kind of stamp-the-floor paroxysm, shouting, *"Out! Out! Out! Out!"*

"So screw the bitch" was the Cowboy's summation, while lo Scenarista scrambled into his clothes.

"Maestro," he began.

"Niente," said Ercolani. *Don't*, as he sorrowfully waved lo Scenarista away.

Then the doctor arrived.

"There is nothing wrong with me!" Adriana began, dangerous and resisting. "But just maybe you movie technicians should examine your wonderful colleagues who hobnob with low-lives and copulate like dogs in the street for all to witness."

"Fuck your opera," said the Cowboy, casually, admiring himself even as he began to lose full boost.

"The hatred of justice," said Adriana, while she straight-armed the doctor, just saying it right out like that, and letting it hang there.

Then she said, "Attacks on the Father."

"Yeah, well, *this* is the father," the Cowboy answered, stroking himself back into form as he marched over to her with a grin. "Take a gander, lady," he added—to her, though he was looking right at me.

Lo Scenarista, fully dressed, left us.

"Each act," Adriana went on, weary again—well, just about spent, as it soon turned out—"creates all other acts." She lay back as the doctor began to fuss and heal.

Suddenly the Cowboy lunged at my dresser, pulling open a drawer and tossing my clothes into the air.

"See now?" he cried, laughing. "Circus time!"

"These secret loves," Adriana breathed out, paling. "Doctor . . ."

"Hush," the doctor replied, getting out his instruments.

"Exit Agamemnon," said Ercolani, pointedly, to the Cowboy.

"Oh yeah, pardner? Is that the case?"

"Leave the hospital!" Ercolani urged him. "In the name of mercy!"

"*You* want me out, Marky?" the Cowboy asked me.

"Yes."

"Take me some souvenirs first," he announced, riffling the contents of another drawer. "Oh, what's this, our miraculous tape recording, now?"

"Hey—"

"Yes, Marky boy, yes," he crooned at me, keeping it out of my reach as I battled for it.

"Come on, Dave, this is too important to—"

"You *must* leave," Ercolani insisted, using the plural form of the verb.

When I was younger, you would taunt someone the way the Cowboy was taunting me, snatching what was his and holding it out of reach, everybody on the scene eagerly siding against the one person, isolating him in that instinctively crushing maneuver that tells the subject he is utterly and irredeemably alone, a figure of fun. "Saluggi," they called this game.

"Marky, now," said the Cowboy, playing one-handed saluggi with me. I grabbed at it, he pushed me away, I ran at him, he pulled the box open.

"Uh-oh," he said. "What if it gets wrecked?"

"Let me have it, Dave," I begged him. Behind me, I heard Adriana groan. "It's nothing to you and . . . Please?"

"What's it to *you?*" he countered.

"A doctor attends me," Adriana got out, her head turning from side to side on the pillow as if she were raving, "and meanwhile it is inverts everywhere, creating a monstrous atmosphere."

"Not monstrous, *different*," I said, still trying to get the tape from Dave.

"Am I a monster, Marky?" he asked.

"No more than I. Dave . . . please, now?"

"What's so special? Tell me, Marky."

I turned to look at Adriana; she was absolutely white, eyes closed. The doctor, concerned but methodical, was examining. Ercolani was looking on.

"Hey, Marky," the Cowboy sang out. "Don't you want your tapey-tapey?"

I turned back to see him spinning the plastic reel on his finger as he unraveled the tape, grinning, jumping back from me as I tried to grab it, switching his grasp to the tape itself to hurl the reel about the room as Ercolani shouted and the Venice *Adriana* went all to pieces in his hands, tearing, furious, handfuls and bits and every part of it, again and again and again, till the room looked like Christmas morning, overrun with waste. I was so angry that I leaped upon him, but he caught me and threw me onto the bed and held me down, panting, his eyes black ice; and he said, "Give me a reason to hurt you."

"Beasts of hell!" Adriana cried out, in a strangled voice. "Unforgiven for all eternity!"

With fastidious calm, Ercolani told the Cowboy, "I must advise you that I shall lose all admiration for you if you do not show respect for your colleague in her distress."

"Yeah, she's some real rooty-toot," replied the Cowboy, still holding me down.

"The insult to God," Adriana murmured, screaming out in pain as the doctor touched something somewhere. "The black mass of the inverted!"

At this, I shoved the Cowboy off me in a surge of will and, jumping up, shouted at Adriana, "I am not inverted! I am what you are—*human!*"

Adriana, whispering prayers as the doctor fished in his bag, gave a start, looked at me, and cried, "Keep the witch away!"

There was a moment.

"The *witch?*" I asked.

She went on praying, oblivious, in Greek.

"Your brother says you're not religious," I went on. "Does anyone know what you are?"

"She's some screwy dame," said the Cowboy, from the other side of the room.

"Now I'm a witch?" I asked. "No, you're . . . you're kidding, right? A *witch?* Like burned at the stake because I don't agree with *you?*"

Ercolani held up a warning palm; and I knew that this was the wrong time to take issue. But I was too angry—yes, mild-mannered Mark. I was so mad I was shaking.

"The burning of the witch," Adriana said, as the doctor looked through machines into her eyes, ears, and heart. "The torment of justice."

I just stood there, and I was furious, and this idiot bigotry just *has to stop*.

"Have you been taking extraordinary remedies?" the doctor asked Adriana.

"There is no remedy," she laughed out. "No," as she grew serious. "A *curse* on *all* of you! May *you* have what *I* have!"

The Cowboy, having slipped on shirt, shorts, and sandals, called out "See you, Marky boy!" and "You, too, Madame Opera," as he married his way out.

"Well, I've lost my precious tape," I said, trying to be reasonable. I shrugged—at Ercolani, I suppose; no one else in the room was even dimly aware of me. "Lost and nowhere to go," I added. "Except away from here. You know, I probably should not have come to music—I mean, to Europe." Funny slip. "You know?"

"Taci," said Ercolani. Shh.

"Right," I said, pulling out my valise to get my stuff together. Reasonable: what's reasonable is showing bigotry what you think of it. So, yes, I was packing; I was leaving; I was striking; I was punishing; I was waiting for a voice behind me to call me back, to undo it all, but none came, and I was on the rapido that afternoon and never saw her more.

22

The Venice
Adriana

Hugh was subletting a floor and a half of a palazzetto in Cannaregio, and he insisted that I bunk in with him in my last days in Europe. What a change from Adriana's little house!: a splendid old Gothic mess overlooking a noisy canal, with ceilings high enough for a pope and great dashing stairways that made one feel like Sarah Bernhardt making an entrance. Also, in the style of the Venetian sublet, Hugh's share of the building was not closed off by lock and key, and members of the landlord's family occasionally wandered in to talk or even just to stare, as if he were not a tenant but an attraction.

The palazzetto stood in a weird part of Venice, way to the northwest near the railway station, a sestiere that few tourists knew of. It was not famous, this part of town. Not colorful. Not surprising. Not historical.

Venice is where one goes to be bewitched; Cannaregio is where one goes to retire.

Hugh loved it. "It's the most authentic Venice of all, lad," he said. "Because it's never been in the guidebooks, never had to perform for foreigners. It doesn't style itself, like gondoliers in those beastly costumes. It is what it is."

"I like you," I said.

We were having lunch at a "little place in the campo" that Hugh frequented, and I was at a crossroads in my life—in Dante's selva oscura, one might say. Because I couldn't bring myself to go home yet didn't dare stay, even though my boss (remember the book I was never writing?) declared himself as intent as ever on publishing Adriana's story.

"You'll apologize to her," Hugh said, "or she'll apologize to you. She's not stone, in the end, shocking though that be. You'll make it up."

"Not this time," I said sadly. "Something went really wrong with the whole thing—and don't tell me how great artists can't be held accountable."

"Of course they should, lad—for their art. As for the rest of it . . . Well, it's all their infernal tantrums and turnabouts, isn't it? They'll always disappoint us if we hold them to average standards of etiquette."

"Are you saying that they're more special than we are?"

"Well, aren't they? No, don't go all misery on me, now. We're speaking of people touched by God. They've the wild magic, and they're all barking mad. How can you ask them to say thank you, and to be punctual, and order a seemly dinner?"

I gave my spaghetti a twist, forked it up, looked around the square.

"Look, lad: someone or other slipped something into her that made her radiant and angry at the one time. That's what genius is. Was Beethoven a love?"

I grunted.

"What have you on for the evening?" he asked. "I've a late tea with the Fenice's master of the house. Well, un 'ombra at Harry's Bar, I suppose.

Venetians love it when you order the local drink. A *shadow*—so odd, that, though one supposes it's simply because one takes it in the afternoon."

"I'm busy, too," I said, wiping up my plate with the last of the pane. "I have to see il Professore on a personal matter."

"Yes, it's the boyo, isn't it? His young fellow. Moving out, is he?"

I shrugged.

"Hooked up with Signor Ercolani, I shouldn't wonder, given his penchants."

I have to say, though, that I was very unhappy to run this errand. Vieri was still shooting in Pisa, to return any day now, and this was surely the indicated time to catch il Professore's ear. Still, who wants to be the one to tell some likable old man that his rock of life is ready to roll on? Parting from Hugh, I took the vaporetto to Salute, wondering precisely what sort of successor would most destroy il Professore: Federica? another Professore? or another Vieri, boy unto boy? Yet did il Professore not tell me, long before—so very long before, it had begun to seem—that when the time came he would nod and accept? Did he not say that?

He and I had arranged to meet at Cici, a pensione a few doors down from number 127. He was there when I arrived.

"Bene!" he cried, rising from the table to greet me. "Ecco il mio e anche di Vieri l'amico più onesto." Here's Vieri's and also my most reliable friend. "Eh," he called to the bar, "un altr 'ombra, sì?"

We did ten or twelve minutes on il film, Ercolani, lo Scenarista, Pisa. We sedulously avoided any mention of Vieri—both of us, I noticed. Did he anticipate, and fear, what I had to say? After all, I must bear a message of some import—or why had I asked to meet him? I also failed to mention Adriana's treachery, the Cowboy's trashing of my prized tape, lo Scenarista's hypocrisy, or my Heimleiden. Homesickness, ja? I was too full of Europe; I could feel, mounting by the minute, too much ombra and courtyard and Siora Varin and this tumult of crafty old-world grace. I gotta get outta here.

So, at the next available caesura, I set my glass on the table in a businesslike manner, looked at il Professore dead-on, and said, "I need to break some news to you."

"Prego."

"It's about Vieri, actually."

"Ben certo," he smiled. "It is always Vieri. When he is not breaking the televisione, he is . . ." A gesture.

"Well, it's more . . . serious."

"But he is not hurt? Not in official custody? I would surely have heard."

"It's nothing like that."

"Meno male," he replied, with a thankful glance at heaven.

"I'm sorry to be coy with you. I don't . . . know the words for this. Vieri wants me to tell you that . . . well, he has met . . . una fia." A girl.

Il Professore was still. Then, holding my gaze, he said, "Ben certo. The most beautiful Italian boys are always meeting someone. Always le fie, as you say. The most incorrigible boys, but they are the more beautiful for that. So young, so touched by the divine—and all they want is to squander their gifts on those who cannot possibly . . ."

He was still again.

"Mi fa pena," I said. I'm sorry. "I hate to be the messenger, but Vieri . . . for some reason unknown to us both . . . felt . . ."

"Sì, the sympathetic other party who brings reason and calm to the theatre of passion. One recalls the last days of Clyto the Frenzied, when his physician had to bribe a kitchen boy to . . ."

He could not face me; he gazed downward. "Un altra?" he whispered, holding his empty glass. Order me a refill?

I called out to the waiter, and we sat silently till he said, as fastidiously as one can with but four syllables to work with, "Una fia?"

"But surely you were prepared for this? Didn't you even tell me you were planning to . . . well—"

"Passare sopravento?" Weather it?

"It had to happen sooner or later, no?"

"Sì, già. *Ah!*"—as the wine arrived. "Un sorso, beviamo." Let's drink;

and he did. "Sì, with beautiful Italian boys it is often not sooner but later, because they want to stabilize their situation. They deceive you; they do not leave. Perhaps the very beautiful Italian boys cannot deceive, and the most beatiful Italian boys will not deceive. He must be what he is, el mi Vieri, eh? So he has, yes, told you, and now you tell me. This girl, you have met her?"

I shook my head.

"What," he asked, "does one know of her?"

"I don't have the details. Vieri wanted me to warn you, so he . . . well, so you . . ."

"È veneziana, la?" Is she local?

"Yes. Si chiama Federica."

He nodded abstractly, not entirely listening.

"I'm sorry," I said, gently laying my hand upon his. "I know how well a man could love Vieri. He is amazing."

"You know this, so young così, my American guest?"

"Some things we learn in time," I offered. "But some things we know instinctively, quite early on. Vieri is one of those things."

"Sì, Vieri," he agreed, his head wagging a bit. Could he have been drunk? "The simplest pleasures," he said. "Sometimes, so out of reach. Or now here, now gone. The simplest love, essential. The quiet life, a peace between the generations. A boy without a father. Tutto questo. I knew he must have a secret friend, but I had been hoping it must be another young man, for then he would not leave me. Someone like you, Sior Foresto, no? For you could not take him away, not in any certain reality. . . . Yet he might learn from you, as beautiful Italian boys must. They have skin as smooth as an infant's, and eyes of the tempter. So solid yet so affectionate. So, so loving. There is always more in them. More love. More resentment. More energy. More truth. More worry. More beauty. The giving of power. The return of power . . ."

"Let me see you home," I said.

He was weeping now.

"Please. Let me . . ."

"Home?" he said. "Is that home? Vieri leaves, sì? You have said so. This girl . . . That must always happen to a beautiful Italian boy."

"Is love so devastating?" I asked. "So draining?"

"It is life itself," he told me. "Who lives without love?"

Well, I finally got him out and helped him home—he *was* drunk, clearly, the poor guy, probably having fortified himself in anticipation of my announcement. Then, having settled him down in an armchair with the *Gazzetino*—certain that I'd done nothing but harm—I gave a knock on Adriana's door to see how Deodata was coping; no answer came.

Strange, I thought. She's *always* in at this hour.

I got back on the vaporetto, but not heading back to Cannaregio and Hugh's. It was odd, magical, voluntarily fortuitous: but I rode all the way east to Sant' Elena and walked up the big canal there to the Public Gardens and down the back streets to San Pietro di Castello, one of the very oldest parts of Venice and maybe my favorite part, because it *looks* old. It isn't even paved: It's grass and mud, as Venice must have been when it was young and had no idea what history was going to say of it.

It's also borderline Venice: beyond it is lagoon, clouds, sky. You stand upon the edge of habitable land gazing out at the wider world. What are you? Where are you headed? You feel this in Venice, the only city in the world that is one great harbor, one pier, all aboard, what next. You feel free of the roots that clutch; the past is nothing. You have no father, no family, no curse. You are purely, even infinitely you, here, ever, now.

I took a more direct route on the way back to the boat, down the Viale Garibaldi, one of the biggest and busiest streets in the city, dotted with merchants and flooded with strollers. There were the inevitable news sellers, their slates chalked with the day's headline. So often it was KENNEDY CONTRA KRUSCIEV or IL VATICANO SOMETHING OR OTHER. Today, it was È MORTA ADRIANA GRAFANAS.

I stopped, staring at the words, thinking, She *can't* be dead! Isn't that what everyone thinks, at the moment of annunciation? Then I thought,

Well . . . she *could* be dead, but I maybe won't buy that newspaper. I was moving, but not to the boat now; I was going nowhere, easy to do in Venice, where every turning leads to another turning. Stupidly, I thought, I'm hurt. I'm guilty. I could be dead, too. These are the clichés of the One who Hears the News: including the pathetic hope that somehow it is all a mistake.

Yes, *of course!* The papers were always lying about Adriana, making up things, you know? Yes . . . it's another of those . . . In that series of unbelievably dishonest stories, they have invented a death in order to sell papers, *yes*, and Hugh will fire off certain angry letters . . .

I wandered from Castello to Cannaregio—the length of Venice—in a daze. Or no: I let my mind lead me on, telling me that her name was Dee Anna, that she was the queen of myth and newspapers, the most unserene protagonist of a screwball tragedy in which I played a shy walk-on part in the last act. I thought of her singing of *La Sonnambula*, to my mind her greatest role. "Inspire me," I said aloud, walking those streets. My eyes went wet a few times, for I was young and of a tender disposition; but did I cry for her or for myself?

And this odd thing: Adriana could hate and damn but not in any real sense outlive her mother. She could survive the Father yet rage that He abandoned her, for he'd broken the chain of life. Human life is unnatural, I decided, somewhere in the vicinity of San Canciano. Men are grasping and hungry where true nature is simple, accepting. The love of the tree; what does that *mean*, anyway? Catholics enjoy these conundrums and poesies because they know that the certainty of death means that all life, all glory, is absurd and hopeless eccentricity. All death is all an ending. Even love dies, first of all things. And fame. Byron says:

> *There's glory again for you, gentle reader! All*
> *Ends in a rusty casque and dubious bone.*

I just managed to gain Hugh's palazzetto before I broke down in sobs, making quite a picture for Hugh's landlords, who collected in a worried group as I read the note he had tacked to the wall just outside our sublet: "Meet me at her house *immediately*."

Death makes all else trivial: one resolves feuds, ignores bills, wastes money. I hailed a passing motorboat and raced to the back entrance of Adriana's house, on the Rio dei Fornaci, hurrying into the garden to find the place in chaos. The police were there, and bustling Siora Varin (occasionally retreating to the courtyard to call updates on the news to her mother at the window), and a furiously anguished Deodata, and strangers taking charge with papers and writs, and Hugh, patiently arguing with the cops.

Workers were bringing crates into the courtyard, packing up stuff in the house, checking with the strangers with the writs.

"Some of that must be mine," I said, in a minor sort of shock. Who, suddenly, were these executors of the will she'd never signed?

"Mark!" cried Hugh. "Come help me explain to these gentlemen of the law about the highly disquieting methods being employed by these..."

"Agents," said someone I didn't know.

"Managers," said another.

"Representatives of Signor Ambarazzi," said a pair of... what, lawyers? The carts kept being packed and piled.

"Hugh," I said, coming up to him. "Is it true?" and he looked at me and nodded.

"But *how?*"

"Physically, of a stroke. Emotionally, of a broken heart. Culturally..." He shrugged. "Of unemployment?"

"But where did all these vultures suddenly—"

Hugh turned to stop somebody from dollying off with the piano.

"Mare!" Siora Varin called up, explaining to her mother the objections I was now making to this all-too-swiftly proceeding foreclosure. "Sto fio diga che no vuol—"

"Ma zo!" old Signora Varin exclaimed, marveling at all the activity. "I fai sti massaria?" Are they moving out?

"No, la zentildona xe mora." The noblewoman is dead.

"Ai!" sighed the old woman in her homemade dialect as she crossed herself. "La vita, l'amare, la morze, la vita." Life, love, death, life.

The lawyers and whatever were clustering around and producing documents. "The official stamps," they explained, more or less at once. "It is legal, it was planned. One views the signatures."

"Nothing was planned," I said, to no one. "The whole business was desperately improvised."

"The liberty of narcissism," said a lawyer, contemptuously.

"The truly selfish know no one," said I don't know who.

"Fame consists in having relations with oneself," said another minion, bringing on a warning from one of the cops on his "reckless choice of words." The minion apologized, then went among the crates, chalking numbers on them.

Hugh, still striving with the law, signaled me over, as a solvent with which to blend his opera-house Tuscan into the cops' Venetian. Siora Varin assisted. But there were so many papers, so many parties of the first, second, and third parts. It was that kind of life, that sort of art: a tumult.

"Who are these people?" I asked. "I've lived with Adriana Grafanas for over a year and I never met or even heard of them."

"Xe una battagliola da ponte," said sage Siora Varin—literally: It's a bridge war, referring to the territorial fistfights held at various bridges throughout Venice's history.

I caught sight of someone taking possession of the scrapbook I had put together. I went up to him and said, "That's mine," and retrieved it without argument.

"What's there, lad?" asked Hugh, nodding at it as I rejoined him.

"Her life."

The dispute went on interminably, with the police listening to our side, listening to their side, examining documents, and siding with them till the sky went quietly, suddenly dark. Very, very, dark: and a great wind began to rise. All over the town, smart people ran indoors, store marquees were hastily lowered, dogs howled. This wind has a name. The Malvoglia? The Viagrande? Historically, Venice has suffered Adriatic convulsions at such times; whole islands have sunk beneath the penetrating surf. But this day no worse occurred in Adriana's garden than the breaking of two windows, the uprooting of the breakfast table, and the upheaval of a pile of boxes, one of which seemed to fly right at me in the black terror of the sky and the wind and the rushing people and struck me right on the head. It was a square box, about ten by ten, maybe an inch thick, and it read clearly on the top face, "For Mark Trigger from Adriana Grafanas."

"I got it," I said, quietly, and no one heard me in all the uproar. "Hugh, she *had it after all!*"

The wind died with astonishing speed. The clouds flew off. People were looking skyward, laughing ironically, righting their messed-up hair. The garden was a garden again.

"She had it after all," I repeated, as Hugh came over to me. *"Look!"*

"What?" he asked, still grave and irritated at the invasion of Adriana's garden by these adventurers and crooks.

"That will be confiscated," said the lawyers, of my box. "That will be considered. That will be inventoried."

"I'll kill who touches it," I said, snarling. Bravado; but they backed off. "Oh, man . . . She *told* me she would give it to me."

Hugh, gazing distractedly up at the sky, shook his head unhappily. Looking back at me, he said, "You're wounded, Mark," and he put a hand on my head above the left ear.

"I'm fine."

He showed me his fingers: blood.

"I'm *telling* you," I insisted.

"What's in the box?"

"The Maltese Falcon. She promised it to me, you know."

"The what?"

"Music," I said. "That much will never stop. Right?"

"You're delirious, lad."

"No, I'm . . . I'm contemplating the great life, you see." I held my tape close against me, beaming at him as, around us, the enemy host bustled and looted.

You might imagine a camera's crane shot drawing us up out of the garden, rising to a survey of all Venice, la Serenissima. In voice-over, I hear . . . well, me, to pose the ultimate of the tale's many questions: Who's right, Dante or Byron? That is, which of us, if any, is free? I'll never know, but here's a thought from the Maestro:

> Lo duca e io per quel cammino ascoso
> Intramma a ritornar nel chiaro mondo;
> E sanza cura aver d'alcun riposo
> Salimmo su, el primo e io secondo,
> Tanto ch'i' vidi delle cose belle
> Che porta 'l ciel, per un pertugio tondo;
> E quindi uscimmo a riveder le stelle.

Or, in other words:

> My guide and I unearthed a hidden road,
> Together to regain the world of truth;
> We made no rest, but steadily upward strode,
> He first and I behind, befitting youth,
> Till, through an opening ahead, I could descry
> The glow of heaven's wisdom, love, and truth,
> And thus came forth to see again the sky.

That is the end of the *Inferno*, and the end as well of my story.

Well, all right, there is one last bit, back in New York. There I became totally American again, eating hamburgers and skiing and scrabbling for the rent and playing the Venice *Adriana*, which my tape colleagues declared the greatest of all Grafanas performances: so in charge yet so tragic. Yes.

"She didn't believe her own life," I told Hugh, who was often in New York and who always, at my insistence, stayed with me. I said, "She was the greatest, yet she acted as if she were some swindle, dunning the world for attention."

"When do you start the book?" he asked.

"After all this? Forget it."

"A dramatic ending," he replied. "All the better."

"I'm not her scribble."

"You're her patron saint. Adriana's San Marco."

"No, you . . . See, it's all about how no one's free and we're all doomed. It's a . . . a bad life."

"Oh, Mark," he said, sitting next to me on my thrift-shop couch with a mug of coffee in his left hand and the back of my neck under his right. "You brew a most telling cup, but—"

"She was *squeezed*, don't you see that? The *whole time!* She spent her life trying to impress people, buy off their contempt. She lived in fear of their opinion. This is not free! This is *tilted* and *false*. Just like . . . well . . . *yeah,* all the guys like *us,* so poised and fearful and quiet in our ways. Ooh, what if the others should *know* of us? The terror, right?"

"Mark, there are no others. We're all the same species."

"No. We're *different.*"

He set down his coffee and looked at me. "How?" he asked.

"Europe really is a study, you know? Because now that I'm back in the States I realize what's really going on undercover. I'm detecting codes. I'm starting to see where and how the . . . the meetings take place."

"Much more liberty in Europe, lad. As long as you don't challenge the standards by which—"

"You think you're free because you've been taught how to lie so well you think *you* devised the system. What kind of freedom is that?"

Wryly, he sipped the coffee, asking, "What would you have, a homosexual revolution? Boys kissing boys in the street? Scandalous Bildungs-romane of young men discovering Who They Are? Parades?"

"Maybe. It's no more than what Adriana did, in a way. She was her own revolution. She *made* them accept her. Oh, sure, there's a price to pay—a loss of love for a return of power. But she freely chose, no? She took power and made them cheer. Yes, she was hard. Limited. Self-absorbed. Yet Western music would be incomprehensible without her. She stands at the center of something and I ask you now, Is this not true? Is this not all true as I tell it?"

He smiled. "Will she be Serenissima at last?" he wondered.

"Listen, it may be strange to say, but I miss her. Not just the singing. I really miss *her*—stingy and crabby and suspicious and unreasonable and idiotically obsessed with that stupid drug. Take away her singing and you describe a hopelessly unpleasant woman, and yet . . . how could you take away her singing and still describe her?"

"That drug it was that killed her, you know. Her heart went numb."

"She would take out the box with the hypnotized wonder of someone in a fable. She rubbed it, as if summoning the genie of a lamp."

"What of your boss and the book?"

"Oh, he forgives me."

"Does he *want* the book?"

I didn't answer. Instead, I brought out a letter that I had received from il Professore. I read it aloud, translating (from Tuscan, Venetian, and the academic's punctuational Latin) as I went along:

My dear young friend;

It has been a festal week for all of us here in la Serenissima. Serving as compare ["best man" was the closest I could come to an ancient Venetian term that means "patron" as well as "confi-dant"], I gave a wedding supper for Vieri and his Federica at Taverna la Fenice.

Yes, a profligate you will call me. But the novizeta looked very lovely, and our youthful yet most confident Vieri was so clearly in love with her that it took one's breath away. At the presentation of the "hidden pie" (a tradition local to Federica's relations, from some dim corner of Castello), cherubs came grimacing out and even ballerinas made themselves known, to the serenade of a quartetto. The pie itself—bananas, paste, and a ladder—was a terror, but then one saw our original Vieri run a fond finger down the cheek of la noa siora and the brand-new dama touch our Vieri's nose. Each so besotted. Not knowledgeable but trusting. *They do not care who knows.* Such love. Such belief in themselves.

The family are undistinguished if acceptable, though the rinfresco at the Fenice brought out a deplorable plethora of cousins from Burano.

Perhaps I surprise you, my young American friend, to seem so spirited at the prospect of marrying Vieri off. I still recall how I failed to far bella figura [how am I to translate this phrase now?: "to maintain a handsome style"?] when you broke the news to me. But I restored myself with the knowledge that as long as Vieri lives, he remains my friend. Even now that he has married, we speak often by telephone, and see each other for an ombra now and then. Vieri says that he slept for two days after the wedding night. We learn why at last: Federica awaits their firstborn.

You must wonder about the disposition of the movie in which our Vieri played so imposing a role. (Though, myself, I have always imagined him as the ideal Patroclus.) Maestro Ercolani had to work around the Madonna's death with the employment of doubles in masks, extreme panoramas, and other such nuances, and is now in the editing season.

Vieri is most excited. He tells everyone of his experiences, but when one asks, What do you play?, he says, "A gangster."

He grows more lovable with each day, and will seem a most

handsome father, full of devotion to his child, the splendid issue of his flesh and love.

Last week, I honored myself with a trip to Rome. The Opera gave Bellini's exquisite *Sonnambula* and a strange Russian piece about someone who travels the world only to return to the place where he began. The museums were rich with art. And Rinaldo, a young man from Cerignola who had ventured north for a visit, proved a most agreeable dinner companion. A very understanding young man with eyes like a firestorm. He has been quite willing to adapt to our Venetian ways, and unlike Vieri, he never breaks the television. Indeed, he is very placid of composure and, like an exotic flower, must often be considerably encouraged of an evening before he blooms.

Siora Varin, her unending madre, and la Deodata all add their salutes to my warm wishes for your happiness.

Il vostro devotissimo Professore Lunardo Tron

Putting the letter away, I asked Hugh, "Don't you love that? Rinaldo, I mean. Il Professore just . . . he just goes on, indomitable. Tiltless."

Hugh fixed me with a ceremonial look. "You have to write that book," he said.

"I want a hero."

"You have, if I may put my oar in, the most spectacular hero in the history of music."

"How can anyone write someone else's story? We scarcely write our own."

"Write yours, at least—she's in it. She's in all our stories. The intrigues and the backstage and the highest art . . . We nose in. We all become bedazzled young Americans up in a balloon over mad old Europe."

"Write my story? Wouldn't that be insufferably arrogant?"

He smiled and shrugged. "*Pretend* it's about you. One of those Bil-dungsromane. Lovely coffee, as always."

"Write my story?" I repeated, as he moved to leave. "But that's not what—"

"*Nothing's* what, lad," he replied, getting on his coat. "Each step we take brings us to a crossroads. New choices. Revelations."

After seeing him off, I hauled out Adriana's scrapbook for the hun-dredth time, turned the pages, and thought about her fire and headlines. Her power. Her beauty and plangent misery, so telling because we all knew she really was suffering. She made opera true.

Yes, of course, it's not my story—but the purpose is mine, to tell her what she never understood: that the applause was love, the one thing she believed must be absolutely and permanently beyond her reach.

To have had it, unwittingly, all along: what an American story that is! There's no place like home.

I was turning pages when my eye fell upon "NEW YORKER EXCELS." I sensed something click on inside me, and I took up notebook and pen and started in:

> There was a church school on the Zattere that I liked to walk past in the warm half of the year, for through the open windows I could hear children reciting those now inspiriting, now bewilder-ing mottoes that Catholics are raised on. I would catch the nun's wearily officious "The love of the tree," followed by the class's merrily dutiful repetition. "The sorrow that is heaven," the nun would continue, to the kids' echo; and "The mortification of van-ity," "The tears of the olive," "All fear what is true," and, the nun's voice rising in the confidence of one made sensible of a great riddle, "Repentance is infinite."